Climates of Competition

Studies in Global Competition
*Edited by John Cantwell, The University of Reading, UK
and David Mowery, University of California, Berkeley, USA*

This book is part of a series. The publisher will accept continuation orders which may be cancelled
at any time and which provide for automatic billing and shipping of each title in the series upon
publication. Please write for details.

Climates of Competition

Maria Bengtsson
Umeå Business School
Umeå, Sweden

Routledge
Taylor & Francis Group

LONDON AND NEW YORK

First published 1998 by
Harwood Academic Publishers

Published 2014 by Routledge
711 Third Avenue, New York, NY 10017
2 Park Square, Milton Park, Abingdon, Oxfordshire OX14 4RN

First issued in paperback 2014

Routledge is an imprint of the Taylor & Francis Group, an informa business

Originally published in Swedish in 1994 as KONKURRENSKLIMAT OCH DYNAMIK: EN STUDIE AV INTERAKTION MELLAN KONKURRENTER by Umeå Universitet, Umeå. © 1994 Umeå Universitet, Umeå.

British Library Cataloguing in Publication Data

Bengtsson, Maria
    Climates of competition. — (Studies in global competition
    v. 5)
    1. Competition   2. Competition, International
    I. Title
    338.6'048

    ISBN 978-9-057-02257-9 (hbk)
    ISBN 978-1-138-00225-8 (pbk)

Table of Contents

List of Figures

List of Tables

Preface

This book contributes to an increased understanding of competition by including relational and attitudinal aspects of competition (intensity in competition, symmetry between competitors, the attitudes of competitors towards each other, their perceptions and values), on which interaction between competitors is (partly) based. Different contexts of competition arise over time, and the concept 'climate of competition' developed here is used to illustrate how dynamics in industry are dependent on different contexts of competition. The nature of the climate of competition can explain why competition in some cases stimulates and in others hinders firms in the creation of new solutions and innovativeness. The question of how and why dynamics in competition develop and function is therefore central to this book. The studies included in this book, then, highlight and give meaning to aspects of competition that are not included in traditional theories of competition.

Competition is often defined as being the rivalling relationship between firms in an industry, where the traditional interpretation of competition rests on the assumption that a perfect market with its many manufacturers and consumers and with price as a regulatory mechanism, can over time achieve an equilibrium between supply and demand. Most markets, however, do not reflect this somewhat ideal situation, giving rise to theoretical explanations of competition in oligopolies and duopolies, where so-called imperfect market structures are included in economic theory. Such an approach aims to explain the state of a market and how this state can be described and analysed. There are other theoretical approaches that have been developed, which, realising that imperfect markets are the dominating form of market, question how such markets arise, how they develop over time, and how firms function in relation to each other and other actors in the market. Time, different processes of development, dynamics and change are central concepts in this group of theories. Competition as a concept has thereby been broadened to include the process through which competition develops, the dynamics created within firms, industries, or strategic groups, and the contents of the interaction that occurs between firms. This book aims to contribute to such a tradition. A central contribution of this book lies therefore in the contents of competition and how competition changes over time.

Competition is not purely one single state or type of relationship, but can exhibit a number of different characteristics, such as degrees of distance, surveillability and acceptance leading to various degrees of stability, harmony, dependence and relative positions. These attitudinal characteristics are expressed in various ways, from, for example, active move and counter-move and rivalling attitudes towards each other, to a tacit collusion and co-existence. Some of these characteristics of the climate of competition are developmental and others debilitating to the dynamic development of industry. Moreover, a certain climate of competition may change in that the nature of the relationships between the competing firms changes. The force behind such changes can be the drive for dominance in the market, but can also be the result of interaction in itself. The above discussion is reflected in the explanatory model presented in this book.

I alone must be held responsible for the contents of this book, but, in cases where the reasoning presented here becomes interesting, part of the merit must be ascribed to others. The analyses of competition and climates of competition presented here have been discussed with colleagues within the framework of the research project 'Competition and Competitiveness'. Associate Professor Örjan Sölvell, Institute of International Business, Stockholm School of Economics, the project director, deserves my particular gratitude for his valuable contribution in discussions of the analyses of the climates of competition. This book appeared previously in the form of a PhD thesis published in Swedish, and Associate Professor Carin Holmquist, Umeå Business School, and Professor Leif Lindmark, Jönköping International Business School, were both active as supervisors in that phase of the research. Andrew Baldwin, PhD student, translated the text and also contributed further with advice for reworking the thesis into the form presented in this book. Anders Söderholm, PhD, Umeå Business School, and Associate Professor Sören Kock at the Swedish School of Business in Vaasa, Finland, were active in discussions of the analyses of the book on several occasions. Professor George Tesar, University of Wisconsin at Whitewater and Owe R. Hedström, university lecturer and Director of Studies at the Umeå Business School have in a number of different ways encouraged and supported the work on this book. Katarina Pousette, secretary at the Department of Business Administration, Umeå Business School, has contributed to the book in the form of layout and indexing the text. In his role as editor for this series, Professor John Cantwell, University of Reading, made valuable contributions and comments during the transformation from thesis to book. Last but not least, the participation of the companies involved in the studies is most gratefully acknowledged, for without their participation and support, this book would not have arisen. The research has been financially supported by Tore Browalds research foundation, the research funds of the Swedish Competition Authority, and the Department of Business Administration at Umeå Business School, which are hereby gratefully acknowledged.

1. Domestic Rivalry

Why is competition desirable? The most common response to that question is that competition is needed in order to obtain an effective allocation of resources and to govern consumer interests. A third reason has been put forward during the last decade, but one that can be traced back to Adam Smith (1776; 1976), namely that rivalry is an important driving force behind innovativeness and development within firms and industries. However, the dynamics of competition may vary between different types of competition; competition in some cases can provide the pressure and dynamics that are needed for the development of new solutions and innovations, whereas in others it can hinder development within an industry. The above question can therefore be rewritten as two questions; 'What characterises different contexts of competition?', and 'How does the nature of competition affect the dynamics within the industry?'.

Different contexts of competition have been distinguished within economic theory based on the structural conditions of an industry, but the dynamics of competition have not been researched further. During recent years, more process oriented studies have been able to state that proximity between competitors is of importance to the dynamics of an industry, but the question of how and why such dynamics develop and function has not been fully considered. This question will be treated in this book, and it will be shown that different climates of competition emerge in different contexts of competition, and that the character of the climate can explain why competition in some cases stimulates and in others hinders firms in the creation of new solutions and innovativeness.

1

INTERNATIONAL INTEGRATION
AND NATIONAL COMPETITION

The background to this book can be found in the debate that has arisen about the importance of national conditions for the development of companies and industries. During the last few decades, the industrialised society has become integrated internationally, and both the development of firms and the development of industries are often described from an international perspective. Empirically this can be exemplified by the increased integration within Europe, by increased direct investment abroad, deregulated capital markets, etc.[1] Theoretically, and to a greater extent now than previously, company development is linked to a company's opportunities of exploiting the advantages that are on offer in the global environment (cf. amongst others Lamb, 1984; Bartlett, 1986; Hood and Vahlne, 1988; Reich, 1991 and Taylor, 1991).

Thus, the discussion on the restructuring of industries into interdependent international systems, as well as its consequences for company action and for the development within the industry, can today be found in literature that focuses on the increased internationalisation or globalisation of industries. To the extent that different national conditions and their importance for the development and the competitiveness of industry have been considered, these discussions have mostly concentrated on interest rates, the level of wages, and other macro-economic variables. National conditions are thus limited to being a variable that is not possible to affect by the strategic action of companies within an industry.

The national industrial environment, and its importance for the development of the firm and industry has then almost been ignored. Leontiades (1989), for example, considers that industrial globalisation implies that the conditions of the national market almost completely lose importance as a result of the increased competition across borders. National solutions for companies are replaced by international solutions. However, as will be shown here, it is not clear that international integration results in the decrease in importance for business of the national industrial environment. Rather, there is cause to consider the importance of national conditions for the development of industry in more detail.

---

[1] See for example Bengtsson and Bonnedahl (1993) and Bonnedahl (1991).

To emphasise geographical proximity and national conditions for industrial development in a world that is becoming increasingly globalised may seem paradoxical. However, a partly new train of thought has emerged during the last few years which claims that national conditions are of crucial importance for companies' international competitiveness, even though companies and industries are internationalised to a high degree (cf. Enright, 1992; Lagnevik et al., 1992; Lagnevik, 1993; Porter, 1990; Sölvell et al., 1991 and Zander and Sölvell, 1991). Porter explains this in the following way;

> The home nation influences the ability of its firms to succeed in particular industries. The outcome of thousands of struggles in individual industries determines the state of a nation's economy and its ability to progress ... nations fail where firms do not receive the right signals, are not subject to the right pressures, and do not have the right capabilities. (Porter, 1990:xiii and 1990:68)

Porter (1990) argues that geographical proximity is of great importance for development within a country or an industry. He shows that a dynamic and challenging industrial environment contributes to the development of competitive advantages. If the dynamics of the industrial environment are weakened, companies will to a greater extent locate strategically important functions to other countries with more favourable conditions. The importance of considering the industrial environment as a whole is emphasised, as the different constituents of an environment support each other, giving rise to synergy effects.[2]

Geographical proximity between actors in an industrial environment means that these actors operate under the same cultural and geographical conditions. This contributes to the development of advanced and specific factors of production (cf. Porter, 1990). Openness and proximity between companies give rise to synergy between industries and technologies within a country. Proximity to domestic competitors can become a subtle driving force behind action consisting of prestige and pride relative to an actor's competitors. Proximity to customers within the domestic market, which in most of the industrialised western world demands advanced solutions, stimulates product development in the company.

---

[2] Porter's position has, however, been criticised by researchers such as Dunning and Cartwright (1991), Reich (1991), and Wilson and Bålfors (1993).

The importance of studying the conditions of the national market increases at the same rate as the increase in international integration. However, the focus of this book does not lie in the development of international competitiveness or in industrial development. What is interesting here is Porter's (1990) conclusion that proximity is of importance for the dynamics of internationally competitive industries.

PROXIMITY AND DIVERSITY IN COMPETITION

Domestic rivalry is considered the most important explanatory factor in Porter's (1990) analysis. Through the demands and the pressure brought about by competition in the home market, companies are stimulated or forced into taking innovative action that results in the development of companies and industries. Companies develop strength and competitiveness by exploiting specific and advanced national factor endowments, by satisfying sophisticated and demanding home buyers, by establishing relationships with internationally competitive suppliers in a nation, by sharing activities in technology development, and by manufacturing with related industries. The presence of domestic competitors in the national arena can lead to domestic rivalry, which creates a pressure for the individual companies to explore these national advantages better than their competitors do. The core of this type of reasoning is that vigorous domestic competition between geographically proximate companies gives rise to a pressure to improve and innovate, i.e. to dynamics. Diversity in competition is also seen to be central. Porter (1990) considers that in the presence of many local competitors, the pressure to create improvements and innovations in operations relative to competitors becomes greater.

These are effects of competition that can be observed externally. Internal effects, as pre-conditions for the external effects, consist of increased information, and knowledge and awareness of one's competitors. Porter (1990) is of the opinion that both geographical proximity and diversity are necessary for both internal and external effects of competition to arise. Proximate competitors are able, within a short space of time, to observe each others' moves and counter-moves, enabling them to rapidly imitate each others' products. Information about and surveillability of competitors (i.e. the ability to keep watch over the actions of one's competitors) also becomes more efficient, as the mobility of individuals increases insights into the competing companies. Psychological factors, such as prestige and pride, also stimulate companies to compete actively and to be innovative in their actions. In this way, proximity sharpens the 'struggle' between competitors, and therefore increases the dynamics within an industry. Without domestic rivalry, companies become passive.

The argument that creativity and innovativeness are stimulated by factors that are fixed locally, and which are therefore immobile or impossible to replicate can be found in Porter (1990), but appeared previously in Marshall's (1920) discussions on the localisation of industry.[3] Ethno-geographical theory also sees specific social and cultural conditions that stimulate the exchange of information and spreading of technology between companies as developing in the local environment (cf. Asheim, 1991).[4] The importance of cultural proximity is stated, for example, by Törnqvist (1990), who claims that proximity eases the exchange of information, which is crucial for creativity (see also Sangenburg and Pyke, 1991). Krugman (1991) offers a similar reasoning, stating that the spreading of technology is stimulated if the information flow is facilitated in local environments. Törnqvist (1986) describes the information that is necessary within creative environments in the following way;

> Information that is not well structured and homogenous, that does not follow well established, formal information channels, and where the transference of information cannot be considered a flow

---

[3] Marshall (1920) and others include geographical space and its importance in their treatments of external economies.

[4] Based on Marshall's (1920) discussion, Asheim (1991) claims that, as well as the social and cultural advantages linked to the local environment, other advantages can be gained through the division of labour between companies within a region. Production systems and the organisation of such systems change parallel to international integration, from the economies of scales and standardisation that characterises 'Fordism' to a more flexible system of production. Many feel that the possibility of co-ordinating operations or distributing tasks and/or functions between actors within the same geographical area will increase in the future (cf. Asheim, 1991). The advantages that exist in the local environment cannot be considered to be solely territorial, but can also comprise functional advantages. However, opinions differ on the consequences of development for the future importance of regional and local industrial environments (cf. Oinas, 1992; Asheim, 1991 and Sangenberg and Pyke, 1991).

of information, leads to creative processes. This type of information requires direct personal contact in continuously new combinations and unexpected constellations. It is the opportunities to link together fragmentary pieces of tacit information in new ways that are important.

(Törnqvist, 1986; page 381, translated)

Törnqvist means that the density and openness of the national environment are important because, through these characteristics, the national context offers meeting places for random contacts. These random contacts provide opportunities to combine new pieces of information and fragments of new ideas, which in turn stimulate creativity. The opportunity to combine new fragments of information is central in bringing about innovative action.

The development of competence is also facilitated and stimulated by geographical proximity between competitors.[5] If a technological foundation is developed in one country, for example through higher technological education, experience, and an ability to solve technical problems, this knowledge is difficult to copy, and is therefore geographically bound, despite technology in itself being mobile. Dahmén (1988) follows a similar train of thought, in that the core of what he calls development blocks is difficult to imitate, and therefore cannot be assumed to be mobile.[6] In the stimulation of innovative action due to proximity, the location of competitors' strategic bases to advanced and demanding industrial environments is of importance, according to Porter (1990). The term strategic base is used here to indicate the crucial strategic functions of a company, such as strategic management or product development.

One consequence of the proximity argument is that the advantages of proximity gained within a country cannot be gained interna-

---

[5] Competence here concerns the ability of the individual to exploit knowledge in the pursuit of goals.

[6] The core of the development block consists of creative groups of manufacturers, research institutes, customers, etc. Dahmén, who takes Schumpeter as his point of departure, is of the opinion that technological development is stimulated if such development occurs in a number of related industries simultaneously. A drive to develop is thus generated within a development block. In a similar way, Melin et al. (1984) explain development and restructuring by describing the dynamism that arises in industrial fields. The core of these fields consists of the industrial network and the relations between actors. That industrial fields stimulates development is explained by the dynamism that arises as a result of the effects of the actors' actions on each other within the network.

tionally.[7] Competition in national markets is therefore, according to
Zander and Sölvell (1991), of great consequence for companies that
have achieved a high degree of internationalisation. If a company is
operational internationally, the advantages that a company can
receive from its home base can be expressed in a wider geographical
area. Geographical proximity in areas that could be described as a
company's strategic base is therefore of particular importance for
the company, whether or not the company competes within a
national or international market.

THE NATURE AND DYNAMICS OF COMPETITION

It can be concluded that proximity between competitors is considered to be of particular importance for the dynamics of competition. However, Porter (1990) does not scrutinise the concept
'competition' to any great depth. He claims that proximity and
diversity are important, but the variety of industry-specific competitive conditions in general have been excluded from his treatment
of competition. Previous studies that I have been involved in indicate that the nature of competition shifts between different internationally competitive industries, and this has inspired me to further
study industries with a large degree of internationalisation in order
to obtain a deeper understanding of the nature and dynamics of
competition. Competition can vary as a result of both structural
conditions and the process of competition, and it is therefore of
interest to further analyse such variations.

---

[7] The delimitation of the industrial environment to one country can be criticised in a
number of ways. Krugman (1991) focuses on the local or regional environment rather than
the national environment, as there can be greater variations between local environments
within the same country. According to Krugman, what separates countries is rather the
political approaches of those countries and the support and obstacles that arise from political decisions. The argument supporting the importance of the local industrial environment
is based for the most part on factors such as culture, climate, religion, and value structure.
The factors give rise to proximity between actors. Most countries can also be distinguished
from each other by such factors, and the local variations that may exist within a country can
be described as sub-cultures within an overall social and value structure. It is proximity in
the national environment that forms the core of the reasoning behind the delimitation of this
study. It should, however, be pointed out that this delimitation is not self-evident, and that
consideration must also be given to the degree of proximity that can differ within a country.

The Structure of Competition

Industrial Organisation Theory (IO-theory) distinguishes between different types of imperfect markets by relating a number of structural variables to action within an industry. By analysing the structure of an industry based on variables such as the industry's costs structure, the degree of vertical integration, the intensity of research and development and the degree of differentiation, the prediction of behaviour in an industry is assumed to be possible. Dependence between actors in an imperfect market, however, means that the result of action is not completely predictable, even though it can be assumed (based on IO-theory) that structure affects the individual company's action, and thereby has importance for the interaction between competitors.

Less importance is ascribed within IO-theory to the national or international geographical space in which competition is conducted, or to changes over time. The fact that time as a variable is not included in such studies means that competition is not placed within its historical context (cf. Lazonick, 1991), and that the dynamics that arise from the action of competitors over time are not studied. It should be mentioned, however, that the dimension of time is considered to some respect by the inclusion of Game Theory in the theoretical reasoning (cf. Tirole, 1988). Even so, companies are assumed to act rationally after a number of periods, based on the game rules that emerge. This means that it becomes possible to identify connections between the structure of competition and competitive behaviour.

Based on the discussion so far, it can be stated that different kinds of connections can be identified between different contexts of competition and the effects of competition. The structure of an industry is related to behaviour within an industry, and proximity between competitors is related to the emergence and growth of international competitiveness. However, understanding of how competition functions is limited, i.e. which inherent mechanisms exist in different contexts of competition and how these may change over time. The following research question is therefore addressed in this book:

What characterises different types of competition between proximate competitors, and how does the nature of competition affect the dynamics of different contexts of competition?

The Process of Competition

To increase understanding of the nature of competition and its inherent dynamics, it is not sufficient just to distinguish different types of competition. The process aspects of competition should also be considered. Three such aspects, which are part of what here is termed the process of competition, can be assumed to be of importance for the structures and behaviour patterns that can be observed at an industry level. These three aspects are 1) the interpretations and conceptions of competition that develop within the individual company, 2) the individual company's actions, its competitive moves, which directly or indirectly affect the company's competitors, and 3) the interaction between competitors, i.e. the competitive plays that occur within an industry.

It is important to base an understanding of company action on the *perception of competition*. Company action is described within economic theory as rational, which is possible only if it is the connection between structure and behaviour in an industry that is described. The study at the heart of this book, however, requires that consideration be given to the fact that individuals act under uncertain conditions. Not only the present, but also the past and the future affect action. The future is uncertain, but earlier experiences reduce this uncertainty (cf. Weick, 1979). It is therefore of interest to gain an understanding of competition through the interpretations and experiences of individuals regarding competition. There are a number of methodological problems with transferring thoughts on the importance of interpretation and experience from the level of the individual to the level of the organisation, but the reasoning is applicable in principle. It is the interpretations of individuals that ultimately lie behind what is observed to be company action. The actions of competitors are interpreted by individuals within the company, and these interpretations are expressed in the kind of interaction that takes place between companies.

Besides the perception and experience of competition, the *competitive moves* that are undertaken by individual companies are also important in building an understanding of competition. It is not entirely self-evident which action follows from the interpretations that develop within an organisation. Action is based on a great number of considerations, and individual measures can be interpreted differently internally and externally. It is therefore of interest to relate individual competitive moves both to the perceptions of the company concerned and to those of its competitors.

It is, however, not sufficient to solely study individual competitive moves without studying the interaction between competitors. The term *competitive play* will be used in the discussion of interaction between competitors in order to distinguish the companies' interaction with other actors in the industrial environment. The core of interaction consists of the actions of individual companies, i.e. competitive moves, in relation to each other. Interaction therefore accumulates to form different expressions of competitive play. An interactive perspective on competition must therefore be assumed. The inspiration for this train of thought can be found in network theory, where interaction is dealt with in terms of co-operative relations between competitors. Interaction also occurs between actors that compete with each other, and this gives rise to relationships between competitors, where those relationships that develop can be assumed to be of great importance for continued interaction and for the actions of the individual companies (cf. Easton, 1987, and Easton and Arajou, 1992). Competition can therefore be described as a process of interaction over time, where competitors develop relationships with each other through a number of competitive plays.

It has been stated above that competition can be understood better by studying individual companies' perceptions of competition, their competitive moves, and the competitive play that occurs. These three parts are integrated and interdependent. Competitive play is affected by both perceptions of competition resident in the individual companies and by individual competitive moves. In the same way, the perceptions in the competing companies, together with a description of competitive play, can describe individual competitive moves. Perceptions within individual companies develop both as a result of competitive play and of perceptions of the actions of the company in question. These three elements can therefore be seen as integrated aspects of the same process, which

THE PROCESS OF COMPETITION

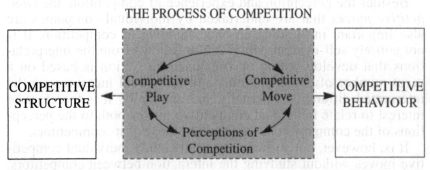

Figure 1.1 Factors which Constitute Part of the Process that Forms National Competition

is termed the process of competition in the figure above. It is this process, somewhat of a 'black box' within economic theory, that contributes to forming competition.

THE AIM OF THE STUDY

Previous studies of the importance of national competition for development within an industry encapsulated in an increasingly internationalised business environment have been based on Porter's (1990) study, amongst others. A number of ethno-cultural theories support the assumption that proximity in the national environment contributes to creativity and innovativeness within a company. It has also been stated that types of competition can differ in other respects, and can exhibit different structural characteristics. Figure 1.1 illustrates, with the help of the white boxes and the arrows, the connection between the structure of competition and behaviour within an industry. This book analyses the process through which the above connection arises, rather than the connection in itself. The overall aim of this book is therefore *to analyse the process of competition in industries where the actors exhibit great geographical proximity to each other. In this way, the book aims to increase understanding of the nature and dynamics of competition.* To make the overall aim more concrete, the following two sub-aims are identified:

1. To identify and distinguish between different contexts of competition, and to develop a terminology through which the nature of competition can be described.
2. Through the generation of theory, to increase understanding for the dynamics that develop as a result of competition.

THE STRUCTURE OF THE BOOK

The discussion of the research question and the aims of this book as presented above leads naturally to a presentation of the theoretical points of departure for the study in Chapter Two. Chapter Two comprises a number of sections, and in the first three sections, traditional theory regarding competition is discussed, together with the contribution that it can provide towards an increased understanding of the research question of this book. The schools of theory are in many respects static and/or normative by nature, and are based on the assumption of rationality. The necessity and implications of considering perceptions of competition that develop within a company, how these are expressed in interaction, and how they change over time, concern the fourth, fifth, and sixth sections of the chapter. Chapter Two concludes with a discussion on how the different schools of thought contribute to an increased understanding of the research question posed by this book.

Chapter Three deals with the methodological considerations involved in the study and the research process. The method that lies closest to the ambitions of the research question and the research perspective that have been chosen is characterised by the generation of theory. The case-study method seems therefore most advantageous. A description is given of the emerging research process, i.e. how data is collected and analysed continuously over time, and how this is related to existing theory. The second part of the chapter presents a discussion on the variables that have been used to distinguish different contexts of competition that have appeared during the different phases in the history of the three industries studied in this book. Two dimensions are identified from the discussion of theory as being most suitable; the degree of symmetry/asymmetry between actors, and the degree of activity/passivity in competition. The empirical studies provide further determination or definition of the inner meaning of symmetry between actors and activity in competition. These two dimensions are presented and discussed in Chapter Three, to then be used in the description of competition as found in the three industries under study. Chapters Four, Five, and Six provide case-descriptions of the competition in these three industries.

Competition in the Front-loader industry, as described in Chapter Four, involves two equally strong and relatively comparable competitors during the 1980s. In contrast, the competitors in the Lining industry, presented in Chapter Five, differ from each other, both in size and area of operations. The third industry under study, the Rack and Pinion industry, is described in Chapter Six, and is characterised by one individual company dominating the industry. The structure of these three chapters follows the same pattern; the first section describes the industry, the second section provides a presentation of the context of competition found during the different phases in the history of the industries, and the third section describes in more detail the process of competition during the most recent phase, the 1980s.

The description and analysis presented in Chapters Four to Six result in a theoretical and conceptual development, from which four climates of competition are identified and their characteristic natures are discussed in Chapter Seven. A model of the dynamics of the climates of competition and the changes to them over time is developed in Chapter Eight. The aim of this book to generate theory is realised in the grounded descriptions of the climates of competition. The mechanisms that bring about dynamics of the different climates of competition are identified and analysed, and the nature and dynamics of the climates of competition are related to the changes and development within the industries over time.

Chapter Nine provides a summary of the conceptual apparatus of the nature of the four climates of competition, together with the model that describes the dynamics of these climates. The findings of the study are related to the aims of this book and to the theoretical points of departure for the study. A number of theoretical and practical implications of these findings are discussed, as is the need for further research to increase understanding for competition and to improve the generalisation of the theory generated in this book.

2. The Process of Competition

Based on the discussion in the previous chapter, the key to an increased understanding of the nature of the climates and dynamics of competition rests in the process of competition. This chapter discusses possible points of departure within existing theory which can be of use in the study of the competitive process. The first part of the chapter deals with existing theories of competition regarding structure and behaviour in an industry. The different schools contribute valuable understanding of structural and behavioural aspects of competitive pre-conditions within an industry, and how these pre-conditions may be interrelated. These different schools help distinguish a number of dimensions from which competition can be described. From the description of competition it then becomes possible to determine different contexts of competition.

To understand the processes of competition that occur in different contexts of competition, an interactive perspective is necessary. This means that the contents of the interaction between competitors are emphasised. The description of the actual action that takes place between the competing companies should be completed by studies of the relationships, flows, and links that develop between competitors as a result of the interaction. The experiences or interpretations of competition should also be taken into consideration, as it is the interpretations of competition that ultimately guide action. This is discussed in the second part of the chapter.

Competition changes over time. The processes of competition which exist at different points of time can explain the changes that occur, and, conversely, can also be seen to be a result of these changes. Change can occur in different ways, both incrementally and/or radically. This is discussed in the third part of the chapter. In the fourth part of the chapter, the theoretical points of departure for this book are summarised.

COMPETITION AS STRUCTURE AND BEHAVIOUR

Competition can be described as both structure of and behaviour in an industry. The structure and behaviour of an industry provide the framework or pre-conditions for the process of competition. The theory-based description of the industry as structure and behaviour takes its points of departure partly in economic theories about com-- petition at the industrial level, partly in theories about strategic groups at the inter-organisational level, and finally in theories on competitive strategies at the company level.

Economic Theories of Competition

Neo-classical micro-economic theory assumes that the actions of buyers and sellers are based on rational considerations. The ideal market situation, i.e. perfect competition, consists of a large number of buyers and sellers that are anonymous to each other, with homogenous or near homogenous products. Competition is considered to be synonymous with price competition, and, over a period of time, the mechanisms of the perfect market lead to an effective allocation of resources. Cost-effective companies survive, and prices stabilise at a level where supply and demand match each other. Micro-economic theory is normative, and has come to serve as a model for anti-trust legislation. It is clear, however, that the theory of perfect competition is insufficient as a description of actual competition, and that other theoretical approaches are therefore required.

Without abandoning the rational approach to how companies within an industry behave, Industrial Organisational Theory (IO-theory) includes market imperfections in its model of competition. The inclusion of market imperfections in the analysis of competition means that parameters other than price and quantity are taken into consideration. Bain (1959), for example, developed the 'structure-conduct-performance' taxonomy, which relates market structure in imperfect markets to a wider definition of company action (conduct). Conduct in turn is related to the overall performance of the market.[1] Bain defines market structure as the pattern in which elements of the system are organised and put together. He argues that technological conditions, cost conditions, and the sales process within the industry to a great extent determine the structural conditions of that industry. Bain describes market structure from market concentration, the degree of product differentiation, and the existence of entry barriers.

Scherer (1980) develops Bain's arguments further through an empirical survey of American industry. He discusses action in four imperfect markets that are distinguished from each other by the number of buyers and sellers, and by the homogeneity of the product — monopoly, homogenous oligopoly, differentiated oligopoly, and monopolistic competition. The goal of the company is assumed to be the maximisation of profit. Combined with the structural conditions of the market, the maximisation of profit is assumed to explain company action.

Followers of Bain include other structural and behavioural variables to explain actual competition, resulting in a theory of imperfect markets comprised of partly disparate theories where distinct structural characteristics are related to company action. Despite the fact that there is no uniform theory of competition in imperfect markets, several common aspects or assumptions can be discussed.

One common aspect is that competition is described as *structure* and *behaviour*, and that the analysis of competition is based on the connection between these two factors. Scherer (1980) uses the concept 'rivalry' to describe the actions of competitors. Individual actors strive to gain leading positions, thereby becoming rivals. Schmalensee (1988) argues that it is rivalry that occurs in imperfect markets rather than competition (which is found in perfect markets). The concept of rivalry therefore distinguishes between action in imperfect markets and action in perfect markets. The description of imperfect market structure is based on variables such as concentration, vertical integration, cost structures, intensity of R&D, and differentiation. These variables can contribute to the occurrence of different kinds of entry barriers. By identifying these entry barriers, an industry can be defined and demarcated.

Another common assumption is that companies act rationally. This assumption, together with the assumption that a company's primary

---

[1] This study ignores effects on society and focuses instead on the relation between structure and behaviour.

goal is to maximise profit, reduces the importance of the individual in organisational action. Dependence between companies is also reduced, as is the consequential lack of predictability of action. It becomes possible, therefore, to ignore the effects of time (or the process through which the connections between structure and behaviour in an industry develop). Scherer (1980) points out that although social structures are important for company actions, these variables are impossible to include in traditional economic analysis.

Recently, attempts have been made within the "new" industrial organisational theory to take into consideration both time and the fact that company action relative to competitors is the product of choice. Tirole (1988) includes game theory in order to develop dynamic models of competition, and he points out that the choice of company strategy is expressed in company action. Despite his criticism of Scherer's (1980) cause and effect treatment of the relationship between structure and behaviour in an industry, much of Scherer's reasoning is reflected in Tirole's writing.

Competition is described in the 'new' IO-theory as a game or a competitive play that takes place over a number of periods or phases. Structure determines the rules of the game, but as the game is complex, there is a number of strategies from which companies can choose.[2] The importance of strategic action (which is based on strategic choice) decreases as a result of the determination over time (by the rules of the game) of which action is appropriate (cf. Tirole, 1988). Instead of seeing company action as a result of the expectations of individuals, it is assumed that individuals in a company will eventually act rationally, resulting in optimal moves and subsequent counter-moves. Even if companies act irrationally during the first period, the rules of the game will force companies to act rationally after a number of periods (cf. Gilbert, 1989). Therefore, imperfect markets can, in principle, be treated in a similar way to perfect markets. The assumption of rationality thus effectively ignores the processes of competition mentioned in the previous chapter.

---

[2] A cautious approach is established, called the maximin approach. The opponents are assumed to attempt to reduce each others' market share or profits or other goals to a minimum, which in effect means that in order to minimise damage to themselves, companies must adopt a strategy that maximises counter-moves against competitors.

Structural Dimensions

As mentioned above, economic theory makes use of a number of dimensions of structure to describe different markets. Although this study does not focus on the connection between individual structure dimensions and behaviour, these dimensions can indicate differences between contexts of competition. A number of structure dimensions is discussed below.

The *degree of concentration* can be described in terms of number and size distribution. If no individual actor is dominant, but the degree of competition is considerable, companies will tend to adapt their actions to each other. Knickerbocker (1973) uses the concept 'oligopolistic reaction' to describe this type of action in oligopolistic industries, meaning that competition often emerges between competitors in the form of action and reaction. Yo and Ito (1988) express a similar argument, stating that competitors in oligopolistic industries tend to avoid intense rivalry, and become defensive in their actions. Scherer's (1980) explanation of action in oligopolistic industries is based on Chamberlin's (1933) theory that companies adapt to each other without explicit collusion arising between them. Companies are aware both of the prevailing interdependency and of the fact that conflicting action worsens the situation for all companies involved. Companies set monopolistic prices despite the fact that they are competitors, and in this way, they gain the best results.[3]

According to Kwoka (1979), co-operation is possible in concentrated industries with as few as two companies. Scherer (1980) argues that oligopolistic co-ordination ceases when the number of actors increases, or when the competitors' share of the market becomes asymmetrical. It is then probable that one of the actors may choose to ignore the effect of their decisions on rival actions, or that the competing companies may have differing views on what constitutes the most advantageous action for all concerned.

---

[3] Both Knickerbocker (1973) and Yo and Ito (1988) study companies' direct investments abroad, whereas Scherer (1980) relates structural conditions to company pricing. This book does not focus on the connection between structural conditions and action in specific areas. It is probable, however, that similar patterns of behaviour can be valid for types of action other than those studied by the above authors.

If the relative strengths of the companies are asymmetrical, a company can, through its strength and power (monopolistic power), manipulate the other companies in the industry (cf. Porter, 1983 and Scherer, 1980). Knickerbocker (1973) holds that, in a similar situation, the other companies will react only to the actions of the leading company(ies), without considering other factors. However, these companies do not necessarily need to adapt to the leading company, but can instigate measures that in the long run may mean that they themselves become leading companies. Worcester (1957) proposes that the leading company must have specific advantages in costs or advantages in customer loyalty for its position not to be undermined by the actions of its competitors.

Vertical integration and *contracts* between different actors in an industry affect the structure of competition and behaviour in an industry. Transactions between vertically related actors can occur in various forms from direct market solutions (i.e. purchases determined by price mechanisms) to hierarchical solutions (where the actors are integrated into one and the same organisation). There are a number of different forms of contracted transactions that lie between these two extremes (cf. Carlman, 1986; Coase, 1937; Leblebicic, 1985; Williamsson, 1975 and 1981; Williamsson and Ouchi, 1981). According to Williamsson (1975), transaction costs determine company choice to purchase from actors in the market, or to integrate vertical actors in the hierarchy (i.e. in the organisation). Gadde and Grant (1984) emphasise the technical and financial advantages that arise from the integration of different phases in the production process. It can be strategically important to control critical inputs and/or customers. However, complete integration and the drawing up of contracts lead to greater uncertainty and greater risks. Long-term contracts involving joint investments and mutual adaptation also reduce company flexibility (cf. Tirole, 1988).[4]

The *costs structure* in an industry is related to the production technology used, to the volume of a single product manufactured,

---

[4] There are, however, ways to reduce risk-taking and to increase flexibility. Gadde and Grant (1984) discuss 'semi-integration' as being the situation where a certain share of the total demand is purchase by the company itself. The advantage of this type of integration is that it gives rise to competition between the internal unit and external actors. It also provides the company with increased power in negotiation. Furthermore, both the internal unit and the external actors contribute to technological development and knowledge, which increases the transferral of technology from one company to another. Similar advantages and an increased flexibility can also be obtained through written contracts with a number a suppliers (cf. Tirole, 1988).

and to the size of the company (cf. Scherer, 1980). Product specific advantages can be obtained through large-scale production. Advantages that arise from having a large range of products can be achieved if several products within the range of products exploit the same production resources. Synergy effects arise between several units within the company that manufacture products in different product areas — so-called 'multi-plant' advantages. The first two types of advantage arise from the ability to create volume in operations and in that way reduce costs. This can be described in terms of the so-called 'experience curve'.[5] The ability of a company (or the opportunities that the company may have) to reduce costs and increase production efficiency affects company action and the development of competition in an industry.

Research and development, i.e. the development of more efficient production technology and new products, change the structure of an industry continually. Rivalry between competitors and the opportunities of imitating innovations are two important driving forces behind intensive developmental action. There is a paradox in this, in that these two forces are also the greatest obstacles to profitable product development. By patenting new products, companies attempt to obstruct their competitors from imitating new products. The importance that is given to patents in theoretical literature does not, however, match their importance in actual competition. The advantage that is gained as a result of research and development can be described in terms of the time that it takes competitors to copy the product. In order to sustain advantages gained from its own product development, the company must develop a leading technological position by continually developing new products (cf. Chandler, 1991).[6]

---

[5] Porter (1984) criticises the use of the concept 'experience curve', meaning that two separate concepts are mixed together; economies of scale due to volume, and learning through development in product and process technology. Porter distinguishes between three ways of describing learning within an industry. Learning can be described as a function of the cumulative volume through which those companies that expand most rapidly are also those that reduce their costs fastest. Learning can also be considered as being a function of time, i.e. the longer a company has existed within an industry, the greater the number of opportunities that company has to reduce the costs of its operations. Learning can also be seen to be a function of the exogenic development of technology by which new machines and materials increase the opportunities for achieving economies of scale.

[6] For a survey of empirical studies in this area, see Kamien and Schwartz (1982) and Stoneman (1983).

According to Schmalensee (1988), there is a connection between the amount of capital that is invested into research and development and the amount of successful project developments. A company in a dominating position can generate capital for development projects by extracting monopolistic prices. A company's product development is therefore linked to company size and to the degree of dominance in the industry. Opinions differ, however, on how company size affects product development. Arrow (1962) argues that the incentive to develop new products decreases when a company has achieved a dominating position in the industry. The other companies, on the other hand, are stimulated by the opportunities presented through the 'relaxation' of the leading company to develop new products and to gain a dominating position themselves, with subsequent profit opportunities.

The degree of differentiation in an industry is another dimension that affects the intensity of competition. Through the development of product or market niches, competition can exhibit certain monopolistic elements, which provide greater possibilities for companies to act independently (cf. Porter, 1980). To use Scherer's (1980) terminology, heterogeneous products make oligopolistic co-ordination difficult. Scherer argues that if the products are completely homogenous, it is only price that can vary between competitors, and that decisions about price must therefore be co-ordinated. If the products are heterogeneous, on the other hand, co-ordinative decisions become complex and more difficult, which can result in a more active rivalry between the competitors. According to Scherer (1980), a company can differentiate itself from its competitors in four ways; through location, distribution, service offered, and through physical characteristics or created product image.[7] Unlike price, differentia-

---

[7] Companies can also differentiate themselves from each other through their market communication. Friedman (1983) views advertising as a tool with which to affect demand: Through advertisements and other market information, a company can differentiate its products and thereby develop a monopolistic situation within certain segments. If the companies operate in areas where a close connection between the amount of communication and the company's market share exists, advantages can be gained by developing economies of scale in market communication. Opinions are also voiced that contrast with this view, stating that advertisement and market information contribute to the negotiated strength of the customer. Schmalensee (1988) argues, however, that advertisement and market information can give rise to both effects. Market communication also occurs through different information channels, for example via retailers (cf. Porter, 1979). The choice of distribution net also affects the opportunities for differentiation.

tion is difficult to imitate, often requiring considerable investments in the improvement of quality and brand loyalty.

A number of dimensions have been discussed above that affect the structure of competition in an industry. These can give rise to entry barriers which in turn demarcate the industry. The actors within an industry are distinguished from other potential actors outside the industry by these entry barriers. Potential actors established outside the industry can also be described as being competitors, but the interaction that occurs between established actors and potential actors is described as being indirect. If there are considerable entry barriers 'guarding' an industry, not only is the entry made more difficult, but so is the exit. Consequently, actors become more dependent on the market in which they operate, and therefore have fewer alternatives for action to choose between.[8]

Despite the fact that IO-theory assumes that competitors act rationally (which has meant that the analysis of processes of interaction is not based on the competing companies' interpretations and experiences of competition), this theory, or rather these theories, are nonetheless useful in the description of competition at an aggregated level. This argument is supported by studies of competition that show the connection between structure and action in an industry.

However, if the process of competition is to be understood, analysis must be taken to an inter-organisational level. Hunt (1972) for example achieves this by highlighting the heterogeneity between actors within an industry, launching the concept 'strategic groups'. He argues that the analysis of symmetrical groups of companies within an industry can better explain rivalry in an industry. The inclusion of strategic grouping, in the discussion of structural and behavioural dimensions discussed above can be used in order to describe competition at an inter-organisational level. The next section will therefore discuss the occurrence of strategic groups.

Strategic Groups

Research on strategic groups has developed rapidly over the last few years, and can be described today as a multi-disciplinary area of research. Strategic groups have been highlighted in IO-theory, in organisation theory, and in strategic research (see McGee and

---

[8] Cf., for example, Aghion and Bolton, 1987; Sölvell, 1987 and Yip, 1982.

Thomas, 1986 and Thomas and Venkatraman, 1988 for a review). Studies of strategic groups within an industry are described in strategy literature as attempts to combine theories based on structural conditions prevalent in an industry with theories based on company-specific pre-conditions. In this way, the heterogeneity of an industry and the uniqueness of the company are both taken into consideration. Theories on strategic grouping are based on the assumption that intra-industry firm heterogeneity exists. Heterogeneity is a prerequisite for the building of strategic groups; i.e. *groups of companies that differ from other groups in the same industry with regard to at least one vital strategic dimension.*

The Identification of Strategic Groups

Strategic grouping of companies can be identified from similarities and dissimilarities in the companies' strategic action in different areas, and from the companies' relative strengths (cf. Barney and Hoskisson, 1990). In their survey of research on the subject, Thomas and Venkatraman (1988) state, however, that there is no uniformity in the treatment of strategic groups in empirical research settings. Hunt (1972) identifies groups of companies within the same industry based on symmetry in cost structures, on the degree of product diversification and differentiation, and on the degree of vertical integration. Newman (1978) also includes the degree of vertical integration in determining strategic groups. McGee and Thomas (1986) argue that the companies' product and market diversification, their geographical diversification, and the occurrence of horizontal and vertical integration, constitute important dimensions in the determination of strategic groups. Hatten and Schendel (1977) determine the boundaries of strategic groups from the relative actions of companies within the same product or business area.

Studies of strategic groups therefore differ from each other in the choice of dimensions for drawing up the boundaries of strategic groups. In many studies, the traditional dimensions used to demarcate industries are generally considered to be of importance for competition within strategic groups. Cluster or factor analysis is then undertaken to discover strategic groups that differ according to the chosen dimensions (cf. Barney and Hoshisson, 1990).

This approach can be criticised, in that the predetermination of strategic dimensions important for the development of competition within a strategic group is doubtful. An alternative method would be to identify strategic groups from both superficial and in-depth knowledge of an industry that is well-grounded empirically. Such an approach is not appropriate for the generalisation of findings or generated theory, but is better suited for the description of actual competition within an industry (cf. Barney and Hoskisson, 1990 and Bogner and Thomas, 1993). It is the individuals, the companies, and the strategic interaction between the actors that determine which dimensions are relevant for competition.

Rivalry Within and Between Strategic Groups

One of the arguments for studying strategic groups is that the dependent relationships that characterise the imperfect market can be more evident in smaller groups within an industry. Hunt (1972) states that the asymmetrical action of companies reduces the potential for tacit agreements between the actors in the entire industry. Departures from 'expected oligopolistic action' are usual, considering the asymmetry involved. Tirole (1988) comes to the same conclusion, and describes interaction between competitors as a game that occurs in conflict between competitors, rather than in collusion. McGee and Thomas (1986) state that collusive action occurs within smaller strategic groups, rather than within an industry as a whole.

Two types of competition can be distinguished if the prevalence of strategic groups is considered; competition within strategic groups, and competition between strategic groups. Caves and Porter (1977) argue that companies within strategic groups tend to avoid rivalling action, taking measures that, combined, aim to contribute to mobility barriers and thus maintain and strengthen the strategic group. They suggest that strategic groups are delimited by 'mobility barriers' that make movement or mobility within an industry more difficult. Company action causes barriers or obstacles that make entrance into a strategic group difficult. Within the same strategic group, a company can develop a greater understanding for the mutual dependency that exists, and thus come to consider mobility barriers as shared assets in the competition with actors in other strategic groups. Members of the strategic group foster implicit understandings; symmetry between a smaller number of actors therefore reduces active competition within a strategic group.

Kwoka (1979) and Kwoka and Ravenscraft (1986) come to slightly different conclusions. They argue that problems of co-ordination can arise between a smaller number of companies, and that symmetry in company size produces active competition. Cool and Derrickx (1993) express similar thoughts, stating that if high mobility barriers exist, competition can be more considerable within a strategic group than between strategic groups. Entry into, and exit from, strategic groups thereby becomes more difficult. If the resources and abilities to act are equal between the companies (i.e. symmetry between actors), the companies are able to contest each other's product and market positions. No individual company owns a specific competence that is difficult to imitate. In this sense, active rivalry develops between companies that ought to have the pre-conditions to act in collusion. A strategic group can also be asymmetrical in certain dimensions, but symmetrical in others (cf. Barney and Hoskisson, 1990). However, no unambiguous response to the question of how the degree of symmetry between competitors in a strategic groups affects competition has yet been provided.

Rivalry between strategic groups is described as being more considerable than rivalry within a strategic group. Porter (1979) writes that the degree of rivalry depends on "the number and size distribution of groups, the strategic distance between groups and market interdependency among groups" (Porter, 1979:218). Rivalry increases if the industry consists of many strategic groups equal in size and if there is a strategic asymmetry among groups. Asymmetry does not have the same impact upon rivalry if the groups differ due to their positions of the industry. However, strategic distance (i.e. asymmetry in the strategic actions of the companies), other things being equal, increases the rivalry among strategic groups, in that tacit co-ordination is more difficult. Asymmetry in action affects the degree of rivalry to a greater extent if strategic groups operate within the same markets. Rivalry decreases if strategic proximity exists between the strategic groups. This is because proximity gives rise to an increased awareness of the mutual dependency that exists between the companies.

To summarise, it can be stated that the same variables used in discussions of structure within an industry are used in discussions of structure within strategic groups. The major difference is that existing theories of strategic groups analyse competition at an inter-organisational level, i.e. at a level between the industry as a whole and the individual companies. The greater part of existing literature is, however, both structural and static. Interaction over time is not discussed to any great extent.[9] The issue at the heart of this book

---

[9] A process perspective has been used in a few studies of strategic groups within an industry. These studies will be discussed further in the section '*Competition and Change Over Time*'.

emphasises the necessity of studying competition as a process over time. Theories of strategic groups are therefore not sufficient to achieve the purpose of this study.

However, knowledge about strategic groups within an industry can be helpful in distinguishing and describing the conditions of competition in which the process of competition takes place. The discussion so far emphasises that the degree of symmetry between actors and between groups of actors is of importance for competition. A common thread in studies of competition within and between strategic groups is that the degree of activity in competition is related to the degree of similarity between companies and their actions. There is, however, no unanimous theory of how symmetry and activity are related to each other.

It is agreed that symmetry between companies and the degree of activity in competition is of great importance for the context of competition that develops within an industry and within a strategic group. The descriptive structure variables discussed earlier can be considered to be variables with which to describe symmetry between actors. There are no generalisable assertions or models that à priori state which strategic dimensions are decisive for the determination of the extent of activity in competition within an industry. Empirical identification of dimensions that can describe competition within a specific industry is therefore needed. Individual companies, and their actions relative to each other, must be used as points of departure in order to understand which dimensions are of importance for competition (cf. Aharoni, 1993 and Rumelt, 1984).

Barney and Hoskisson (1990) are of the opinion that companies and their unique characteristics, rather than groups of companies, ought to constitute the points of departure for gaining an understanding of strategic action. Companies act relative to each other in an environment that is characterised by uncertainty and multiplicity of meaning, which leads to the necessity of making strategic choices. Through their own efforts, companies can develop new resources and new pre-conditions for competition. Companies therefore both affect and are affected by their structural conditions. The next section discusses competition from a business strategy perspective.

Competitive Strategies

There is a considerable amount of strategy literature, differing both in focus and in fundamental theoretical assumptions (for a survey of literature regarding strategy and management see Chakravarthy and

Doz, 1992; Gabrielsson and Paulsson, 1991; Quinn, Mintzberg and James, 1988 and Wåhlin, 1993, amongst others). In the strategy literature that directly discusses the competitive strategies of companies, two slightly different points of departure can be identified; the analysis of competition from IO-theory models, and the use of the war metaphor to describe both the competitors' relative positions, and the threats and opportunities provided by the environment.[10]

Despite the fact that these points of departure may differ, they are strongly deterministic by nature, in that the analyses of threats and opportunities in the industrial environment and internal preconditions result in the determination of successful action and of strategies that provide the best result (cf. Ansoff, 1965 and Hofer and Schendel, 1978). Companies are assumed to develop a planned strategy arising from a number of individuals in leading positions within the companies formulating strategies that the rest of the organisation is assumed to implement.

Caves (1980) indicates the importance of using economic models in the analysis of the external environment, and Porter (1980) transfers arguments from IO-theory to the area of strategy environment (see also Montgomery and Porter, 1991). Both Porter (1980) and Scherer (1980) make use of a number of structural variables to discuss companies' competitive strategies, and analyse competition within an industry based on what Porter calls competitive forces. These forces are composed of the intensity of rivalry, the bargaining power of suppliers, the bargaining power of buyers, the threat of new entrants, and the threat of substitutes. As both suppliers and customers affect competition, they constitute an important part of the context of competition. In this respect, Porter is very close to network theory's approach to the description of an industry's environment as a system consisting of a number of actors that, in a number of ways, are related to each other. However, Porter's focus still lies in competition, and companies' strategic actions are determined from structural conditions.

The use of the war metaphor takes its point of departure in the company's position in the market, and discusses different attack and defence strategies. By focusing on relative strengths and by discussing suitable strategies for the different categories, Kotler (1991) distinguishes between market leaders, challengers, followers, and

---

[10] For a more thorough discussion of different types of strategy, Bengtsson and Skärvad (1988) is recommended.

niching companies. His point of departure lies in military attack and defence strategies that have been used in various situations of war throughout history. The use of the war metaphor in discussions of competitive strategies is based upon the assumption that companies strive to develop dominance within their industry (cf. Quinn, 1988).

The competitive strategies that are discussed are to a great extent comparable with the behavioural patterns discussed in IO-theory. If one company dominates the market, and if a challenger exists within the market, a pattern of move and counter-move can be expected to occur where the challenger attacks and the dominating company defends its position (cf. Durö and Sandström, 1985 and Kotler, 1991). If the dominating company develops competitive advantages by being more cost-efficient or by differentiating itself from its competitors, other companies are enabled to find their own niches by focusing on core competencies. In this way, dependency decreases between the actors, and they can act independently to a greater extent. A company that is not a market leader and that has not found its own niche can become a market follower by imitating and adapting to its competitors.

Although the analyses of competition discussed above can provide valuable understanding of the situation in which a company acts, the determination of company action based on structural conditions can be criticised. Aharoni (1993) argues that the school of theory based on structure and relative positions treats the companies as 'black boxes' and assumes that the environment is stable. Uncertainty and ambiguity in competitive relations are discussed, but the analysis of competition is assumed to make the reduction of uncertainty and the determination of action possible. The processes that occur internally and/or externally are not discussed. The dependency between companies in imperfect markets implies that competitors affect each other through their actions. The interaction between competitors is therefore of central importance.

To summarise, theories dealing with competitive strategy can provide indications of possible patterns of interaction in competition between companies, such as move and counter-move, attack and defence, adaptation and imitation, and independent action in well-delimited niches. Patterns of interaction can be used to distinguish and describe different types of contexts of competition. However, an understanding of how these patterns of interaction emerge and affect the continuing competition within an industry or within a strategic group must include the dimension of time (discussed in the next section in terms of the process of competition).

THE PROCESS OF COMPETITION

The schools of theory discussed above focus on the connection between competitive structure and competitive behaviour without analysing in more detail the relationships, interpretations, and experiences that develop and affect interaction between competitors. The competitive process in itself (see Figure 1.1) is only discussed in passing. To understand how interaction and competitive play between competitors is built up, the assumption that individuals (and consequently organisations) act rationally must be abandoned. The identification of a company's choice of strategy (the definition of the strategy a company should chose relative to its external and internal environments), is not sufficient to be able to understand competition. Interaction between competitors must be seen as a process over time, where individual competitive measures are undertaken, interpreted, and reacted to.

Unlike the structural theories discussed earlier, evolutionary and Schumpeterian economists view competition as a dynamic process that changes over time. Interaction between competitors is described as the motor in an evolutionary process that brings about changes on many different levels, from products to companies, from industries to nations (see for example Schumpeter, 1942; Nelson and Winter, 1982; Dosi, 1988 and Loasby, 1991). It is therefore important to study interaction and the conceptions or interpretations of competition if an understanding of the development and dynamics of competition is to be gained. These aspects of competition are discussed in more detail in the following sections.

Interaction and Relationships Between Competitors

An alternative approach to competition and interaction between competitors is to focus on the relationships that develop through interaction. Network theory focuses on relations among actors (cf. Håkansson, 1982 and Hägg and Johansson, 1982, amongst others), but it is primarily the relationship based on economic exchange between vertical actors (i.e. between buyer and seller) and the co-operative relationship between competitors that are discussed (cf. Nilsson and Nilsson, 1992).

When competition is discussed from an interactive perspective, two slightly different trains of thought can be identified. Competition is described as being indirect relationships within a network (cf. Yamagishi, Gillmore and Cook, 1988) or as competition between networks (cf. Jarillo, 1988). Jarillo (1988) states that by taking advantage of the opportunities that the building of networks can provide, actors can develop competitive advantages relative to other actors. Competition can thus be described in terms of strategic networks as a competitive advantage. Competitiveness depends upon the company's ability to interact with the most efficient suppliers, in order to obtain the best resources.

Jarillo's (1988) description of networks as partly closed systems that compete with each other can be questioned, based on the fact that many competitors interact with the same actors. Networks of companies do differ in certain respects, geographical location for example, but they are integrated in other respects. Although certain competitive situations could be described as competition between networks, networks are integrated and difficult to separate.

Competitive relationships are also described as a result of indirect interaction between competitors. Indirect interaction arises, for example, from two competitors interacting with one and the same customer. Direct interaction (i.e. when a competitor instigates measures primarily aimed at affecting other competitors) is not discussed, though direct relations between competitors must be assumed to exist as they actively undertake measures relative to each other. Relations among competitors therefore cannot solely be described as resulting from competitors' relations with vertical actors. Although direct economic exchange does not occur between competitors, more subtle social and psychological factors can be included in relationships among competitors (Porter, 1990).[11]

In an attempt to consider direct interaction between competitors, Easton (1987) and Easton and Araujo (1992) have distinguished five types of relationships among competitors.[12] Easton (1987)

---

[11] Mitchell (1973) discusses the contents of direct relations, and argues that relations are composed of three elements; communication, exchange, and expectations. Johansson and Mattson (1987) point out that relations are built on a mutual preparedness to interaction, in mutual knowledge and respect of each other, and on the desire of the actors to effect reciprocal investments in the relationship. According to Håkansson (1982), a relationship between two actors arises when they interact, and interaction between two actors occurs when an exchange has taken place. Relations are therefore linked directly to the exchange of different types of resources. In the interaction between competitors, no exchange takes place in the traditional sense, which is why interaction and relationships between competitors are described as indirect.

[12] Easton also describes the structural relationships that can be linked to the different types of competition.

bases these relationships on the motives for interaction and on the intensity of the relationship. The five types of relationship are termed conflict, competition, co-existence, co-operation, and collusion. *Conflict* and *competition* are described as being active relative to competitors, though they differ from each other in that conflicting competition is object-oriented (i.e. competition is centred on destroying or incapacitating the opposing counterpart). Easton argues that a competitive situation is conflicting when it consists of only a few actors and where one of those actors dominates the situation. Competition, on the other hand, is goal-oriented, i.e. is not intended to inflict damage on other competitors, but is intended to achieve other goals, although reaching these goals may affect other competitors negatively.

The three other types of competition are more passive by nature. *Co-existent* competition occurs when the actors do not consider each other as competitors, and therefore act independently from each other. Competition through tacit *collusion* arises in the agreement between actors to avoid any active competition which can be regarded as being destructive. This form of competition includes such practices as illegal pricing agreements. *Co-operative* competition is passive, in that the companies involved strive towards the same goals. Despite this, they do compete with each on a fundamental level, and only when both parties can achieve their goals better through co-operation, do they chose to co-operate. Competitors can co-operate by working together and by different kinds of strategic alliances. However, co-operation can also be part of a more active form of competition. If competition between a number of actors is very intense, which in itself speaks against co-operation, individual companies do tend to form alliances with one of their competitors; two companies can together compete more successfully against a third (cf. Leontiades, 1989). Although companies may co-operate in some areas of the market or in some areas of operation, they can still be each other's competitors in other areas.

Easton and Araujo (1992) discuss the issue of when a relationship can be considered to have arisen between competitors. To base a relationship solely on interaction would mean that no competitive relationships arise between actors that co-exist. Easton and Araujo argue that the competitors' relative positions should be the basis for deciding on the existence of a relationship between actors. If one company's position is relative to another, a form of relationship can be considered to have arisen between them. In this sense, competitors that co-exist can be considered to have potential for interaction. By defining competitive relations from companies' relative positions, action that is independent of other actors can also be included as part of a competitive relationship. Awareness, another dimension of company interaction, therefore becomes interesting. Competitors can both consciously and unconsciously act independently from each other.

Network theory's discussion of the nature of relations among actors emphasises closeness, or proximity between actors as being of particular importance (cf. Kock, 1991). This can be related to Porter's discussion about the importance of domestic rivalry, in that proximity between competitors increases dynamism within an industry. According to Kock (1991), closeness between actors increases in that they interact with each other. Proximity also increases through the development of different kinds of bonds between the companies, and through acceptance of the prevailing pre-conditions for interaction. In the same way, proximity between national competitors can be assumed to vary according to which types of relationship that develop between them.

In summary, it can be stated that relationships, which differ in their inherent qualities, can develop between competitors that interact. Relationships differ from each other because companies' positions and goals are to a varying extent relative to the positions and goals of their competitors. The intensity of interaction and the proximity between competitors also affect relationships among competitors. To achieve a greater understanding for the interaction between actors and the relationships among competitors, an analysis must therefore not only include relative action, but also expectations, interpretations, and the way that a company's own positions and goals are related to those of its competitors. The next section will therefore present a discussion on the pre-conceptions of competition that exist and develop in companies.

Conceptions About Competition

Decision-makers in organisations scan the environment to determine which actors constitute the company's competitors, to interpret their actions, and, from previous interpretations and experiences of competition, to instigate different kinds of competitive moves. Thus, conceptions of competition at both individual and group level are related to an organisation's competitive moves and to the competitive play that develops between competitors. How individual and organisational conceptions that arise as a result of individual perceptions affect competitive play within an industry must therefore be discussed further.

The Effects of Individual Perceptions on Competitive Play within an Industry

Competitive plays arise through strategic interaction between competitors. The question of what drives a company to act in a specific way therefore becomes interesting to study. Mintzberg (1988) states that a company's strategic action cannot solely be described as the formulation and implementation of strategy, because individuals do not act completely rationally, and because unforeseen events occur that change the chosen or planned strategy. By taking the individual and the uncertainty that characterises the environment into consideration, as Mintzberg (1988) does, unforeseen events, the actions of others, and internal processes can lead to a realised strategy that differs from the intended strategy.

The figure below illustrates the relationship between intended strategy and realised strategy. Mintzberg and Walters (1984) state that realised strategy consists of both intentional (deliberate strategy) and unintentional (emergent strategy) actions. Intended strategy is based on expectations of the future nature of pre-conditions for action. As it is impossible to predict with certainty how the company itself will act, or how competitors, customers, and other actors will act, the pre-conditions for competition change, and new situations arise. Both intentional and unintentional actions therefore take place and are integrated into the realised strategy.

Mintzberg (1989) argues that action can precede thought, and that the realised strategy is formulated afterwards. In this sense, the assignment of meaning is an important part of the realised strategy. The meaning that is assigned to the situation within an industry and

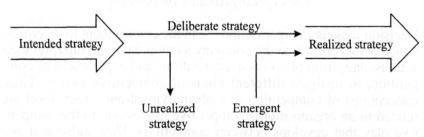

Figure 2.1   Different Types of Strategy (Mintzberg and Walters, 1984; p. 258)

to the company's own opportunities is expressed both as plans for the future (i.e. intended strategy), and as meaning assigned to action after the event (i.e. realised strategy). Mintzberg (1989) argues that formulation and implementation of strategy is interwoven in a continual process of learning, resulting in the development of creative strategies.

According to Weick (1979), pre-conceptions, or cause maps, about the environment are generated through a process of learning that transforms data into information, and action into experience. Pre-conceptions and/or experiences of, in this case, competition and organisational pre-conditions are manifested in action, according to both Mintzberg's and Weick's reasoning. In this sense, mental images and concrete action can be seen as two sides of the same coin. Weick (1979) describes this relationship by presenting the idea that an individual acts while thinking, i.e. that action and thought occur simultaneously, or that a dialectic relationship exists between action and thought.[13]

Is it the Individual or the Organisation that Acts?

If Mintzberg and Walters' (1984) reasoning is taken as a point of departure for an understanding of competitive play as realised strategic interaction (which consists of actions that partly are planned and partly emerge), a number of important questions arise. One issue concerns how interpretations and experiences of competition are related to the companies' relative actions. This issue implies a second question, which focuses on whether it is the individual or the organisation that thinks and acts.

If an individual's experiences of competition are considered to affect the competitive play that occurs within an industry, the individual's perceptions of competition must then be considered to be

---

[13] Other authors, for example Isenburg (1986) and Downey and Brief (1986), argue that thought precludes action, and thought steers or influences action. Describing thought and action as being simultaneous can be considered to be more accurate, however. It is not possible to ascribe meaning to an event before the event has taken place. Rather, one can talk of expectations or intentions, which can be compared to what Mintzberg meant with strategy. It is only when events can be consigned to history that they can be given meaning. Through the ascribing of meaning, action gives rise to experience, which in turn affects action. Strategic thought and strategic action can therefore be seen as two parts in a process of reciprocal effect. The development of strategy should therefore be seen as a continual process, where experiences and historical behavioural patterns are integrated with the plans and goals that set up for the future.

expressed in the company's competitive moves. According to Cyert and March (1963), it is the individual and not the organisation that thinks, formulates goals, develops images and visions, and acts. Thinking and acting individuals within the organisation differ from each other. Individuals at different levels and in different departments in the company meet different environments, which provide them with different experiences (cf. Lawrence and Lorch, 1967). The meaning that is ascribed to competition can therefore vary from individual to individual. Consequently, competitive play is complex, and cannot be described in terms of rationality.

> Strategy-making also takes up the complex issue of collective intention — how an organisation composed of many people makes up its mind, so to speak.
>
> (Mintzberg, 1989; p. 25)

To base the discussion of a company's action on the individual's perceptions and interpretations of competition gives rise to a number of problems,[14] such as how individual interpretations of competition can produce collective (or company) action. A certain degree of consensus or legitimacy for the interpretations must be present, if these interpretations are to lead to collective strategic action. The interpretations that most of the organisation can hold to be 'true', or that a few individuals (because of their legitimacy in the organisation) can gain a hearing for, do not necessarily have to be held by every individual in the organisation. The organisation can be said to live its own life, acting without that action being necessarily linked to individuals. (cf. Gioia and Sims, 1986)

Brunsson (1985) defines organisational action as those measures that are taken by several members of the organisation in co-operation with each other. The individual must feel motivated to act, he must have certain expectations, and must commit himself to participate in action, for collective action to develop. Louis (1981) and Smircich (1983) argue that individuals in the organisation act in concordance with each other, in that experiences they have in common lead them to develop similar interpretations of, in this case, competition. This has led to the development of an approach

---

[14] The meaning that individuals ascribe to their own operations can differ from one individual to another, and this can be explained by the fact that individuals exist and act in different contexts. This can lead to internal conflicts and to the development of sub-optimised goals in different functions of the organisation.

that sees the organisation as a system of shared meanings. The above discussion indicates that consensus is required for collective strategic action to occur. There are, however, a number of contrasting opinions on the effects of conflict on development.[15]

Weick (1979) is of the opinion that both differentiated interests and experiences and common collective action can exist simultaneously, which can be explained by the internal processes between individuals in the organisation. He describes the processes whereby individuals with differing goals can come to an agreement over means, and can then act in a specific way. When this has occurred over a period of time, the goals of the individuals tend to become increasingly similar. However, the creativity of an individual that, over time, develops ends that are common to those held by other individuals leads to individuals that develop different means to achieve these ends. This in turn leads to goals that once again come to have different meanings for different individuals. The individuals then have to agree again on means to achieve their (different) goals. In this way, the process is continual. Based on the above, individuals can be in agreement or disagreement over goals yet at the same time agree to act in a specific way.

Another important explanation for the development of collective strategic action is the power or legitimacy that certain individuals can wield in the organisation. Weick (1979) argues that a minority that is part of the majority acts and forms the actions of the organisation. It is the legitimacy or authority in terms of legitimate power of this minority that is important. Conflicting perceptions do not obstruct collective action if a minority that has developed legitimate power in leading position exists. Weick is of the opinion that meaning is often retrospective, and, in this sense, groups in organisations ascribe meaning to collective action after the event, giving rise to shared meanings.

The reasoning outlined above is also true of the occurrence of a rationalisation after the event by individuals with leading positions in

---

[15] Burns and Stalker (1961) argue that the relationship between individuals in the organisation span between competition and co-operation. Organisations develop this polarisation as a result of their hierarchical constructions and functions. It is evident that conflicting pre-conceptions do exist. Lawrence and Lorch (1969) claim that conflicts are more evident in environments that, as a result of their multiplicity, create uncertainty. They argue that the ability to solve these conflicts by integration is a prerequisite for the organisation to achieve good results. Others argue that conflict is necessary for innovativeness and creativity to develop.

the organisation. This contributes to the explanation of why it is the leaders in the organisation that to a great extent participate in the formulation of organisational action. Spender (1989) suggests the occurrence of an organisational rationality, which can be compared to Weick's (1979) reasoning that meaning is retrospective. He criticises the total rationality of 'Economic Man' and the bounded rationality of 'Administrative Man', suggesting an organisational rationality that can be described by the concept 'Choosing Man'. Based on Barnard (1968), Spender is of the opinion that a leader's primary task is to reduce the uncertainty that meets the organisation.[16] By making use of their roles as co-ordinators, leaders can, to a great extent, affect the perception, interpretation and creation of meaning that follows from action. Leaders can affect organisational rationality.[17]

It therefore appears relevant to understand competitive moves and competitive play within an industry from the point of view of the leaders in the organisations. The 'Choosing Man' can steer strategic action, either as a result of legitimate power or as a result of being an intimate part of the common values, the organisation's rationality. Depending upon the structure of the organisation and the degree of decentralisation and control, the leaders of different departments within the organisation can be of varying importance. As different parts of the organisation meet different environments, and therefore can develop different perceptions of competition within the industry, 'Choosing Man' (or the leaders of the different sub-systems) should be studied in order to gain an understanding of the process through which collective action develops. This in turn facilitates an understanding of the competitive play that takes place in an industry. Collective patterns of interpretations also develop as a result of interaction between several companies. This type of collective or common pre-conceptions can also be of importance for competition within an industry.

---

[16] Barnard (1968) links uncertainty to three different sub-systems or economies. These are the physical resources, the individuals that are employed, and the relationships between the organisation and its environment. Spender terms these the physical, the motivational, and the social sub-systems, which all incorporate parts of both the environment and the organisation. By co-ordinating these three sub-systems in meaningful and co-ordinated activities, a self-preservational system can emerge, i.e. the organisation and organisational action.

[17] This can be compared to March and Simon's (1958) discussion about man striving for rationality, despite not being able to be considered completely rational. 'Rationality' can only be achieved by individuals post-reconstructing rationality.

Collective Conceptions at An Aggregated Level

A number of different concepts have been used to describe collective conceptual frames among actors that operate in the same environment, such as 'industry recipes', organisational fields, industrial wisdom, and atmosphere. Powell and DiMaggio (1983) argue that organisations develop common mental models by directly or indirectly imitating each other, which can explain the similarity between the companies' competitive strategies. These common mental models can also be likened to what Nelson and Winter (1982) describe as routines. The occurrence of collective conceptions has also been highlighted in recent developments of theory about strategic groups (cf. Bogner and Thomas, 1993; Fombrun and Zajac, 1987 and Reger and Huff, 1993, amongst others). Porac et al. (1989) suggest that if an understanding of the action of competitors is to be gained, it is important to base studies on cognitive groups within an industry rather than on normative descriptions of strategic groups from an IO-theory perspective.

Spender (1989) suggests that so-called 'industry recipes' developed by decision-makers within an industry lie behind action. These recipies can be considered to be a set of collective norms or rules that govern competitive action within the industry. Porac and Thomas (1990) argue that it is the managers' perceptions of whom their competitors may be and of which strategic dimensions that are central for the companies that determine action. Conceptions of which action is successful or expected in the industry can also limit the number of opportunities that are perceived to be available for the companies.

Porac et al. (1989) identify both collective and conflicting conceptions within the same group, and come to the conclusion that collective conceptions or mental models developed in the group affect the companies' strategic action.

Network theory describes the overall atmosphere within a network as a major aspect of relationships between actors. The interaction that arises, combined with the nature of the relationships, gives rise to more subtle interpretations of interaction. The concept 'atmosphere' is used to describe these experiences and the climate in which the exchange between buyer and seller occurs. Atmosphere is described as a number of interwoven variables that are defined according to the environment, to companies that interact, and to the process of interaction between companies.

One of the main aspects of the relationship which may be affected by conscious planning is the overall atmosphere of the relationship. This atmosphere can be described in terms of the power-dependence relationship which exists between the companies, the state of conflict or co-operation and overall closeness or distance of the relationship as well as by the companies' mutual expectation.

(Håkansson et al., 1982; p. 21)

The use of the atmosphere concept centres primarily on the discussion of the relationships between buyer and seller, and not the relationship between competitors, which means that the concept is not directly applicable to this study. However, the idea of an atmosphere existing in a network can be transposed and used to describe the climate that develops in different contexts of competition. As with atmosphere, conceptions of competition can be affected by the actors that participate in competition, by the interaction that develops between them, and by the context of competition within which this interaction occurs. The nature of the relationships (whether they are characterised by conflict or by harmony), the proximity or distance between actors, and individual and collective expectations of the competitors are examples of a number of factors that can characterise the different climates of competition.

To summarise, the conceptions or experiences of competition are expressed in the companies' competitive moves, which in turn constitute part of the competitive play that develops in specific contexts of competition. Although individuals are taken into consideration, it is not the aim of this study to focus on the process through which the interpretations of these individuals develop. To understand the nature and dynamics of competition, the conceptions and perceptions of individuals must be related to company action. It is the conceptions of interaction and of competitors that lie behind the companies' competitive moves. By relating the conceptions that develop within an industry or strategic group to action over time, an understanding of the nature and dynamics of competition can be gained. Two alternative ways of approaching competition are discussed above, specifically to approach competition from interaction and the relationship between competitors, and to study the conceptions of competition. The third part of this chapter deals with the changes in competition that arise from interaction between competitors.

COMPETITION AND CHANGE OVER TIME

Competition in an industry can change and take on different characteristics during different periods or phases in the history of an industry. The dynamics of a specific context of competition are expressed in the mobility that develops as a result of competition, but also as changes in competition. It is therefore of interest to study changes in competition over time.

According to Fiegenbaum and Thomas (1993), changes can arise as a result of the strategic action of companies, or as a result of the process through which companies progressively adapt to their environments. Nelson and Winter (1982) follow a similar line of reasoning, and state that routines and changes to routines are a vital part of the dynamic evolutionary processes that successively change the industry. Routines are described as certain accepted ways of doing business which both limit and facilitate the individual companies' strategic action. Routines can also be considered to be common conceptions on how things ought to be done, which develop and change over time through interaction between the companies (cf. Loasby, 1991). In discussing changes in companies' choice of strategy or accepted routines, a number of issues become interesting, such as "What is the driving force behind change?", "Does change occur gradually or through dramatic redirection?", "Does change involve a company moving from one industry or strategic group to another, or does it consist of actors within an industry or strategic group changing their relative positions?".

Change and Inertia to Change

The driving force behind change within an industry is usually described as differences in profit potential in terms of long-term return on investment (cf. Caves and Porter, 1977 and Porter, 1980 amongst others). Profit rates vary between different industries and strategic groups, and this provides the incentive to change strategy to areas of operation that offer a higher profit or return. Porter (1980) is of the opinion that intensive competition[18] forces the

---

[18] The forces of competition that Porter (1980) discusses are the threat of new entrants, the power of negotiation of buyers and sellers, the threat of substitute products, and competition between competing companies.

level of profitability to a minimum level, which can be compared to the profitability in a situation of perfect competition. Companies then seek new opportunities and higher profit margins in new areas, in this way stimulating strategic change.

In discussing a company's competitive strategy, its position in the market is considered to be an important driving force to change. Competitors attempt to conquer a better position in the market through different offensive strategies, while leading actors defend the position that they have already conquered. A company's strategic action is based, however, both on the pre-conditions within the industry, and on the company's goals and internal resources. Rumelt (1984) argues that the point of departure for understanding the differences in competitive positions between companies must be the company and its assets. It is the company's ability to develop its uniqueness and its resources which gives rise to change.

A number of arguments can be put forward that criticise the idea that change occurs as a result of differences in profitability between industries or as a result of companies striving for better positions. A company's operations can be based on goals other than profit maximisation or the gaining of leading positions in the market. Changes can also be obstructed or delayed due to the company's resource allocation and to the process through which change occurs (cf. Fiegenbaum and Thomas, 1993).

This raises another issue, namely the characteristics of processes of change. Nelson and Winter (1982) and Dosi (1988) describe the restructuring and development of companies and industries in terms of an evolutionary process that is driven by technological development. The evolutionary standpoint is shared by Quinn (1980), who describes the companies' adaptation to changing conditions in the environment as an evolutionary process. Companies adapt successively to changes in the environment. Contrary to Quinn, Miller and Friesen (1980; 1982) are of the opinion that changes in the strategic actions of companies are dramatic and infrequent. An innate inertia exists in companies, which means that they tend to 'continue as before'. These companies therefore do not instigate measures to adapt to ongoing changes in the environment until they are faced with acute crises. Change is therefore dramatic.

Inertia to change is also related to the process through which mental models of market relations develop and change (cf. Loasby, 1991). Collective conceptions and knowledge develop successively within organisations and strategic groups, and these conceptions are hard to change, which is why action and the formation of groups are often stable over time. Fiegenbaum and Thomas (1993) state that;

> These groups have distinct recipes and are bound together by such forces as mobility barriers, institutional forces and social enactment mechanisms. Consequently, groups will also tend to exhibit momentum over time particularly in regard to the key strategic decision variables.
>
> (Fiegenbaum and Thomas, 1993; p. 74)

When it is discovered within the organisation that the organisation's strategy is not suited to the conditions that prevail within the market, competitors are observed, not only within the strategic group but also in competing strategic groups. By observing the actions of competitors, a limited number of alternatives for action, or 'industry recipes', can appear. These are perceived as being possible alternative strategies. Companies are thereby able either to develop action that differs from that of their competitors but that is in accord with the action that occurs in other strategic groups, or to seek out new alternatives for action.

Fiegenbaum et al. (1990) argue, however, that there is a number of competitive positions, and that these are stable over time. Change consists primarily of actors moving between these different positions. Öster (1982) is of a similar opinion, arguing that mobility between strategic groups may be minimal, but despite this, actors within the same strategic group can still act more or less successfully (cf. Hatten and Hatten, 1987). Despite the similarity between actors in certain important strategic dimensions, and despite the fact that these actors form a strategic group, their profitability and return of investment differ. Such differences can become incentives to change within the strategic group.

Patterns of Change

Apart from determining the causes of change and the reasons behind inertia, patterns of change can also be discussed at a higher level of aggregation. Strategy literature describes the life-cycle of an industry based on the assumption the companies strive to maximise profits. With the help of the life-cycle of an industry, Porter (1983) describes how industries emerge and develop as a result of the potentially high levels of profit margins that attract new entrants to the market, and how these industries concentrate and eventually disappear as new industries develop and replace them. During the process, the number of competitors decreases both as a result of mergers and acquisitions, and also because actors withdraw from the arena. The saturation of the market also results in the concentration of customers and suppliers, which gives those remaining a greater bargaining power. The threat of substitutes increases, the technology used is well-established, and the risk of new technological solutions appearing also increases. This can be compared to organisational ecology's cyclical descriptions of the birth, life and death of organisations (cf. Hanna and Freeman, 1989).

If the description of the life-cycle of an industry is related to the previous discussion of action under different structural conditions, action during the first phase of an industry's life-cycle can be assumed to be active. The industry is fragmented and action is active, which means that the possibility of manoeuvring becomes considerable. During the process of maturity of the industry, the degree of structuring and concentration increases. In industries with only a few actors, companies are assumed to undertake direct moves and counter-moves relative to their competitors. If the degree of concentration increases further so that the structure of the industry can be characterised as a duopoly, competition can involve an increasing degree of co-operation, and become more defensive and more passive.

Based on structure-related theories, strategic interaction can be assumed to develop from independent active action, via move and counter-move, to more defensive action between competitors over time. However, this description of the development of an industry can be criticised, both because the point of departure is not based on the individual, and because the theories are too deterministic. Development is described as transition, where the industry changes from one stage to another, which can be compared to the neo-classic focus on equilibrium.

Håkansson (1992) chooses a network perspective, and thus takes into consideration the relationships that develop between actors. He describes the processes of change in a network both as continual and partly random processes of interaction, and as processes that more systematically change the network over time. Håkansson (1992) has identified a number of developmental processes within networks, but is of the opinion that these are not predictable, rather the strength of the processes is determined from the human forces that support the processes. Over time, however, more general patterns of change can be identified.

Changes in networks can be described as two general developmental processes of combining resources and activities — structuring and heterogenising — and two process involved in the struggle for control within the network — the tendency to hierarchisation and the process of ectriction. The structuring processes arise from the attempts to develop existing ways of combining activities and resources, which leads to the strengthening of relationships that are already established in the network. The process of heterogenising, on the other hand, is a result of the arrival of new actors, and the breaking down of old relationships. The process of building hierarchies is related to the structuring process, but this process is formed by the actors' attempts to control existing relationships. The number of actors that control the network decreases at the same rate as the process of building hierarchies takes place, whereas the process of ectriction involves the distribution of power to an increased number of actors.

Håkansson (1992) argues that the above processes are interwoven, and that combined, they form a pattern of change in the network as a whole. In areas where the structuring of the network increases, the process of building hierarchies also increases. The concentration over time, described in the discussion on the life-cycles of industries, can be compared to with the processes of structuring and the process of building hierarchies. Håkansson does not see the process of change as having a start, several steps and an end. He argues that the structuring process in turn can lead to new actors entering the market, and to a process of heterogenising, which also means that control over the network is extricated. Consequently, the development of these processes cannot be predicted or foreseen. In the above discussion of the importance of the individual, it was noted that human commitment to the different processes determines how change in the network will be expressed.

The chapter so far has presented a discussion based on different perspectives on patterns in the process of change. The industrial life-cycle metaphor provides a description of change within an industry at an aggregated level, but provides only limited understanding of the mechanisms that operate in change. It seems more relevant to treat change as an unpredictable process over time. By analysing competitive play in an industry and how it changes over time, an understanding of the dynamics of competition can be gained.

THEORETICAL POINTS OF DEPARTURE OF THIS BOOK

Chapter One stated that the purpose of this book is to provide an increased understanding of the nature and dynamics of competition by analysing the process of competition (see Figure 1.1). Different points of departure have been discussed earlier in this chapter. These seemingly disparate points of departure can, however, contribute to an increased understanding for the issue at the heart of this book. Despite the fact that these schools of theory differ from each other in their approach, it is the same phenomenon (i.e. competition) that is studied.

The first part of the chapter dealt with the schools of theory that relate competitive action to structural conditions in an industry in order to determine action. Explanations at different levels can be found. Firstly, behaviour at the industry level is explained by analysing a number of dimensions of structure and relating them to competitive behaviour at specific points in time. Secondly, studies of strategic groups do not focus on the industrial level or on the organisational level. Research in this area attempts to integrate an industrial perspective with a company perspective, thus focusing on competition at an inter-organisational level. Most of these studies can be described as being structural. Thirdly, strategy literature that deals directly with companies' competitive strategies is based on the company and its actions, and discusses possible strategies based on the company's pre-conditions in relation to the surrounding environment.

The schools of theory named above only marginally take into consideration the interpretations and conceptions that develop about competition and the process through which interaction between competitors arises and develops over time. According to Lazonick (1991), three important factors are vital in understanding change over time, namely the individual, the importance of what he calls the 'business organisation', and the importance of the past.[19] Another limitation is that parts are studied rather than the whole, in that individual variables are analysed in isolation. This study, however, focuses on the nature and dynamics of competition, which means that the isolation of individual structural variables and the

---

[19] Lazonick discusses the development of entire nations' economies, but bases this on company action and the ways that companies join together in industrial systems. Although Lazonick analyses development on a macro level, his criticism of economic theory is transferable to analyses at industrial and organisational levels.

analysis of them relative to the companies' actions is insufficient for further understanding.

Structural descriptions of competition do not contribute to an understanding of the process of competition as such, but can provide valuable information on structural and behavioural dimensions by which different contexts of competition can be described. Structure and the actions of the competitors are interpreted and expressed in the actions of the individual companies, and in the interaction between the competitors. Therefore, the process of competition cannot be considered as being essentially different from structure or behaviour in an industry or strategic group (as is illustrated in Figure 1.1 in Chapter One by the white boxes).

It has been stated that the degree of symmetry between companies and between strategic groups affects competition. Therefore, *symmetry between actors* is of interest to study in order to achieve an increased understanding of the process of competition. Structure in an industry and the existence of strategic groups have been described with the help of factors such as vertical integration and costs structures. These dimensions can be considered to be variables with which to analyse symmetry/asymmetry between actors. The companies' actions relative to each other can also differ. In the discussion of competitive strategies, competition is described as being more or less active. The degree of *activity in competitive play* can therefore be assumed to vary and to affect the process of competition. Using the degree of symmetry between actors and the degree of activity in competitive play, different contexts of competition can be distinguished (see Figure 2.2 below).

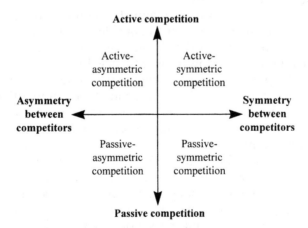

Figure 2.2 Different Contexts of Competition

There is one aspect of competition that has not been discussed in any great depth within traditional theories of competition; the process through which competition is formed over time. To be able to understand how different contexts of competition operate, described in terms of the degree of symmetry and the degree of activity, a more in-depth analysis of the processes of interaction between companies is needed.

In the second part of this chapter, a number of alternative approaches to competition were discussed, making it possible to study the process of competition. It was emphasised that studies of interaction between competitors ought to take into consideration the relationships that develop between competitors. An alternative approach to the study, aimed at increasing understanding of the process of competition, would be to analyse the relationships that emerge through the interaction between competitors in different contexts of competition.

The second part of the chapter also pointed out the fact that the conceptions that develop within companies and within the industry affect the process of competition. Studies of the actions of individual companies, and the interaction that develops between competitors should take into consideration the individuals that participate in the interaction. Individuals interpret and ascribe meaning to competition, which is expressed in the conceptions that develop within the company and in the actions of the competing companies. It is therefore important to describe the processes of interaction between competitors and to analyse them based on the interpretations of competition that are specific to the company and on those that are commonly held within the industry.

In order to be able to understand the nature and dynamics of competition, it is also important to consider change in competition over time. The third part of the chapter discussed change in competition, and Figure 2.3 below illustrates the link between competition at specific points in time to change over time in competition. It has been stated earlier that different contexts of competition can be distinguished from structural and behavioural dimensions; i.e. the degree of symmetry between competitors, and the degree of activity in competitive play. When these two dimensions are added to the figure first presented in Chapter One and represented below, competition at specific points in time can be illustrated as cross-sections in a continual process of change. By identifying the elements that constitute competition at a specific point in time, a static representation of the pre-conditions and frameworks within which the process of competition proceeds is possible to give. However, without com-

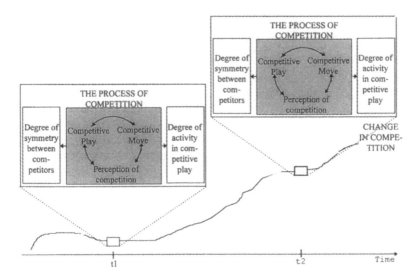

Figure 2.3 The Processes of Competition in Different Contexts of Competition at Different Points in Time, and the Change in Competition Over Time

parison over time, a static description of competition cannot provide an increased understanding of the nature and dynamics of competition. The process of competition is affected by the competition that has been previously pursued, just as the competition that will be pursued in the future is affected by a continual process of change.

To summarise, traditional theories of competition state that competition can differ depending on the degree of symmetry and the degree of activity in interaction, which make possible the distinction of different contexts of competition. However, to gain an increased understanding of the nature and dynamics of competition, alternative points of departure are needed. It appears necessary to analyse the processes of interaction, and to take into consideration the conceptions of competition that develop within the company and within the industry. Competition and its development ought also to be analysed from a historical perspective, thereby making possible the identification of patterns of change that can be understood based on the process of competition at different points in time. It is with this perspective on competition in mind that a number of industries will be described and analysed in the following chapters of this book.

3. To Study Interaction between Competitors

The discussion in the previous chapter showed that the degree of symmetry between competitors and the degree of activity in interaction between competitors were related to each other. Four separate contexts of competition can be identified from these two dimensions; namely *symmetric-active* competition, *symmetric-passive* competition, *asymmetric-active* competition, and *asymmetric-passive* competition. Industries with similar structures can therefore be studied based on differences in the degree of symmetry between competitors and in the degree of activity in competition.

However, the theoretical discussion presented in Chapter Two does not fully answer the research question at the heart of this book. Existing theory does indicate that symmetry and activity are important dimensions of competition, but does not determine how competitors interact within a specific context of competition and thereby stimulate the development of industries. Nor is it possible to determine from existing theory what specific aspects of symmetry and activity are important for competition within a particular industry. These specific aspects must therefore be identified empirically, based on interaction among competitors within different contexts of competition.

ABOUT THE STUDY

To answer the research question posed in this book, I decided to study a small number of industries in-depth, this for two reasons. Firstly, the case-study method provides the opportunity to gather a lot of data on a small number of study objects, which in turn makes possible multifaceted descriptions of competition (cf. Glaser and Strauss, 1967). Such an approach is needed if new qualities of reality are to be uncovered and if understanding for the interaction among competitors is to be increased. Secondly, an understanding of how competition stimulates development in internationally competitive industries requires not only knowledge of the histories of the industries, but also knowledge of how changes in competition over time have led to the development of companies' current positions. The case-study method is therefore appropriate, in that it allows both the description of structures at specific points in time (contexts of competition) and the description of processes over time (interaction between competitors) (cf. Normann, 1976).

Thirdly, individual interpretations of competition that arise in an industry and the way that individuals relate their own actions to those of their competitors are important aspects of competition. These interpretations can be accessed through interviews or conversations with managers in the studied companies, which necessitates establishing a close relationship between researcher and representatives from the studied companies. In that the analysis of competition focuses on the interaction between competitors, individual interpretations should be related to each other, both within and between competing companies, which in turn requires repetitive comparison. The above requirements can be fulfilled by the case-study method.

THE CHOICE OF INDUSTRIES

Which are, then, the three industries that are analysed in this book, and why have these particular industries been chosen?

An important criterion in the choice of industry is that the industries should be limited to those companies that compete with each other in the same product area. This allows their actions and reactions, i.e. their interaction over time, to be studied relative to each other. Hence, the term industry is used here to denote the sub-industries that are composed of competitors within the same product area (which includes manufacturers of close substitutes).

Another criterion of choice is that the companies in the chosen industry have developed prominent positions in the international market. The importance of national, or domestic, competition for companies that operate to a great extent in international markets is a pertinent element of the study of competition. The study of if, and why, national competition is important in the development of internationally competitive industries therefore becomes interesting. One sampling criterion that has been used here is that the export share of a company's total operations should exceed 50 per cent, and that these companies should be market leaders in a number of foreign markets. As international statistics are not always available for individual product areas, the companies' own assessments of their market share in other countries have been used.

A third criterion in the choice of industry lies in theoretical relevance, i.e. that the industry should contribute to the continued development of theory (cf. Burgess, 1984 and Glaser and Strauss, 1967). The first industry, the Front-loader industry, was chosen because this industry was assessed to be a good example of the phenomenon under study (cf. Glaser and Strauss, 1967). This assessment was based on previous knowledge of the industry from earlier contacts with the companies involved.[1]

Glaser and Strauss (1967) also state that the choice of further case-study objects should aim to maximise differences in order to be able to discover further qualities of the phenomenon under study. The advantage of this approach is that theoretical relevance increases, as does the number of opportunities for comparison among cases. In this study, the maximisation of differences through the study of other industries was based on the initial analysis of the Front-loader industry. The comparison of different contexts of competition requires the study of industries that exhibit different characteristics of competition. The Front-loader industry comprises two main companies, Ålö-maskiner (Ålö) and Trima, which are comparable to a great extent, and which actively compete with each other within a homogenous product area. Symmetry between the competitors in this industry was therefore considerable.

To maximise differences between the case-studies, the Rack and Pinion industry and the Lining industry were chosen. The Rack and Pinion industry consists of one main competitor, Alimak and three very minor competitors, namely Tornborg, Tumac and Malmqvist. Alimak dominates the industry, which to a great extent signifies that there was considerable asymmetry in the industry. The Lining industry consists of two competitors, Skega and Trellex (part of the Trelleborg corporation). This industry differs from the other two in

---

[1] Bengtsson 1987, SIND 1988:1, SIND PM 1988:7.

that there is considerable symmetry between competitors in certain respects, but also considerable asymmetry in others. A major difference from the Front-loader industry was that the competing companies were operative in a heterogeneous product area.

A number of former employees and persons that were assumed to have knowledge of the industries were contacted. These confirmed the assumption that there were major differences between the three industries, and that the competing companies in these industries had developed strong international positions.[2]

THE COLLECTION OF DATA

The data that has been collected and analysed has been of a mainly qualitative nature. Each case-study began with the collection of data at one company in the industry, and progressed to subsequently include the other companies. Data-collection began with an interview with the company's managing director and with a review of different kinds of documents. At the initial interview, the managing director was asked to describe the company's organisation and the history of the industry, and to describe the company's relations with customers, competitors, and suppliers. This interview, combined with yearly accounts, newspaper and journal articles,[3] the minutes of board meetings and other internal documentation, resulted in a chronological reconstruction of company action over time. The study of documents that were produced at the time provided information about the exact timetables for individual actions.

After this first step in the data-gathering process, the main collection of data was carried out in the form of interviews that were more structured than the initial interviews. To begin with, these interviews were of a more in-depth nature, but towards the end of the data-gathering process, interviews served as a forum to check details linked to specific events. The decision to proceed from a broad base of data-collection, through in-depth interviews to interviews with very specific and detailed questions, reflects the approach that

---

[2] A preliminary study was also conducted in the Lining industry, Delmar (1990).

[3] Articles concerning the Rack and Pinion industry covered the last 20 years and the articles concerning the Lining industry covered a period from 1947 to 1985. The ambition was also to gather secondary data from Trellex, but as Trellex is part of a larger corporation, information about its operations is not normally presented separately in the corporations annual accounts or in other internal material.

Glaser and Strauss (1967) consider necessary to make the generation of theory possible.

Interviews were carried out with departmental managers at the companies. The companies studied were mainly organised functionally, and some of them were also divided into product and/or market areas. The ambition of the study was to interview the managers of every department of the company, as well as individuals with overall responsibility for the management of the companies, but for practical reasons, certain departures from this ambition had to be made. At Trima, the construction, product, and development managers have not been interviewed because they had only recently been appointed to these positions. The production manager at Trellex was also not interviewed, as production is integrated with other companies or departments in the Trelleborg corporation.

Interviews were carried out with fifteen managers in the Front-loader industry, sixteen in the Lining industry, and ten in the Rack and Pinion industry (these managers were all managers at Alimak, the dominating company of the industry). The annual financial reports of the other Swedish companies in the Rack and Pinion industry were also studied. The collection of data began in 1984. The study of the Front-loader industry continued until 1992, though the most intensive period of data-gathering occurred between 1986 and 1990. The Lining and Rack and Pinion industries were mostly studied during 1991. Studies of secondary material regarding the companies were carried out during 1990, with follow-up interviews in 1992. The same individuals have been interviewed up to six times during the data collection period. Due to geographical distance, Trellex and Vreten were only visited once, which is why repeated interviews have only been carried out with a few managers. The interviews in all three industries have taken two to four hours, but the initial and unstructured interviews sometimes lasted up to six hours. In that no one objected, each interview could be recorded on tape. Complementary interviews in all three industries and a couple of initial interviews with managers at Trellex were carried out over the telephone. These telephone interviews were also taped.

Apart from interviews with individuals inside the organisations, interviews were also carried out with individuals that had previously worked in the industry. Two individuals that had left Skega were interviewed; the son of the founder, who had been Managing Director until 1980 (and had consequently had a great influence on the company), and another former Managing Director (in this position for most of the 1980s), who had worked for the company for many years. An individual that previously worked at Trellex with product development and market penetration was also interviewed. The above interviews have primarily been used to assess the correctness of the interpretations presented in this book.

ACCESS TO MANAGERIAL INTERPRETATIONS AND OPINIONS

The choice of interviews as a method of data collection accentuated the problem of which individuals to interview and how these interviews should be approached. The assumption made in section 'Do Individual or Organisations Act?' in Chapter Two, where departmental managers are assumed to be representatives of collective action and of the interpretations and opinions that lay behind measures taken by the firm, is reflected in the decision to interview every departmental manager in the studied companies. The issue of how the researcher should best gain access to these managers' interpretations and opinions about competitors and competition is of paramount importance, in that access is a fundamental pre-condition for the collection of qualitative data.

To gain access (according to Lincoln and Guba, 1985), the researcher, must first create or build a trust-relationship with 'gatekeepers' in the organisation, and then build trust between himself and the representatives of the companies. This is of particular importance in a study such as this where the method of study in itself can directly affect the relations among competitors. For one thing, it was impossible to grant anonymity to the companies involved, as they are known by their competitors. For another, it was assumed that a certain amount of doubt or suspicion would initially arise within the company, primarily due to the inclusion of the company's competitors in the study. Therefore, the initial contacts with each company presented, orally and in writing, the purpose and aim of the study for the companies' managing directors. To minimise any perceived risk with the researcher's contacts with competitors, each managing director was guaranteed the opportunity to read the material prior to any presentation for competitors and other interested parties, thereby providing him with the opportunity to correct errors and the right to erase anything in the case-descriptions that may be considered to be internal 'secrets'.

As well as access to the company, Lincoln and Guba (1985) consider that personal trust must be established at every new contact or interview. In a study such as this, trust is particularly important, as it is the opinions and interpretations of the individual that are central. As competitive relations comprise interpretations that are full of attitudes and values, it is important to maintain trust, and to provide the interviewee with security in the interview situation. Throughout the data collection in this study, the individual was guaranteed anonymity in the sense that he or she would not be directly referred to, or named, in the case-descriptions. Direct quotations have therefore not been used to any great extent, and no listings are given here of the individual respondents. Trust in itself is ultimately a result of personalities that meet and of what takes place in that meeting. The degree of perceived trust in the relationship built up with the respondents in this study can therefore be assumed to vary. Building trust takes a long time, which can explain why those persons interviewed a number of times provided more information over time, which in turn increased the depth of this study.

THE FIRST STEP — IDENTIFYING CONTEXTS OF COMPETITION

The main purpose of the empirical study is to scrutinise how competitors interact within a specific context of competition and thereby stimulate development within an industry. The context of competition that has prevailed during the different periods in the history of the industries must therefore be determined. To achieve this, the data must first be organised and systematised to give meaningful information, and second, dimensions have to be determined through which it is possible to identify contexts of competition that differ with regard to the degree of symmetry and activity in competition.

The Systematisation of Data

As suggested by Lincoln and Guba (1985), the data material has been coded and categorised to represent self-contained and independent meaning. This means that the researcher's own interpretations of what should be considered a self-contained meaning have steered the coding, and are therefore an important part of the analysis (cf. Johansson Lindfors, 1989). The primary systematisation of the material was based on the individuals that had participated in the interviews. In this way, it was possible to assess if the interviewees shared the same values and interpretations of one and the same event, and also to assess which individuals, and how many of them, expressed opinions on any one subject.

The descriptions given by the interviewees in the Front-loader industry did not differ from each other to any great extent. The descriptions given in the Lining and Rack and Pinion industries showed greater differences, as interviewees sometimes expressed completely conflicting opinions on certain subjects. Additionally, knowledge of certain events in the Lining industry was considerably greater within the departments that had been involved in them. Common to every company was that a small number of key individuals gave a rich level of detailed information regarding every event. Their opinions normally concurred with each others.[4]

The second systematisation of the material was based on the year that the specific events took place. This chronological classification is not without problems. Despite access to documents that provide exact dates, it is difficult to clearly determine when certain measures were undertaken. Product development is a case in point. When a specific point in time is given for the development of a product, it can be difficult to establish whether it is the start of the development work that is referred to, or when the patent was awarded, when the product was tested on the market, or when the product was finally launched. The same reasoning holds for the establishment of subsidiaries and co-operation with agents, etc. It has therefore not been possible to completely avoid ambiguities in the chronological descriptions. The competitors' somewhat contrary opinions on exactly when a product was launched is, however, just as interesting as exact dates. Conflicting opinions can reflect the struggle and the climate that exists in relations among competitors.

By analysing the chronological descriptions of events during the history of the industries, it was possible to identify of a number of periods or phases in the development of the industries. Processes of change are continuously present within industries, but these

---

[4] To convey this information in the case presentation in chapters Four, Five and Six, different words have been used depending on how many respondents have provided the information given. If the data only relates to descriptions made by one person, this is made clear in the text. The wording "the company considers that..." expresses an opinion held by 90 % or more of the interviewees in that company. The phrase "many..." is used when more than half of the interviewees hold the same opinion, and the use of the word "some..." indicates that less than half of the interviewees hold the same opinion. In those cases where opinions are not shared, and that can be referred to conflicts that are important to the competing companies, this is clarified by the text.

processes can be more or less stable. Change over time can therefore be described as comprising a number of stages with periods of stability that are interrupted as a result of considerable structural or behavioural change, as is illustrated in the figure below. One period or phase illustrated in the figure can also be split into several smaller periods, which in turn can be separated into further periods. Drawn to its limits, every individual event can be described as a period, as is also illustrated in the figure.

Each individual measure or structural change affects and influences the conditions for competition. The competition that occurs at every specific point in time can therefore be said to be unique. Consequently, the conditions for competition in the three industries have undertaken major changes several times. The interviewees also describe competition and development in the history as different stages. In the case descriptions that are presented in Chapters Four, Five, and Six, the descriptions of the histories of the industries have been based on the different stages in the industries' history of competition as described by the interviewees. As the character of competition is an expression of the actors' experiences and interpretations of the relationships that develop between them, the most important criterion for the division into phases is that it concurs with the actors' opinions on how the conditions for competition have changed over time. The division into phases has therefore been presented to a number of individuals in the three industries to be tested.

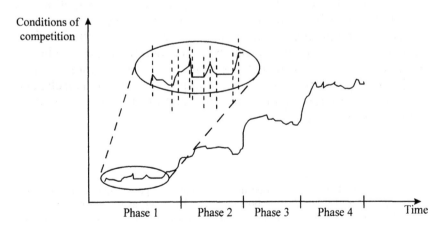

Figure 3.1 Development of Industries Over Time, Separated into Phases

Separating Different Contexts of Competition

As mentioned above, the development of the studied industries and of related changes in competition is described by the interviewees as a number of stages or phases which differ from each other according to the conditions for competition. The transition from one phase to another arises due to changes in the degree of symmetry or in the degree in activity, or in both. Competition during a specific phase can subsequently be classified as one of the four theoretically identified contexts of competition discussed in Chapter Two.

A number of aspects of symmetry and activity in the studied industries have been empirically identified as being of importance for the occurrence of competition. These aspects must be assessed in order to classify which context of competition has prevailed during a particular phase. Due to the approach of this book, it is of little interest to attempt to measure the 'actual' degree of symmetry and activity, (if indeed an 'actual' degree of symmetry and/or activity can be said to exist). Rather, it is the perceptions and interpretations of the actors concerned that are important, as interpretations and perceptions of reality (cf. Weick, 1979) ultimately lie behind human action. The aspects of symmetry and activity that have been found in the three case-studies presented in the following chapters will be discussed below.

1. The Degree of Symmetry Between Actors

By comparing the different phases of competition, it was possible to identify a number of differences of importance for competition in the three industries that are related to the degree of symmetry between actors; primarily, differences in the relative strengths of the companies, the companies' product choice, and their market choice. The interviewees described the companies as being more or less similar during different phases according to these three aspects, and this was considered to influence the conditions for competition within a specific phase.[5]

---

[5] Differences could also be identified in, for example, the purchasing behaviour of the companies, and in their production processes, etc. However, as these aspects were not related to competition and change in competition by the interviewees, they are not included.

1a) Differences in the Relative Strengths of the Companies

The differences in relative strength that are emphasised are related to differences in resources and to the companies' relative positions. There are a number of different reasons that lie behind the development of asymmetry in resources between the companies. Competitors, for example, can be asymmetric in their financial and personnel resources. A dominating actor has both greater personnel resources and greater financial resources due to its size, and this provides the company with greater possibilities for market penetration and product development.

Differences in the companies' resources can provide the pre-conditions needed for the development of economies of scale in different areas, which in turn can lead to the relative strengths of the companies becoming asymmetrical (cf. Scherer, 1980 and Porter, 1983). Diversification into related areas of operation may influence the relative strengths of companies through internal economies of scale in the form, for example, of more and better resources. Furthermore, differences in relative strength can be related to the ownership of the company. In that a competing company can be part of a larger corporation with other areas of operation, advantages over competitors may be gained, such as existing relations with customers, and financial support, resulting in asymmetry.

As well as differences related to companies' resources, the relative strengths of the companies can also be asymmetric if their positions are unequal. Positional differences can be either of a technical nature and/or related to market share. Leadership in either of these aspects confers increased strength to the company through the reputation and image that is innately connected with leading positions. If two competitors operate in several product and market areas, it is possible that both of these companies could be leaders, though in different technical and/or market segments. In such a situation, the companies' positions can be assumed to be comparable, and can be a result of the actors' mutual understanding of the dependency that exists between them. If, however, one company can be described as technical or market leader in significant product or market areas, the relative positions of competing companies are unequal.

Thus, symmetry in relative strength is determined by differences in resources and positions. The assessment of the degree of symmetry/ asymmetry in relative strength is based on the interviewees' descriptions of the conditions for competition. The basis for this assessment is described in Table 3.1 on the next page.

Table 3.1   Rules of Thumb for the Assessment of Symmetry and Activity

DEGREE OF SYMMETRY	Symmetry	Neither Symmetry nor Asymmetry	Asymmetry
Relative Strength R1 = Resources R2 = Leadership	All of the competitors see themselves as being equal, or considers itself leader/strongest	One company and a couple of individuals from the other companies describe a competitor as leader/strongest	Every company considers one company to be leader
Product Choice P1 = Product offer P2 = Product range	The competitors offer mainly the same type of product offer/range	There are some differences between the companies' product offer/range	There are major differences between the companies' product offers/range
Market Choice M1 = M. penetration M2 = M. segments	The competitors have mainly the same market choice	There are some differences between the companies' market choices	The are major differences between the companies' market choices
DEGREE OF ACTIVITY			
Interaction pattern	Move and counter-move, reactionary and conflicting action	Imitative action	Independent action, of which the companies are aware or unaware
Intensity	Frequent and rapid interaction = high intensity	Action is neither frequent nor slow = medium intensity	Slow interaction = low intensity
Scope	Competition in several areas = great scope	Competition in some areas = medium scope	Competition in one area = little scope

1b) Differences in Product Choice

The product choice of the competing actors can include both product offer and product range. The product offer of competing companies can differ despite the fact that they may operate in the same product area. If one company integrates several links of the value chain in its product, the company can be considered to be distinguishable from its competitors (cf. McGee and Thomas, 1986), which means that these companies are asymmetrical. In the same way, vertical disintegration can increase the degree of asymmetry between competitors. The product range of the competitors can also differ. One company may manufacture several versions of the same product, whereas its competitors might specialise in one version of the product. Differences can also be found in the price and quality of the products. One company may offer a wide range of products from simple low-cost products to advanced high-cost products, whereas competitors may concentrate on manufacturing either simple or advanced products.

In discussing symmetry/asymmetry in the companies' product choice, consideration must be given to the importance of the product area in question, as a company can operate within several product areas. If there are considerable differences between the companies' total product offer and/or product range, the actors are assessed to be asymmetrical. If competitors differ only within certain sections of their product offer and/or product range, actors can be considered neither symmetrical nor asymmetrical. If, however, the products are essentially the same, the companies can be considered symmetrical.

1c) Differences in Market Choice

Differences in market choice between the actors are related by the interviewees either to how the market is penetrated, or to which markets to penetrate. Market penetration can differ due to the companies' choice of distribution channel. Exclusive rights to marketing channels or to specific customers, for example, can be obtained by integrating further links of the value chain. Companies can even tie customers and distributors to themselves by contract, which intrinsically excludes their competitors. Market penetration may also differ depending upon the chosen entry mode abroad. The manufacturing and/or distribution of products directly through subsidiary companies, or indirectly via representatives, provides different pre-conditions for operations abroad. The choice of customers and geographical market segment may also differ. Companies can distinguish themselves from their competitors by selling homogenous or near-homogenous products to completely different market segments. Geographical differentiation can arise through either choice of different regions within a country, or choice of different national markets.

As well as focusing on the relative importance of different product areas in the assessment of the degree of symmetry between the competitors, attention must also be given to the extent and relative importance of different market segments. When, for example, an industry is relatively new, containing small companies that operate solely within the domestic market, regional demarcation can give rise to a high degree of asymmetry. As the industry and its companies grow, regional demarcation may decrease in importance, whereas the division of the international market affects to a greater degree the symmetry between competitors. This is explained by the decrease in importance of the domestic market for the total operations of the companies. The assessment of the degree of symmetry in market choice is based on the interviewees' descriptions of their market activities. The basis for this assessment is described in Table 3.1 above.

2. The Degree of Activity in Competitive Play

The style of interaction between competing companies and their experiences of interaction differ between the different phases of the industries studied. The descriptions given by the interviewees emphasise primarily the pattern, the intensity, and the scope of interaction. By focusing on the competing companies' pattern of interaction, the intensity, and the scope of competitive play, an understanding of the different phases and the transition from one phase to another can be gained with respect to the degree of activity in competitive play.

2a) Different Patterns of Interaction

A number of different patterns of interaction can be identified and distinguished in the case-studies; active interaction, neither active nor passive, and passive interaction. Two types of active competitive play (i.e. action-reaction pattern) have been identified. The first type of active competitive play can be described as move and counter-move. This type of active interaction is characterised by companies acting in response to each others' actions either in the same product or market area (move and counter-move), or within several areas (multiple moves). This is described as being reciprocal rather than conflicting.

The second type of active competitive play can be described as reactive and conflicting interaction. As above, this pattern of interaction can be considered an action-reaction pattern of interaction between competitors, but the competing companies interpretation of the action taken differs. Action taken by competitors is described as conflicting (action taken in order to inflict damage), whereas the company's own action is described as reactive (i.e., necessary in order to avoid the damaging effects of competitors' conflicting action). The actions of both individual companies and their competitors are therefore related to each other, though in different ways. Reactive and conflicting action, as seen from the interpretations of competing companies' actions, can be compared to what Easton (1987) describes as conflict. In the descriptions given by the companies under study, issues such as customer needs and the companies' own individual objectives are given as motives for individual company action (i.e. goal-oriented), whereas the actions taken by competing companies are interpreted as being taken in order to inflict damage (i.e. object-oriented).

Competitive plays that are neither active nor passive have also been detected in the studied industries. This pattern of interaction can be termed adaptation through imitative action. When competitors imitate the leading actor without this actor initiating any direct counter-moves, this is neither active nor passive competitive play. The actions of the leading actor are dependent on, for example, his own goals and customer needs, and therefore do not stimulate or necessitate direct counter-moves. Those companies that do imitate relate their moves to their competitors in order to adapt, not to inflict damage or to develop their own positions in the market (as in the two patterns of active interaction described above).

Competitive plays that are neither active nor passive can be compared to Knickerbocker's (1973) distinction between competition through action — reaction, and to competition where companies act solely in order to adapt to each other, as discussed in Chapter Two. The latter pattern of behaviour is described as defensive, whereas the former is described as active. Structure-related theories explain this phenomenon as being differences in the companies' relative positions. In some areas of literature dealing with strategy, imitation and adaptation is described as typical action for market followers, defined as companies that have not found their own niche, and that are not strong enough to challenge the leading actor in their industry.

The third and final type of competitive play identified in the three industries is termed passive interaction. Independent action, such as can be found in the three industries, signifies that competitive plays are passive. This can occur in areas where not all actors operate, and also where some of the competing companies differentiate their business from competitors by focusing on specific product versions. To a great extent, then, companies may act independently, despite operating within the same areas.

This line of thinking can be compared to Industrial Organisation Theory, in that competing companies can become passive in their interaction as a result of differentiation. Strategy literature describes this as focusing, or as the development of niches (cf. Porter, 1980). Easton (1987) states that companies co-exist if they are not conscious of competitors, or if they define them as not being worth attention. What Easton and Araujo (1992) describe as co-operation and collusion can also be considered to be passive competitive play, in that rivalry is only implicit in such interaction. Actors agree not to compete, which signifies that any active competition ceases. These formal or tacit (and, according to Easton (1987), illegal) agreements are, however, under constant surveillance by the actors concerned, to make sure that they are conformed to. No such form of agreement has been observed in the industries under study.

2b) The Degree of Intensity in Competitive Play

The pattern of interaction is not the only dimension that determines the activity/passivity of competitive play. Intensity, i.e. the frequency and speed of competitive interaction, is also of importance for the assessment of the degree of activity in competitive play. If intensive interaction occurs, the competitive plays are perceived as being active. The actions of competing companies in some areas and during some phases in the three industries are described as intensive, where the individual company's actions are experienced as being directly countered by similar moves from the competitors. If, however, companies only act relative to each other after a longer period of time has elapsed, competitive play is described by the interviewees as passive.

In the assessment of the speed of interaction, it is important to consider the time factor required to put measures into effect. For example, competitive play over product development is described during certain phases as intensive, even though counter-moves may only occur after several years. In other phases, delays of this length of time should imply that interaction is slow. This can be explained by the fact that the process of development takes a varying amount of time dependent upon how advanced and sophisticated the products are. A more detailed and, in a sense, more objective description therefore requires more data. For example, more information is needed about the time requirements for different product development projects. The assessment of the intensity of competitive interaction during different periods is based upon the respondents' perceptions and descriptions of the competitive plays that occurred in the studied industries, as it is the perceived intensity rather than an objectively defined intensity that affects actions taken by the competitors.

2c) Differences in the Scope of Competitive Play

Active competitive plays, neither active nor passive competitive plays, and passive competitive plays may occur simultaneously. By including scope in the assessment of activity in competitive play, the extent that a company's operations are exposed to active or passive competitive plays is taken into consideration. Even if move and counter-move occur frequently in one market area, it does not necessarily mean that the competitive play as a whole is active. Competitive play must also be of considerable scope. If companies continuously instigate measures within several product and/or market areas, the scope of competitive play can be considered to be considerable, implying that competitive play as a whole is very active. If, however, companies only compete within one area, the scope of competitive play must be described as limited, and thereby passive.

The definition of competitive play as being of considerable scope, due the number of areas within which companies should be active, has to be contextual. The number of possible areas in which to compete varies between phases and, of course, between industries. The importance of the different areas of operations for the industry may also differ. If competition is pursued within a number of areas of marginal importance, the scope of competitive play is not assessed to be considerable. Similarly, if competition is pursued in several important product and market areas, scope is considerable. Assessment must therefore be contextual, taking into account the specific competitive situation during a certain period in a certain industry.

The Assessment of Symmetry and Activity

To be able to compare the descriptions of the dimensions and changes to these dimensions, a number of rules of thumb have been set up for the studies included here. These rules of thumb and assessment criteria for the degree of symmetry between actors and degree of activity in competitive play are set out in detail in Table 3.1 above.

Three variables are used in the assessment of symmetry; relative strength (R), product choice (P) and market choice (M), and each are described from two aspects (R1 and R2; P1 and P2 and M1 and M2). The assessment of the degree of symmetry during a particular phase is based upon both aspects of each variable. If, for example, one phase in the industry history is heavily dominated by either symmetry or asymmetry (four of six aspects), relations between competing companies are assessed to be characterised by considerable symmetry/asymmetry. If, however, symmetry outweighs asymmetry without dominating, relations between competing companies are assessed to be characterised by symmetry and in the opposite case by asymmetry. If neither symmetry nor asymmetry outweigh each other, relations are assessed as being neither symmetrical nor asymmetrical.

The degree of activity is assessed in a similar fashion, though as each dimension of activity is described in one way only, the maximum number of aspects possible is three. If, for example, all three aspects are active, or if two are active and the third is neither active nor passive, competitive play is described as very active (and vice versa with respect to passive competition). If no aspect outweighs the others, competitive play is described as neither active nor passive. The degree of symmetry and the degree of activity is consequently described on a five-grade scale (see Table 3.2 below).

In order to assess both symmetry between actors and activity in competitive play, each aspect must be rated equally, and be assumed to affect competition to an equal extent. This simplification is not a matter of course, as examples in the case descriptions show, in that certain aspects are discussed more than others. However, due to the type of data gathered, the relative importance of the different aspects has not been weighted.

Based on the two dimensions and the particular aspects that will be used to distinguish different types of competition that have been discussed in this chapter, the context of competition during different phases for each industry can be described in Chapters Three, Four, and Five.

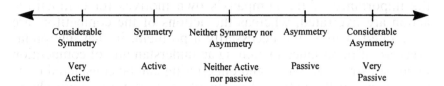

Figure 3.2 The Different Grades of Symmetry and Activity

THE SECOND STEP — UNDERSTANDING COMPETITIVE PLAY

Having identified which context of competition has prevailed during the different phases in the history of the three industries under study, it is possible to analyse the interaction among competitors and compare competitive plays in the different contexts of competition. A third systematisation of collected data based on action and how the competitors relate different measures to each other is therefore necessary.

A number of events or measures that are seen to be important for the companies and the development of the industry have been identified, and the data has been categorised accordingly in order to identify chains of actions i.e. competitive plays. In this way, the categories (cf. Glaser and Strauss, 1967) into which the material is systematised are based on the competitive plays that take place in 'competition in the Japanese market' and 'the development of the front-loader' for example.

Some measures can be part of several competitive plays, and in such cases, the data has been sorted into several groups. By using the interviewees descriptions of a certain event, i.e. their interpretations or perceptions of their own actions, the competitors' reaction to these actions, or the actions of the competitors themselves, the connections between events can be determined. In those instances where interviewees related action in a specific market to their own actions or the actions of their competitors in another market area, this type of competitive play is included within the specific market. In the descriptions of action in the three branches, the following three types of interpretations or perceptions can be distinguished; interpretations of one's own company's motives for instigating a specific measure, interpretations of how the competitors reacted to this measure, and interpretations of the motives and causes that lie behind the action of competitors. There is considerable risk that the importance of the company's own motives for competitive action are overrated, whereas the actions of the competitors are underrated. This is not necessarily a problem, in that interpretations are of importance in gaining an understanding of competition in an industry. Overrating and underrating can be considered to be expressions of the nature of competition during a specific phase. The interpretations of the own company's merits and shortcomings can indicate both how the company relates to its competitors and the nature of interaction. It is therefore important to collect information on the actors' ways of describing their own individual actions and those of their competitors, so that comparisons can be made, rather than to understand the concrete motives that were significant at the point in time of the action itself.

However, a number of problems arise when the point of departure rests in the descriptions and interpretations of historical courses of events by individuals. Gathering information on motives behind action is difficult. Responses to questions dealing with how the interviewee relates his own company's action to that of its competitor is coloured by the rivalry between the companies. It is therefore not possible to achieve a 'true' description of the motives. Nevertheless, perceptions of competitors and their actions and interpretations of how competitors react to the company's own action can describe the climate of competition that develops within and through the interaction among competitors.

Bearing Weick's (1979) and Spender's (1989) arguments as discussed in Chapter Two in mind, it seems probable, however, that the researcher can gain a relatively good understanding of competitive plays and their characteristics afterwards. Weick is of the opinion that differing opinions develop in organisations by groups assigning different meaning to collective action after the event. This can be related to Mintzberg's (1989) description of realised strategy. Spender's thoughts on the created organisational rationality as a basis for company action is yet another argument for focusing on the post-reconstructions that action gives rise to, rather than the actual motives for action. This post-reconstruction of meaning ought to remain in an organisation over a longer period of time than the actual motives for action, and therefore also ought to effect action and be easier to access through information from interviewees.

Another difficulty associated with the historical analysis of competition in an industry is that the actors in an organisation change over time. Only a few individuals have been found that have been members of the organisations during the entire histories of the industries. Memories of events in the past also fade over time, which means that descriptions and understanding of the competition that took place in the early days of the industry become meagre and less detailed. To compensate, individuals involved in the first phases of the industries' history that have left the organisations have also been interviewed. Furthermore, the analysis of data has concentrated on the information gathered regarding competition during the 1980s and 1990s.

This chapter presents certain methodological decisions that have been taken in order to respond to the research question posed in this book. The first step taken in order to analyse the interaction among competitors is to identify different contexts of competition. In the following three chapters, the contexts of competition during different phases in the histories of the three industries, and changes from one context of competition to another, are therefore described. The next step taken is to describe and analyse competitive plays that occur in different contexts of competition in order to understand the nature of competition and how competition stimulates or debilitates company development and industries. The competitive plays that have been identified in the studied industries are also described in the following three chapters, to be analysed in Chapters Seven and Eight.

4. The Front-loader Industry

Chapter Four provides a description of the development of the Front-loader industry, to establish which of the four contexts of competition that were presented in Chapter Two can be identified during different periods in the history of the industry.

The front-loader is a product that can be attached to tractors used in agriculture as an aid to the farmer, and the development of this particular product can be said to be inseparable from the development of the market. There are three companies that manufacture the front-loader in Sweden,[1] of which the two larger companies, Trima/Bergsjöverken (Trima) and Ålö-maskiner (Ålö), both hold strong positions in the international market. Vreten, the third company, manufactures considerably fewer front-loaders, primarily for the Swedish market.

The development of the Front-loader industry is described as four partly separate phases, which can be demarcated by distinct changes in competition at three particular points in time in its history. The first change took place with the internationalisation of Ålö, when the company, which at the time dominated the Swedish industry, almost completely abandoned the Swedish market in order to grow internationally. The second change occurred as a result of the concentration of the market to a few companies, mainly during the 1970s. The third change happened when Ålö

---

[1] Since 1989, a Danish loader has been imported by the Swedish Fiat retailer, Rosenqvist AB.

discovered that it had lost its dominating position in the Swedish market and began to re-penetrate the market, at the same time as Trima began its international expansion.

To provide the reader with an insight into the industry, this chapter begins with a brief description of the product and of the main characteristics of the major regions of the international market.

As ascertained in Chapter Three, an understanding of the nature of competition in this industry requires access to interpretations of competition held by individuals participating to some extent in the competitive play that occurs. These interpretations are presented in the form of a chronological case description, where the four phases in the history of the Front-loader industry are presented separately. It has been stated earlier that a more in-depth description of the most recent phase of an industry can provide greater insight into the nature of competition within that industry, and this phase is therefore treated in greater detail later in the chapter.

THE FRONT-LOADER AND ITS MARKETS — A BRIEF INTRODUCTION

The front-loader is a product attached to agricultural tractors. With the help of a front-loader, a farmer can, amongst other things, load gravel and deal with manure, which makes his work easier. Technically, the product is relatively simple. It consists of lifting arms that can be locked to the sub-frame of the tractor by an hydraulic coupling system. There is a tool carrier at the end of the lifting arms (designed as part of a simple attachment system) to which different tools, such as bale spikes and buckets, can be attached. The variety of tools increases the areas of use for the loader, which is manoeuvred by hydraulics. The front-loader is manufactured in different models with different lift capacities, lift heights and timing, and work angles. The hydraulic system is a strategically important part of the front-loader, as it is through this that the product has its lift and work capabilities. The attachment system is another important part of the product, because the sales success of the product is dependant on the fact that the front-loader can be attached to any type of tractor. It is therefore crucial to develop attachments for as many brands and models of tractor as possible.

The Front-loader industry is limited to those companies that manufacture the product described above (i.e. the front-loader, not the tractor). Internationally, the industry comprises two categories of actor, those that manufacture front-loaders for tractors up to 40hp, and those that manufacture front-loaders for tractors over 40hp. Customers in the Nordic countries mostly use the larger tractor, whereas both the smaller and the larger tractor are used in Europe and the USA. Swedish manufacturers have primarily specialised in front-loaders for tractors over 40hp, and the industry studied therefore comprises the competing actors in this product segment.

The demand in Europe for the product is heterogeneous, due to differences in the level of development of the agricultural industry. A country with a low level of mechanisation demands simpler loaders than countries with a high level of mechanisation, and a rationalised agricultural industry demands loaders that are more technically advanced. Regulations by the Swedish state have contributed to the development of an increasingly mechanised and rationalised agricultural industry, more so than in many other European countries. Sweden, for example, was the first western European country that developed and implemented an agricultural policy.[2]

Other countries in Europe exhibit varying levels of development, leading to varying levels of supply and demand of and for front-loaders. However, the European agricultural industry has developed towards increased mechanisation and rationalisation, and in pace with this rationalisation, the requirements from European customers have also increased. This places higher requirements on the technical and functional qualities of the product. Consequently, research and development in European companies has been driven forward, leading in turn to a decrease in differences between Swedish and European manufacturers.

The Swedish lead in the rationalisation and mechanisation of the agricultural industry has had consequences for the development of the Swedish Front-loader industry. Customer requirements have been high, which has led to the development of more advanced loaders, which in turn has given Swedish front-loader manufacturers an international competitive advantage. Swedish companies have therefore become international market leaders, as well as leaders regarding product quality, primarily Ålö and Trima.[3]

---

[2] Törnqvist, 1986.
[3] For the purposes of readability, Ålö-maskiner and Trima/Bergsjöverken are hereafter termed Ålö and Trima.

Table 4.1   Front-loader Manufacturers in Europe and their Markets

Company	Markets										
Ålö (Swe)	Swe	No	Finl	Den	GB	Ger	Fran	Ital	Irel	Neth	Aust
Trima (Swe)	Swe	No	Finl	Den	GB	Ger			Irel		
Vreten (Swe)	Swe	No			GB						
Veto (Den)	Swe			Den	GB						Aust
Danchif (Den)				Den	GB	Ger					Aust
Vilske (Finl)			Finl								
James (Finl)			Finl								
Tanco (GB)					GB				Irel		
Grays (GB)					GB						
Bamford (GB)					GB						
Stoll (Ger)					GB	Ger				Neth	Aust
Schaeffer (Ger)						Ger					
Frost (Ger)					GB	Ger			Irel		
Baas (Ger)					GB	Ger			Irel	Neth	
Hydrac (Aust)						Ger					Aust
Mailleux (Fr)							Fran	Ital			
Faucheux (Fr)					GB		Fran	Ital		Neth	Aust
Agram (Fr)							Fran				
Audereau (Fr)							Fran				

Source: Agrar-techni (1986) (own re-working)

Together, the two companies served 90 per cent of the Swedish market in 1990, with Ålö's financial turnover reaching 155 million Swedish kronor in 1990/91 (75% of this amount due to exports), and Trima's turnover the same year topped 185 million kronor (65% due to exports). Part of Trima's turnover also comprised agent sales of other agricultural machines and sales of hitch hooks.

Of Vreten's total turnover during the same year, only 16% concerned the front-loader product group.

The international industry is segmented geographically. Those companies that manufacture and sell front-loaders either operate in domestic or national markets within their own continent, i.e. American manufacturers do not sell their products in Europe, and vice versa. There is however one exception. Ålö operates on every continent.

Companies and local smithies oriented towards their own domestic markets manufacture simple mechanical loaders, at low costs and with minor service organisations, and can consequently sell their loaders cheaper than the Swedish companies. Apart from these companies, there are about ten larger international companies operating in Europe, manufacturing mainly the more advanced loaders. The table above presents a number of the largest competing companies in Europe.

North American companies operate only on their own continent. These companies are comparatively larger than European companies, which can be explained by the fact that the agricultural industry is run in a different way. Acreage is greater, and consequently, so are the machines. The technical quality and level of equipment of hydraulic tool-manoeuvrability is not demanded to the same extent as in Europe. Japanese competitors differ from their European and North American counterparts by manufacturing loaders for smaller tractors used in a more intensive agricultural industry, which can most closely be associated with smallholders. The agricultural industry on the Japanese island Hokkaido can, however, be considered to resemble the European and American industries, and in this market, there is a demand for larger loaders. It is to this market that Swedish manufacturers have the opportunity to sell their products. There is a number of Japanese manufacturers of larger loaders in their domestic market, but their efforts in product development have been limited.

DIFFERENT CONTEXTS OF COMPETITION IN THE HISTORY OF THE INDUSTRY

The development of the Front-loader industry can be described as four partly separate phases, illustrated in Figure 4.1 below. This section presents a brief description of the context of competition

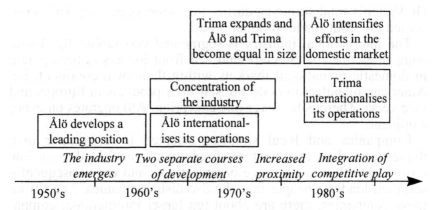

Figure 4.1   The Development of the Front-loader Industry

during each phase. The assessments of the degree of symmetry and activity between the competitors during different phases are summarised in Appendix 1.

Phase One — The Industry Emerges

The first phase of the Front-loader industry comprises the 1950s and half of the 1960s, and begins with the launch in 1947 of the first Swedish front-loader, resulting in the formation of Ålö-maskiner. With the success of the product, it was not long before other companies joined the market, and within two years, another company, Källve (today named Vreten), began to manufacture front-loaders. 1956 saw the establishment of Bergsjöverken AB, to be followed by Trima AB in 1963. The latter two companies were located in the same region in the centre of Sweden, and thereby became competitors within the same geographic area. As well as these four companies, a few other companies were established, resulting in an industry in the mid 1960s comprising approximately twenty manufacturers.

The competing companies were very asymmetric during the first phase, mainly due to Ålö having developed a strong position within the domestic market as a result of being the first company to launch a front-loader. By the middle Sixties, Ålö had a market-share of 35%, while the remaining 65% was divided approximately equally between the twenty smaller manufacturers. Ålö's domination of the industry in resources, technology, and market meant that the relative strengths of the companies were asymmetrical.

Most of the companies only manufactured components of the front-loader, which were then sold further down the chain. Bergsjöverken, for example, produced steel constructions, whereas Ilsbo Industries manufactured the hydraulics and Hellsäters bil handled sales. Ålö differed from the smaller competitors by manufacturing the entire product, which gave rise to asymmetry between the competitors. The loaders that were manufactured during this phase were simple constructions with a small number of versions. The differences between the companies' product ranges were therefore minor.

The mechanisation of the Swedish agricultural industry began in the early 1950s, which meant that farmers became the main customer category for front-loader manufacturers, rather than Trade and Industry. Ålö signed an exclusive contract with Svenska lantmännens riksförbund (SLR), an organisation owned by farmers, which agreed to represent Ålö in the entire Swedish market. SLR operated throughout the Swedish market, and Ålö concentrated their direct sales activities on the market in northern Sweden. Sales via SLR were successful, which partly explains how Ålö developed a leading market position in Sweden. The other Swedish manufacturers sold their products regionally, mainly in southern and central Sweden, selling exclusively via the private retail market. The Swedish competitors were therefore asymmetrical during the first period, both with regards to their market penetration and in their choice of geographic market segment.

To meet the requirements that farmers placed on the product, Ålö developed a new generation of loader, the Quicke. Despite the fact that Ålö patented this system, it took only a few years for other manufacturers to include a fast-coupled loader in their product offers, which Ålö explains as being due to the relatively simple construction of the loader. Ålö considered itself to be technical leader, and to exceed its competitors, the company considered it necessary to continue the development and improvement of the product. In 1964, a fast-coupled loader called the Hydro-Quicke, boasting hydraulic tool manoeuvrability, was launched. This product was also imitated after a few years. The intensity of R&D was therefore high in the industry.

To summarise, competitive play during this phase was both imitative and frequent, and therefore of no great scope, as the companies only competed actively in product development.

Phase Two — Two Separate Courses of Development

The transition between Phase One and Phase Two began when Ålö decided strategically to expand into the international market. This decision involved decisive changes in competition between the Swedish actors. The second phase, from the mid 1960s to the later part of 1970s, came to comprise two somewhat different courses of development. Ålö internationalised its operations at the same time as the industry concentrated and the number of domestic actors decreased. However, the effects on competition from the concentration of the industry mostly appeared later, which explains the context of competition that prevailed during the following phase.

During the first phase, Ålö had developed a dominating position in the Swedish market, and had 'lived its own life' alongside the other competitors. The company was faced with the choice to either continue its expansion in the domestic market, or to expand abroad. Ålö's sales through SLR in Sweden were considered satisfactory, as SLR had an established and stable market. Ålö did not therefore consider its position in the Swedish market to be under threat. A national expansion would have meant that the company would have been forced to compete actively in the Swedish market to gain market shares from the other front-loader manufacturers. This would have required the penetration of the private retail market, a strategy which was obstructed by the contract Ålö had with SLR.

Ålö had previously sold its products abroad on a number of occasions, with good results, and the owner of the company was also interested in expanding into foreign markets. His vision was that 'his' loader should be on offer in Great Britain and Europe, which many individuals within Ålö emphasise as being one of the reasons why the company has considerable export operations today. Ålö decided to internationalise its operations, and more or less 'left' the Swedish market to concentrate their business in a number of foreign markets.

Ålö's efforts abroad exceeded all expectations. By 1967, the quantity of exported loaders had reached the same levels as loaders sold in the Swedish market, and to date, export plays an increasingly important part of Ålö's total business. The goal of Ålö's efforts in internationalisation was to be product market leader. By the latter half of the 1960s, Ålö had contracted retailers in Ireland, Germany, Great Britain, Belgium, Austria, Spain, France, Switzerland, and Canada, as well as in the Nordic countries.[3] In 1970, Ålö was also able to contract a retailer in Japan, which was seen as a great step forward.

Parallel to the expansion of Ålö into the international market, the Swedish Front-loader industry underwent a process of concentration through a series of mergers, acquisitions and shut-downs. As described earlier, there were approximately twenty manufacturers in southern and central Sweden during the 1960s. After the concentration, only Ålö, Trima/Bergsjöverken and Källve remained. In 1969, Karolin Invest bought Trima, and shut down its production of loaders and in 1970, it acquired Bergsjöverken. Trima therefore came to function as a sales organisation for the loaders manufactured at Bergsjöverken.[4] For Källve, the loader product group was only a small part of company's total operations, and no acquisitions or mergers took place in order to increase market shares in the loader market.

Trima's expansion went in a diametrically opposite direction to Ålö's, in that Trima decided to intensify its efforts in the domestic market. Whilst Ålö built up its market organisation abroad, Trima developed its Swedish retail organisation, in order to increase its penetration of the private retail market, selling to farmers. The company also expanded in the industrial loader segment. Ålö, on the other hand, faced a less mechanised agricultural industry abroad, where the customers had fewer requirements on technology. By concentrating product development to the needs of its international customers, Ålö was no longer pressed into continuing product development towards more advanced loaders as before. Ålö's position as technical leader therefore became somewhat weaker. As a result of the concentration of the industry, the degree of disintegration decreased, which meant that the degree of asymmetry in the companies' product offer also decreased. Trima, for example, began to manufacture the entire product.

Ålö met completely different requirements abroad. The company competed with domestic competitors in different countries that did not have the additional costs associated with export. Ålö was therefore forced to reduce costs by manufacturing simpler products. Product development and product adaptation were also needed to meet the different requirements of the customers in the different countries. Ålö increased its range of products with the introduction of loader models that were newly developed to meet the demand from company's foreign markets. For example, extendible lift arms were constructed in 1968 for the French market. Ålö also developed

---

[4] Trima/Bergsjöverken is referred to as Trima in the continuing text.

considerable knowledge in coupling systems for different types of tractor, in order to adapt to European conditions.

The exposure to different requirements on product performance led to an increase in the range of products that Ålö offered to the international market, which resulted in asymmetry between competitors. At the same time, however, products on offer in the Scandinavian market became more equal as several of the other competitors began to manufacture the entire product.

The geographical division of the market during the second phase of the Front-loader industry increased as a result of Ålö's expansion at the international market. This strengthened the asymmetry that already existed between the companies in their choice of market segments. The asymmetry in the companies' market penetration that had existed during the first phase of the industry's history remained, as Ålö still delivered its products through SLR whereas Trima and Källve delivered their products through private retailers.

Despite the concentration of the industry, competition during Phase Two is not described as being intensive. The early company specialisation in the manufacturing of front-loader components meant that mergers and acquisitions were considered to be natural. Those companies that were shut down are described as being local or regional actors that had not succeeded in establishing a strong position in the market. These shut-downs were therefore not a result of intensive competition between the Swedish actors, but rather a part of a process of self-reconstruction within the industry.

Competitive play became very passive during this phase, in that imitative action in product development ceased, and due to competitors acting independently towards geographically demarcated market areas. Ålö had earlier served as a model for the other companies, but in that Ålö changed its strategic direction, this was no longer true to the same extent. Product development was therefore less affected by competition, and took on the nature of an independent course of development. A certain amount of competition did occur between the smaller actors, but the geographical divisions remained. This limited competition in the market.

In spite of the domestic expansion of Trima, Ålö took only limited counter-measures. The indirect penetration of the Swedish market, through a retailer, led to insufficient feedback of information. One other, and perhaps more serious, reason that no counter-moves were taken, was that Ålö's concentration on its international efforts was both time-consuming and demanding in terms of other resources. Competitive play therefore became passive, relative to the previous phase.

Phase Three — Increased Proximity
Between the Two Major Competitors

The period of concentration ceased at the end of 1970s and the effects of the process become clear during the third phase. The competing companies became aware of these effects during 1979 and 1980, which meant that they mentally perceived each other as a competitive threat. The reason that Ålö and Trima did not realise that the competitive situation was undergoing change during the second phase was that both companies were occupied by their own development, and ignored their competitors.

Trima and Ålö became equal in size and comparable due to their resources. They can therefore be described as being potential threats to each other in both international and national markets, although neither of them acted in a threatening manner. Trima became heterogeneous through acquisitions and fusions, which in turn limited its efforts to expand in international markets. Trima´s growth had brought about organisational changes, and its efforts had focused on building up the company and its market organisation in Sweden and Norway. Ålö, on the other hand, had lost its leading position in the Swedish market. The pattern of purchasing changed during the 1970s, and a greater number of farmers bought their loaders from private retailers. In that SLR's share of the market decreased, Ålö also lost shares in the domestic market. Ålö did not instigate measures to defend its leading position in the domestic market, which can be assumed to be due to the intensive process of internationalisation that the company pursued.

Trima had developed a strong position technically in the industry without any counter-moves taken by Ålö. Trima focused on the requirements for strength and quality placed on the loaders by the Swedish market (a market with tough conditions), and developed products to suit these conditions. The market had also developed from small, relatively powerless tractors to large four-wheel drive tractors. The tougher requirements placed on the loader by Swedish farmers were not responded to fast enough by Ålö. Ålö's loader became thought of by farmers to be suitable only for lighter work. Interviewees at Trima consider that their company took over the technical leadership during the third phase, as do some at Ålö (whereas others do not). Differing opinions regarding technical leadership can be interpreted as signalling that a technical leadership did exist, but that differences between leader and follower were not significant. The fact that Ålö had lost its leading position was very worrying for Ålö and the need to undertake counter-moves became obvious.

At the same time, the need to expand internationally became acute for Trima. Trima had expanded in the private retail market, and had thereby become comparable in size and strength with Ålö. Instead of competing with Ålö for SRL's customers, the company planned to intensify its efforts abroad. Despite Karolin Invest's ambitions to internationalise the company's operations, the share of exports during the 1970s remained modest, which is explained by some to be a result of the fact that these ambitions originated with the owners of the company, rather than in the company itself. In order to change the situation Trima introduced its loader in Great Britain in 1978.

Källve, the third company to survive the concentration of the industry, sold its products mainly within its own region, and continued with its differentiated operations (as it had done in the previous phase). The company remained a relatively minor competitor in the front-loader market, even though it had gained approximately 10 per cent of the Swedish market. Källve also began to export, but on a small scale and only to Norway and Great Britain.

In a comparison of the Swedish competitors' product and market choice during this phase, it is possible to conclude that symmetry between them had increased. Trima and Ålö became more similar to each other in their product choices, and Trima and Källve, like Ålö, began to manufacture the complete loader. This meant that the earlier division in manufacturing parts of the product ceased. However, Ålö continued to distinguish itself from its competitors by manufacturing other types of loader for the international market. In the competitors' market choice, all of the companies penetrated the entire Swedish market during this phase. Both Ålö and Trima also operated in international markets, although Trima's international operations were still limited in scale. However, the differences in the choice of distribution channel still existed throughout this phase. Ålö kept its sole rights to SLR, whilst Trima sold its products through private retailers.

Despite the similarities in product choice, and despite the fact that Trima and Ålö had penetrated the entire Swedish market, the competing companies acted independently. Competitive plays differed from each other, in that the companies' choice of their main markets differed. Trima prioritised the Swedish market, penetrating it through the private retailing market, whereas Ålö continued to concentrate its resources and efforts to foreign markets, thus releasing the domestic markets to SLR. As the threat from competing companies increased, signals from the market indicated that Trima's position became stronger. Signals about Trima's strengthened position can be exemplified by the fact that it was Trima's tool carrier that became accepted as being Swedish standard, not Ålö's. At the end of the 1970s, Ålö took notice of a number of occurrences which indicated Trima's strength, as well as the fact that Ålö's loader was perceived by customers as a loader for lighter vehicles. Ålö's awareness of Trima's position grew stronger, but it still took several years before the organisation as a whole came to the conclusion that counter-moves were necessary.

Some measures of a more preparatory nature were taken, however. Ålö took internal measures both to increase awareness that the competitive situation had changed, and to increase interest for the domestic market. Trima examined its opportunities for further international expansion to a greater extent than before. The increased similarity in awareness of competitors, as well as the preparatory and mobilising actions undertaken, explains the integration of competitive plays taking place during the rest of the 1980s. Direct competitive plays therefore remained very passive during this phase.

Phase Four — The Integration of Competitive Play

Competition changed once again as a result of Ålö's re-commitment to the domestic market and Trima's intensified internationalisation. For most of the 1980s, both dominating actors had begun to compete actively against each other in most areas. The awareness of the competing companies of the threats and opportunities resulted in processes that increased the symmetry between the two competitors during the fourth phase.

The relative strengths of Ålö and Trima became equal in that they are described as operating with similar resources and technology in the same markets. Ålö's re-awakened awareness of, and recommitment to, the Swedish market led to a decrease in the company's international domination, at the same time as Trima's internationalisation led to a decrease in its domination of the domestic market in Sweden. Both companies describe themselves as leaders during this phase, which indicates that the competitors were equal in technological and market leadership. Although one company held stronger positions in some markets and the other in other markets, the companies can be described as being symmetrical due to relative strength in the industry as a whole.

Symmetry in product and market choice also increased. Ålö once again concentrated its product development on the demands of the Swedish market, whereas Trima began to develop products for foreign markets. This resulted in the competing companies' product ranges becoming similar. As the smaller companies in the industry answered for only a minor share of the total operations of the industry, symmetry in product choice can be said to have been considerable, relative to the previous phase.

Market symmetry also increased. Ålö's cancellation of its contract with SLR made it possible for both companies to use all of the available market channels. Trima's increased commitment to internationalisation strengthened the symmetry of the companies' geographical market choice, though Ålö's international operations and engagement were still greater than Trima's (Ålö for example crossed the Atlantic and established itself in North America). The companies' geographical choice of market as a whole are therefore assessed to be neither symmetrical (internationally) nor asymmetrical (nationally).

From having previously been passive, competitive play during the fourth phase became active. Awareness of each other, combined with the internal mobilisation, resulted in active competitive plays between the companies, particularly in product development and in the various actions in different geographical markets. Descriptions of action given by individuals in the two companies are given relative to the actions of the competitor(s). The competitive play that occurred in the fourth phase can therefore be described as move and counter-move, which is explained by the endeavours of both companies for technological and market leadership.

Competitive play became both intensive and of great scope during this phase. Between 1982 and 1989, loaders were improved and new series of loader were launched one after the other by the competing companies. Intensive competition also occurred in the market-place. Competitive measures directly related to the action of the competitors were taken every year during most of the 1980s.

Contexts of Competition in the Front-loader Industry — a Summary

The descriptions given so far in this chapter illustrate that competition has shown different characteristics during each of the different phases of the industry, and also that the degree of symmetry between the competitors and the degree of activity in competitive play have varied. The four phases in the history of the industry can therefore be said to comprise four different contexts of competition.

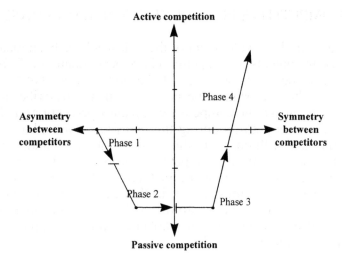

Figure 4.2   Changes in Contexts of Competition in the Front-loader Industry

The points in the figure illustrate the assessment of competition in the middle of each phase, and the lines illustrate the direction of change in competition. In reality, symmetry/asymmetry and activity/passivity has progressively increased or decreased during the phases. Although the different variations and nuances in competition cannot be fully illustrated by points and lines, it is possible to ascertain which type of competition has characterised the different phases. The reader should be aware, however, that the above figure is a simplification of the true state of competition.

During the first phase of the Front-loader industry, the companies found themselves in a context of competition where the actors were very asymmetrical, but where competitive play was neither active nor passive. Competition changed due to the internationalisation of Ålö, and became asymmetrical and very passive during the second phase. The concentration of the industry brought about an increase in symmetry in the third phase, but the competitors proceeded to act independently of each other. This means that competition changed character once again, to become symmetrical and very passive during the third phase. When the competing actors became aware of the symmetry, and of the competitive threat that this symmetry implied, their competitive plays became successively integrated and active. Competition during the fourth phase, therefore, became very symmetrical and very active.

COMPETITIVE PLAY DURING THE LAST PHASE

Four phases in the development of the industry have been identified, and different contexts of competition have been identified. To be able to gain a deeper understanding of the competition that has been pursued by the companies, the next section will describe in more detail the action and the competing companies' perceptions and inter-pretations of competition during the two final phases, but concen-trating on the fourth phase. In this way, an increased understanding of the interaction between competitors can be gained. An increased understanding of how competitors force each other to undertake more innovative measures, which in this case have resulted in the companies' development of strong positions in the international market, is also made possible. A number of competitive plays can be distinguished, and these are described below.

Product Development — A Race?

Product development and the introduction of new generations of loader are considered to be central for each company to retain and develop their market positions. The figure below illustrates the development during the 1980s.

Product development by the companies can be divided into three sections; the development of the loader, the development of tools,

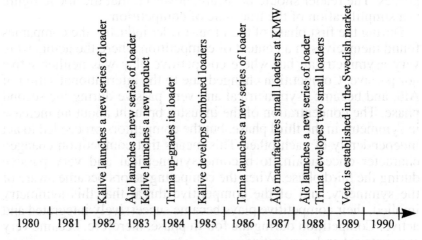

Figure 4.3   Product Development during the 1980s

and the development of the attachment system. These developments are discussed separately in the following.

The Development of New Loaders

Källve launched a new series of loader in 1982, considered mainly to be due to the changed market situation (though comparisons with Trima's loader are made). As Trima had become the largest national company, and operated in the same market segment as Källve, Källve considered competition with Trima to be important. Källve saw itself having a competitive edge over Trima in that it had developed an integrated product concept at an early stage. Trima's product concept (a narrower loader), on the other hand, was not considered to be of the same quality. Trima's narrower loader entailed a number of problems with some of the tools, and these problems are considered to have originated in the fact that Trima developed its product program in stages, and therefore manufactured both new and old loaders with different attachment systems. According to Källve, Trima did not solve this problem until 1986.

The next stage in the development of the front-loader began in 1983, when Ålö launched its new product programme. Ålö's new generation of loader was adaptable to both two-wheel and four-wheel drive tractors, and earlier investments in flexible manufacturing systems made the manufacturing of the new series more rational, as well as increasing the quality of the loaders. Källve also developed a new product during this period, the gripper, which introduced a new direction of operations for the loader. Ålö does not mention Källve's new series of loader in the descriptions of its own product development. The competition with Trima and the changed competitive situation in the Swedish market are, however, considered to be important causes of the development of Ålö's new series of loader (which in itself is a change from the situation during the 1960s and 1970s, where the main cause of development was considered to be the requirements of the international market).

The development of the loader programme is linked by many at Ålö to the image that Ålö's products had in the Swedish market, and Ålö's somewhat patronising treatment of the Swedish market over a longer period of time. To change the image that Ålö's loader had with customers, the company ran an advertisement campaign based on a new loader lifting a tractor equipped with one of the older generation of the loader, implying that 'Ålö' stood for strength. The new series contributed to an improved position in the Scandinavian market for the company.

In 1983, Bergsjöverken bought Trima from Karolin Invest and formed a new company, Trima/Bergsjöverken AB. The greater part of the year was spent in co-ordinating the two organisations and their work routines. This re-organisation took a great deal of time and effort, which, according to several respondents at Trima, explains why it was not possible for Trima to meet Ålö's product development directly. However, in 1984 Trima improved its front-loaders by including new hydraulic valves in the loader. Previously, the company had imported low cost hydraulic components, but that year Trima began to buy valves from Nordhydraulik, the hydraulics division of Trima's sister company, Nordwin. Nordhydraulik had attempted to develop hydraulics suited to the need of the loader over a long period of time, but it was not until 1984 that Trima considered the advantages of changing supplier to be sufficient. The main argument for the use of the new valves was competitiveness. One of Trima's managers was of the opinion that the hydraulics bought from Nordhydraulik were more expensive, but were able to be used in marketing as a competitive advantage over competitors' loaders (and were therefore an argument for claiming that Trima's loader were of higher quality than its competitors).

In 1985, Källve was acquired by Vreten. Problems of re-alignment due to the acquisition led to serious supply problems for Vreten. Consequently, sales of its front-loaders were reduced by two thirds, and sales of the grip-loader sank to one sixth of its previous level. The acquisition of the company also led to product development becoming even more directed towards industrial and entrepreneurial markets. Vreten manufactured snow-ploughs and other tools that could be combined with the loader so that the customer could use several products simultaneously. Similar solutions were also developed by Trima, though on a smaller scale (for example, Trima did not manufacture ploughs, which according to Vreten's managing director was a competitive disadvantage for Trima). Vreten's managing director is of the opinion that Trima saw Vreten as a threat, and that Vreten was put under close surveillance by Trima. Vreten's actions were directly followed by counter-measures, which often were stronger than necessary. The managing director also states that Ålö did not act relative to Vreten to the same extent as Trima, due to Ålö being focused to a higher degree on front-loaders for the agricultural industry.

In 1986, Trima launched a completely new product range, which was comprised of four basic models. Two motives for the development of the new series of loader are given. Firstly, the company wanted to gain a competitive edge over its competitors. Trima considers itself leader in product development, which in turn is considered to be important for competition. This is illustrated by the following quotations.

> I would suggest that it is we and Ålö that push product development forward ... If I were to be honest, I don't know of any area where our competitors have gained an edge over us. It is more a question of how far behind us they are. If they get close, we have to push further forward. But I'd still suggest that all of our competitors, including Ålö, copy what we do.
>
> (product manager)

> If you do want to be market leader, then it is the area of product development that is crucial.
>
> (financial manager, personal interview 1989)

> In that it is a mature product in almost every market, it is important to develop something regularly, so that you can point to something that distinguishes us from our competitors.
>
> (managing director, personal interview 1989)

Secondly, the foreign market had other requirements on the product, which were accentuated when Trima acquired Baas (a German front-loader manufacturer); greater lift capabilities are needed in Germany, for example. In developing Trima's new programme of loaders, customer requirements in other countries were also taken into account. The series that Trima launched therefore made more use of mechanical parallel drive (Vreten does not consider this to have been anything 'new', as Vreten had included mechanical parallel drive as early as the 1950s). Another new element in Trima's series was that the loaders were able to be hydraulically de-coupled, which is considered by Vreten's managing director to be "a hyped gimmick, it has little technical importance to usability".

1988 saw the launch of Ålö's new series of loader. This series consisted of five basic models with a number of variations on the models. With the launch of this series, Ålö went over to mechanical parallel drive in all of its models. Work angles were improved upon, and a number of features that previously could be purchased as special equipment became standard features. Comparisons with other competitors are made when the development of this series is discussed, and the competitive advantages of the new loader over the competitors' products are often mentioned. Customers and their needs are also considered to be a source of, and driving force behind, the development of the product.

Many at Ålö consider that the plans for future operations are the foundations for all product development. Ålö's managing director, for example, states that "We have to live our own life ... we have to work after our own philosophy when we develop our products". Since 1980, five-year plans have been developed for the organisation, and these define the need for greater developments in product range. According to the managing director, new series of loader ought to have a life of five years, as development costs are too high for any shorter span of life.

Although plans and customer needs are important driving forces behind development, competitors also play an important role. Ålö agrees that Trima had previously taken a leading position in technological development, mainly due to the fact that Trima had specialised on the Scandinavian market (which is a market that demands more advanced technical solutions). Many also believe that Ålö's product development profited from Trima's technical leadership; by watching the Swedish market's reactions to Trima's products, Ålö could gather ideas and knowledge for what was in demand. Product development is described by many at Ålö as a race between the Swedish companies, where the company that launched a new series took over the technological leadership. Through Ålö's launch of a new product programme in 1983, some interviewees at Ålö argue that the company had 'caught up' with Trima, but Trima in turn regained the technological leadership in 1986. The effects of Trima's launch of a new programme in 1986 is seen by some at Ålö to have resulted in a reduction in market shares for Ålö, for example in the English market, and that this increased the need for Ålö to launch another new programme. Many interviewees consider Ålö to have regained leadership with the new product series that was launched in 1988, as illustrated by the following quotations:

> Trima takes market shares from us when they launch a new series. It then becomes important for us to lose no time in developing a new series of our own. They probably feel the same way now that we've launched a new series.
>
> (personal interview with product development manager, Ålö)
>
> Ålö and Trima have taken it in turns with being leaders in product development. There have been a number of years when we have

lagged behind Trima, but just at the moment we are ahead of them. Obviously, they watch us very closely, and I presume that they plan to catch up. We'll just have to wait and see what they come up with.

(personal interview with Ålö's export manager)

At Trima, many consider that Ålö have partly imitated Trima's loader. Trima's export manager is the only interviewee that mentions a number of features of Ålö's series that were not found on Trima's loader. However, many of the attributes that could be found on the product are considered to be finesses that were without real value for the customer. There is a general agreement at Trima that Ålö's product name was a copy of Trima's product name, and this resulted in some irritation. Stoll, a German competitor, is also considered by some at Trima to have copied its product, in that the mechanical parallel drive and other attributes that could be found on Stoll's product were part of Trima's series of loader. Trima's managing director is of the opinion that the majority of Trima's competitors have in one way or another been inspired by Trima's products in their product development.

In 1988, Trima launched two new and smaller loaders, in co-operation with its German and English divisions, aiming to increase its product range towards smaller tractors. The volume of these loaders was not particularly large, but the launching of these products was seen as necessary in foreign markets to meet customer requirements, and to cope with the competition in foreign markets. The same year, Ålö acquired an Canadian company, which meant that its product range also increased to include smaller loaders. Ålö planned to export small loaders in the future to Europe from Canada. The respondents from Trima did not consider Ålö's acquisition of KMW to have affected Trima's decision to develop small loaders. Many at Ålö believe, however, that the acquisition did have a certain effect, even though the most important motive for the development was customer needs in Europe.

In 1989, a Danish manufacturer, Veto, established itself in the Swedish market, and this affected both Ålö and Trima. Ålö considers this establishment primarily to accentuate the need to develop smaller loaders (illustrated by the comparison of Ålö's loaders with Veto's in the description of development plans by the head of product development at Ålö). Ålö had come into contact with Veto through retailers in northern Sweden. The awareness that Veto's products showed a number of attributes that Ålö's loaders did not is given as an argument for the development of the smaller loaders. The fact that Veto had succeeded in establishing itself and spreading its products in the Swedish market is seen by many at Ålö to have been cause for reflection.

The Development of Tools and the Attachment System

Ålö's, Trima's and Vreten's policies for the development of tools for the loader differ from each other. Trima and Vreten mainly bought their tools from other manufacturers, which explains the limited amount of development in this area of production. Ålö, on the other hand, manufactured its own tools. The three companies agree that Ålö is the market leader in the development of tools. Trima's export manager compliments Ålö on this, and means that through its experience of the needs of other markets, Ålö has been able to gather an enormous competence in the area of loader tools. Some interviewees at Ålö state that it is not the fact that loaders and/or tools are developed that is paramount, but rather the fact that solutions to the farmer's problems are found. This means that the development of loaders and tools must occur parallel to each other, and must be seen as a whole. It is therefore considered important that co-workers in the company, both national and international, are observant to new methods within the agricultural industry.

Trima does carry out a certain amount of tool development, despite the majority of tools being purchased from other companies. However, the export manager states that it is sometimes unprofitable to manufacture tools, in that tools are bulky, and this leads to high freight charges relative to the value of the tools. It is therefore better in some cases to purchase tools from other companies than to manufacture them. In connection with the intensified efforts in the Scandinavian market, Ålö developed a tool attachment system which fitted both Ålö's and Trima's tools. This meant that the customer that changed from using Trima's loader to Ålö's could keep using his old tools. Patenting rights were applied for in markets where Trima's presence was considerable. Trima then developed coupling joints to facilitate the use of other tools than those manufactured by Trima. These joints were wielded to the tools which could then be attached to Trima's attachment system.

The development of attachment systems were considered to be more of a necessity than a competitive advantage, because they limited the available markets. It is only possible to sell loaders for those tractors on which it is possible to attach the loader. The differences that exist in this area between the two dominating companies can be linked to Trima's previous specialisation in the domestic market and Ålö's early internationalisation. Trima had developed an attachment system that was more suitable for larger tractors and for heavier loads than Ålö's. Loaders in the international market were generally smaller and the amount of lifting power was less important. In that Ålö launched its new product range of 1983, the company included a new attachment system that was adapted to larger loaders to better serve the Swedish market. Ålö produced a greater range of attachment systems in comparison with Trima, which is why it was possible to use Ålö's loaders on a larger number of tractor models (and consequently in a larger number of markets). Ålö's early internationalisation, where the company came into contact with a greater number of tractor models than Trima, seems to be the reason behind this.

Competitive Plays in the Domestic Market

In the description of competition in the domestic market (as illustrated in the figure below), the Nordic countries (with the exception of Finland) are considered by the companies to be a single market.

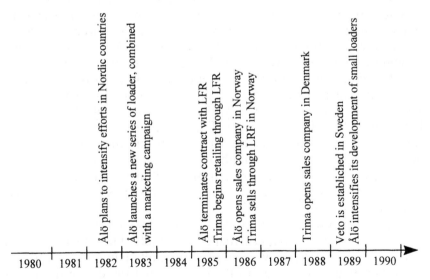

Figure 4.4 Competitive Action in the National Front-loader Market

The struggle between the two companies was slight during the 1970s and at the beginning of the 1980s. The companies cultivated different channels, and did not meet in direct competition. Many at Ålö consider the market share that had been gained earlier to have been sufficient, which is why Ålö intensified its efforts in the export market. Some interviewees at Trima describe the focus on the domestic market as an inability to internationalise Trima's operations, rather than a conscious strategy to build a strong position in the domestic market. During the 1980s, Ålö began to redevelop an interest in the Swedish market, whereas earlier, sales had remained at a constant or decreasing level.

At the end of the 1970s, certain individuals in the company suggested that efforts in the domestic market had been mishandled, and that intensified efforts were required. Plans were developed to increase efforts in the domestic market, both through product development and through an increased cultivation of the market. The managing director remembers this as being a difficult time for the company. Trade conditions were in recession, leading to large stocks of loaders. There was a certain internal resistance to expanding efforts in the domestic market under such circumstances. The first five year plan showed, however, that the planned efforts ought to give good returns. It was therefore decided to implement the plans, and, as already mentioned, a new series of loader was launched in 1983.

Ålö changed its strategy. The contract between Ålö and SLR was terminated in 1985, considerable resources were invested in market analyses of the Swedish retail market, and three new salespersons were employed to cultivate this market. Ålö's actions brought on counter-moves from Trima, which already had a well-developed service and retail network. The company intensified its efforts in the private market, and also began to cultivate SLR, which was made possible by the termination of the contract between SLR and Ålö. Many at Trima interpreted Ålö's actions as direct cultivation of Trima's customers in an attempt to increase Ålö's market shares, although it was felt that Ålö would not succeed in its attempts to expand in the domestic market because Trima had already gained a strong position, a positive image, and good relations with the retailers.

Many at Ålö were aware of the fact that Trima did not appreciate Ålö's cultivation of Trima's market channels, but considered it a necessity because there were no other market channels to cultivate. However, many at Ålö are of the opinion that the use of discounts and price reductions would have been reprehensible, which relates to an opinion that this was just what Trima had done in a number of the international markets. The intensified efforts were spoken of as being the best thing that could have been done considering the situation that the company found itself in. Many at Ålö refer to official statistics available on the industry, and state that Ålö's market shares in the Swedish market increased with 10 per cent as a result of these efforts, and that Ålö became market leader in Norway (an opinion that is disputed, however, by many at Trima).

For a long time, Ålö sold its products through the Norwegian agricultural co-operative, whereas Trima sold its products through the rest of the Norwegian machine trade. When Ålö terminated its contract with the co-operative, Trima had the opportunity to sell through that market channel. Many at Ålö consider that despite this, the company was able to maintain its domination with the co-operative, due to the company's strong product development. 1986 saw the establishment of Ålö's sales company in Norway, so that customers who had not turned to the co-operative could also be reached by Ålö. The co-operative had previously strongly resisted such a move, but by 1986, it could accept such an establishment.

Apart from competing with each other, Ålö and Trima also competed with Vreten and Veto (the Danish company that had established itself in the Swedish market). Some years after the re-construction of the Norwegian market, Vreten developed two new sales channels in Norway, of which, at the time of this study, only one was known of at Trima. Many at Vreten consider that Trima acted directly with counter-measures aimed at crushing Vreten's efforts. Trima competed via the importer that cultivated roughly the same market segment in Norway, offering extra discounts and price reductions. Vreten's managing director is of the opinion that Trima over-reacted and "gave away discount unnecessarily". Vreten's efforts were limited, and the company therefore did not compete in any real terms with Trima. Vreten tried to find small niches and small channels where the company could act alongside Trima. The costs of a wide expansion with high volumes were perceived to be too considerable, and would place too many requirements on production capacity, for example.

The descriptions of competition by interviewees from Trima differ from those given by Vreten. Many felt secure about the smaller company's action, despite Vreten operating in areas where Trima has its strongest foothold, because Vreten sold a very limited number of loaders and had split its operations over a number of different product areas. The head of Trima's finance department is of the opinion that the Front-loader industry requires specialisation.

Trima's experience of specialisation over thirty years cannot be found at Vreten, and this led to competitive advantages for Trima. A number of interviewees at Ålö are sceptical over Vreten's possibilities of surviving in the long term. According to these interviewees, the company had considerable problems with profitability, and however Vreten handled these problems, it operated in areas mainly dominated by Trima. Vreten was therefore not considered to be a competitor in any real terms.

With the changes in Sweden and Norway, Ålö increased the size of its sales force in Denmark, whereas Trima established a sales subsidiary there. Trima considered its establishment in Denmark as a step in its internationalisation strategy. The company's ambition was to expand its operations into other foreign national markets, and the aim in each market was to become one of the three largest manufacturers of loaders in that country. Trima had previously established itself in Holland and Ireland, and therefore looked to other markets. The choice fell on Denmark, where there was no great market for loaders, even though it is geographically close (a reason some saw as the motive for choosing Denmark).

The following year, 1989, the Danish manufacturer Veto (which previously operated in Norway, Great Britain, and Ireland) formed a co-operation with Rosenqvist AB, Sweden, a company that sold Trima's loader. Trima's managing director considers this to be a direct consequence of Trima's establishment of a subsidiary in Denmark. Veto was part of a larger corporation, and therefore had considerable resources available for establishing a position in Sweden, which led to many at Ålö and Trima viewing Veto's breakthrough in the Swedish market to be irritating. Veto's establishment in Sweden was also perceived as being disruptive in that it gave rise to an increased price competition.

Competitive Plays in the International Market

The competitors also met in the international market. The figure below summarises the competitive actions in the international market during the 1980s. A struggle for the British market (one of Ålö's earliest foreign markets) occurred during the 1980s. Trima began selling to Britain at the end of the 1970s via a company that produced its own loaders, but that wished to complement its range by also selling Trima's loaders. This company later ceased production of its own loaders to concentrate on selling for Trima. However, these sales never reached high volumes. During 1984, a new manag-

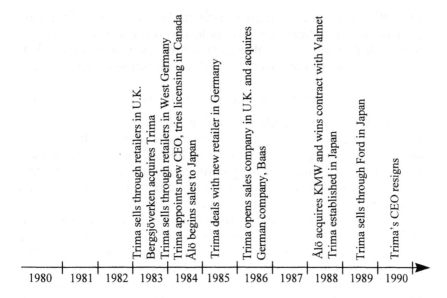

Figure 4.5 Competitive Actions in the International Front-loader Market During the 1980's

ing director was appointed at Trima. This was, according to him, a step in Karolin Invest's goal of bringing about international expansion. The new managing director had previously been export manager at a number of Swedish companies, and had considerable knowledge of international trade. A great deal of the work with international expansion therefore fell under the leadership of the new managing director. The fact that Ålö had succeeded in establishing a position internationally with similar products, was also part of the argument that Trima should also be able to establish itself in international markets.

At the same time that Ålö built up its operations in Scandinavia, Trima decided to establish a sales company in Britain to build a stronger position in the country. This sales company was established in 1986. Ålö was market leader in Britain, but at the time of Trima's intensified efforts in Britain, Ålö had had problems with its suppliers. This meant that the competition with Trima became tangible. Some are of the opinion that Trima purposely attacked Ålö to get even, as illustrated by the following quotation:

> We are market leaders in Britain, and Trima are just getting their own back for us taking their customers in Sweden and Norway

by cultivating our customers in Britain. We have 30% of the customers, which means that 70% is left for others, such as Trima.
We think they should be able to penetrate the rest of the market.
But they seem to have quite a decided ambition to go after our
customers.

(personal interview with Ålö's export manager)

Trima felt that it was an advantage that Ålö was established in the
British market, as Ålö had already 'informed' and 'taught' the cus-
tomer the advantages of the more technically advanced loader.
Many claim that Trima primarily competed with other manufactur-
ers, and that the best situation would have been that only Ålö and
Trima expanded in the British market.

During 1984, both Ålö and Trima expanded their markets internationally. Trima, for example, began on a project basis to export via
Massey Ferguson (MF) in order to reach more distant markets. The
same year, Ålö signed a contract with a Japanese company, Saporov
Overseas, which began to import Ålö's loaders. Saporov Overseas
sold loaders to MSK,[5] which imported MF's tractors, amongst others.
Four years later, Trima also began to sell to Japan through MF, which
led to a 'full-frontal clash' between the two companies, 'fighting'
over the same customer, MSK. This was seen by Ålö as being a
direct attack, whereas many at Trima claim that it was a business
opportunity like any other, and that Trima was unaware that Ålö was
cultivating the same customer. As opinion differ on this matter, both
companies' views on what happened will be presented below.

During the period 1984 to 1988, Ålö had established a continual
and, according to many, sufficient sales volume in Japan. As the
market was geographically distant, and was only 'visited' a few
times a year, an increased commitment was considered to be too
risky. Ålö was relatively satisfied with the situation as it was.
However, in 1988, the retailer in Japan phoned the export manager
at Ålö to inform him that Trima's front-loaders could be found at
MSK. Ålö's export manager then phoned Trima's managing director
to hear how this could have occurred, and received the following
explanation.

In 1988, Trima signed a contract with MF in Britain, which
agreed to sell Trima's loader in Japan. This was considered to be

---

[5] In Ålö's documentation, the abbreviation "MSK" stands for a Japanese company that is
part of the Mitsubishi corporation ("M").

advantageous, as the costs associated with penetrating a distant market alone were too high. Trima was unaware of who its competitors in Japan were, until a previous phone-call from Ålö. By that time, Trima had reached the final stages of working out an offer with MF, and to abandon the business at that stage just because Ålö was also working with the same customer was not considered possible. The contract was therefore signed.

Ålö, however, is of the opinion that Trima knew very well that Ålö operated in the Japanese market, and that Ålö's presence there was rather an incentive to Trima's action. The company's experiences from the British market, dealt with above, are seen to be a basis for this opinion. This opinion is backed up by the fact that Trima sold its loaders via MF, and through this, to Ålö's customers in Japan. This occurred despite the presence of other retailers, and, according to many, the fact that Trima offered loaders at prices 15 per cent lower than Ålö.

Trima's managing director argues that this was unfortunate. He became aware that Ålö had invested considerable resources in Japan, and thereby had created an interest with the Japanese for the type of loader that was manufactured in Sweden. To go from this awareness to direct competition was considered to be unjust, and the managing director pointed out that he did not aim to cause damage to Ålö. The production manager is of the opinion that if Trima were to establish itself in a market such as Japan, the company ought to use a different market channel than that used by Ålö. The insufficient information about Ålö's operations therefore explains the clash with Ålö, which was unfortunate, according to the production manager. As for pricing, Trima's managing director speaks only in general terms about the company's policy.

> We set prices according to the market, and we are not going to enter markets such as France or England and offer similar loaders at a lower price, because that will harm both of us. Here, it is more a question of both companies being healthy companies that earn money. Dumping or any other such means of competition is out of the question.
>
> (personal interview in October 1989 with Trima's managing director)

Japan is one of the markets in which Trima planned to expand, and although the full-frontal clash with Ålö was considered unfortunate, it was the company's ambition to succeed in Japan. Many of the interviewees at Trima are of the opinion that Ålö lost a portion of its sales as a result of Trima's entry, and that through this and other measures, Trima was able to create a position in the Japanese market. Ålö, however, did not consider Trima's actions to be threatening, even though it went against what was considered to be good competition. Ålö's managing director did not think that Trima would be able to build up high sales volumes in Japan, as the company would not be able to retain Ålö's customers. Through the grapevine, Ålö heard that Trima had raised its prices by ten per cent, and in that Trima no longer used price as a way to compete, many at Ålö thought that Ålö's relations with its customers would weigh heavier in the choice between the two companies. No countermeasures were therefore undertaken in the Japanese market.

The clash in Japan differs from the competition normally driven between the Swedish companies. Both Trima and Ålö describe each other as colleagues, and mean that the competition that is driven more often than not corresponds to what is considered good competition. Many interviewees at Ålö consider the action in the Japanese market to have been an exception to the rule.

Company Acquisition — A New Phenomenon

The measures and events that are described above are characterised by the competitors' action relative to each other. In both companies, other actions not directly motivated by or related to the actions of the competitors are also mentioned as being important for their international positions. One such important measure is the acquisition of subsidiaries.

In 1986, Trima broke with the traditional pattern of establishment in the industry by buying up the German company Baas. Germany was a large market with considerable market potential, which, according to Trima's managing director, made the German market interesting. Trima had previously attempted to break into the German market via importers, but without fulfilling the company's expectations. Ålö had worked purposefully towards engaging an importer for every region in Germany since 1980. Trima was about to begin this development. Knowledge of the time it took for Ålö to build up its contact network led Trima's managing director to state that it would require over ten years for Trima to develop a well-functioning distribution net.

Baas was one of West Germany's biggest manufacturers of loaders, but had been unprofitable for a number of years. When the company began to have problems, production was progressively reduced, so that by the time of Trima's acquisition, the company only retained a certain amount of assembly and construction from its previous operations. Trima decided to buy Baas in order to gain both a known name and a market position in Germany. Trima moved all production to Sweden, and re-organised Baas as a sales and service organisation. Baas imported simple mechanical loaders from Danchif in Denmark. Trima did not include mechanical loaders in their product range by this time, which explains why the company continued with the above arrangement. From the time of purchase in 1986 and for a period of several years, considerable work went into integrating the two companies, and into repairing the bad reputation that accompanied the name Baas as a result of the company's previous unprofitability.

In 1988, Ålö acquired a Canadian company, KMW, thereby becoming the first company of the two companies to cross the Atlantic. Ålö assessed North America to be a market with considerable potential. Ålö had been looking for possible opportunities to enter this market for over ten years, without actively working to bring about an establishment. During the 1980s, the Canadian family company KMW began to be profitable, and decided to search for a suitable buyer. Turning to Europe, KMW heard about Ålö, made contact with them, and was acquired by Ålö in 1988. KMW, with a turnover of 60m SEK and 120 employees, had two manufacturing plants; the main plant in Canada near the border with the USA, and a subsidiary in Kansas, USA. The American market alone had a potential annual production volume of 35,000 loaders.

The newly acquired company had a strong position in the market for smaller tractors of 15–40hp, whereas Ålö manufactured loaders of 40hp and above. The Canadian company therefore complemented Ålö's product range. Ålö's managing director and export manager saw the acquisition as an opportunity to increase Ålö's product range, to increase the company's production capacity, and to build a bridge into the North American market. Ålö had noticed that there was a demand for smaller loaders in Europe and in Japan. The company was market leader in several markets in Europe, and an expansion of both the product range and the international market to include North America was considered to be a way of continuing the expansion of the company. The increased production capacity gained through reconstruction in 1982 showed itself to be insufficient during the economic boom, which is why the acquisition (which would provide further production capacity) was considered to be important.

Trima's international commitments were limited up to the time of its acquisition of Baas, but through this acquisition, the company was faced with completely new requirements for adaptation and quality. The German market did not have as high requirements for technical sophistication as the Nordic market, but did have higher requirement for quality, precision, and fitting. This led Trima to instigate improvements in production quality control. According to many interviewees at Trima, the company's acquisition of Baas gave rise to a number of counter-measures from the other competitors, partly in imitating Trima's products, and partly in Ålö's acquisition of KMW. The actions of the German competitors are perceived by Trima as being both a confirmation of the company's relative strength, and an aid in helping Trima with its market penetration. Trima links Ålö's reactions to its acquisition of Baas primarily as a reciprocal race between the two companies. This race is described by Trima's managing director primarily in terms of reciprocal pride and prestige.

Ålö did not consider its acquisition of KMW to be a cause of other competitors' action, or a reason for counter-measures. The acquisition of KMW is not assumed to have affected competition within the Nordic or the European markets. After a while, Ålö also attempted to sell smaller loaders in Europe, but as none of the competitors at the time operated within this segment, competition in these two segments were assumed to be negligible. Trima linked Ålö acquisition of KMW both to Trima's acquisition of Baas and to its development of smaller loaders. Several interviewees at Trima also considered Ålö's commitments in North America as an opportunity to expand unnoticed in Europe (an argument based on Ålö's action in the Swedish market during the company's expansion of its export operations).

Many interviewees at Ålö saw Trima's acquisition of Baas as an opportunity for Ålö to succeed in the domestic market. The company knew from previous experience that the effort needed to build up an export organisation required enormous resources, with the result that other markets often suffered. Ålö's managing director is of the opinion that Trima's acquisition of Baas was peculiar, in that the most important aspect of an acquisition within Europe is that production should also be placed there, especially due to the development of the European Community. Trima's shutdown of all production at Baas made the acquisition less of a threat for Ålö and for Ålö's commitments in Europe. All of the interviewees at Ålö commented that they did not feel that it was necessary to instigate counter-measures against this acquisition.

Meanwhile, Ålö began to negotiate with Stoll, the major competitor to Baas in Germany, regarding a co-operation in production. The two companies visited each other, co-operating in the development of a number of technical details. At the time of the interviews carried out for this study, Trima was not aware of this co-operation, despite the fact that Baas had contact with Stoll, primarily to keep itself informed on the market situation in Germany. A number of French companies were also visited by Ålö, and one of them, Faucheux (France's second largest manufacturer), after a number of years of unprofitability, made contact with Ålö regarding a possible co-operation. However, Ålö's managing director considered Faucheux's financial situation to be too poor for a co-operation to be interesting for Ålö.

In 1990, Ålö intended to acquire its major competitor, Trima. This was due to an idea that the acquisition would lead to advantages of co-ordination, and would improve Ålö's strength relative to its foreign competitors (which had been under development to become stronger competitors). Instead of competing with Trima abroad, it was felt that it would be better to bring about some form of common action. Karolin Invest was prepared at that time to sell Trima, and negotiations became relatively advanced, but the contract was not signed because the financing of the acquisition could not be organised in a satisfactory way. Ålö did acquire, in 1992, a French manufacturer by the name of Agroma SA, and 50 per cent of its sales company Agram Manutention SA. One of the reasons for this acquisition was the possibility of gaining an increased production capacity through the acquisition of Agroma, together with being able to achieve a better market penetration through Agram Manutention.

Competitive plays during 1980s — A Summary

The research question posed in Chapter One, and further defined in Chapter Two, namely, what characterises different contexts of competition, and how do these different contexts contribute to the dynamics of an industry, can be analysed from the description given in this chapter. During the last half of the 1970s and the beginning of the 1980s, the Front-loader industry has exhibited symmetric-passive competition, which changed to be symmetric-active during the rest of the 1980s. By analysing the competitive plays that occurred primarily during the remainder of the 1980s, it is possible to increase knowledge of the nature and dynamics of symmetric-active competition. This chapter will therefore finish with a summarised description of the competitive plays that have emerged as being of greatest importance during the last phase of the history of the industry, as is illustrated in the figure below.

The competitive plays based on the product development of the companies can be described in terms of the companies' moves and counter-moves over time. In the companies' descriptions of product development, there is a high degree of relating actions to the actions of competitors. Competitive play can also be identified in the Swedish, Norwegian, and British markets. Ålö began its cultivation of the remaining machine trade, which made it possible for Trima and Vreten to cultivate SLR. This type of action can also be found in the Norwegian market. Parallels are also drawn between Ålö's actions in the Nordic countries and Trima's actions in Britain.

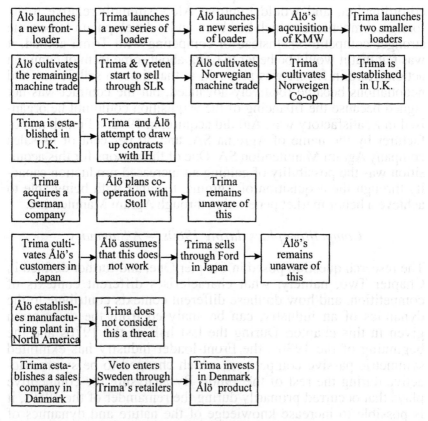

Figure 4.6   Competitive Plays in the Front-loader Industry

Ålö's reaction to Trima's acquisition of Baas was minor, but despite this, attempts to co-operate with Baas' main competitor were instigated, which ought to be considered a counter-move. Trima has not yet reacted to this, and the company's unawareness of the situation explains why it has not instigated and planned to undertake any counter-measures. This unawareness of the situation is due to a lack of information of Ålö's actions.

The companies' action in the Japanese market, the only instance of direct conflict, can also be described as constituting competitive play. Action broke with what both companies agree to be good competition, and it is claimed that insufficient knowledge was the source of such actions. Ignorance characterises this particular competitive play to a greater extent than other competitive plays in the industry, and this can be explained by the considerable geographical distance of the market. In the discussions of the actions in the Japanese and, to a certain extent, in the Swedish and Norwegian markets, the question of which rules-of-play ought to regulate competition is often brought up. Both companies talk about the importance of good competitive ethics, and express the opinion that the best competitive situation would be the expansion of both companies at the cost of other foreign competitors. Both companies would then be able to work together to influence customer preferences and knowledge of the advantages of using technically advanced loaders.

There are also examples of action that was not followed by direct counter-measures from competitors, such as Ålö's acquisition of KMW. Previous experience from the time that Ålö 'forgot' the Swedish market in its attempts to internationalise led to measures being taken in other areas. Both companies invested more resources in those markets they assumed the competitor had 'forgotten'. Entry into the Swedish market by foreign competitors has also given rise to active moves and counter-moves, as is illustrated by the competition between Trima and Veto. Ålö considers Veto to be a possible threat, but has decided to adopt a watchful attitude concerning the company's actions. Veto's actions had not previously aroused the attention of Ålö or Trima, but due to its entry into the Swedish market, this company is now closely watched by both companies. No other similar competitive play between the Swedish companies and their foreign competitors is described.

5. The Lining Industry

Chapter Five continues the description of the three industries under study with a presentation of the Lining industry. This industry differs from the Front-loader industry in a number of ways. Change over time is different between the two industries, as is the context of competition prevalent during the 1980s. Competition during the 1980s in the Front-loader industry was identified as first being symmetric-passive, changing then to symmetric-active, whereas the competition in the Lining industry, presented in this chapter, can be determined as being asymmetric-active. By including a study of the Lining industry in this book, further aspects of the nature and dynamics of competition can be ascertained.

As with Chapter Four, this chapter begins with a brief description of the product and its areas of use and a presentation of the different categories of actor in the industrial environment. The chapter then continues with a chronological description of the history of the industry, separated into the different phases characterised by different contexts of competition. The third phase in the development of the Lining industry is then described in greater depth, this to give a detailed description of the competitive play that occurred in an asymmetric-active context of competition.

THE PRODUCT AND THE ACTORS — A BRIEF INTRODUCTION

Lining products are manufactured to reduce the amount of wear and tear in machines that are particularly susceptible to heavy-duty processing. There are a number of areas of use, such as mill lining, screens, pump lining, lining for de-barking drums, and lining for floatation apparatus, where the amount of wear can be reduced by different types of lining. There are two companies in Sweden that manufacture these types of lining in rubber, Skega and Trellex. Both companies occupy leading positions in the international market, selling their products to the Mining industry, the Pulp industry, and to the Gravel and Stone industry.

The actors that are of importance for the Lining industry can be categorised into final customers, machine manufacturers, and consultants. The figure below illustrates the relations among and between these actors and the companies (those that manufacture the two types of lining — rubber and steel) in the Lining industry.

The Final Customer

The Mining industry has traditionally been a major customer for companies in the Lining industry. The process of ore-dressing in the Mining industry involves the transportation of raw material or ore on conveyor belts into mills to be ground. The ground ore is then pumped out of the mills in order for the minerals to be separated from the mass by floatation or other processes. These minerals are then screened. By lining pumps, floatation apparatus and mills with rubber, and by using rubber screens, the wear and tear of equipment that arises in the refining process can be reduced. Mill lining is the largest product group for the Mining industry, though

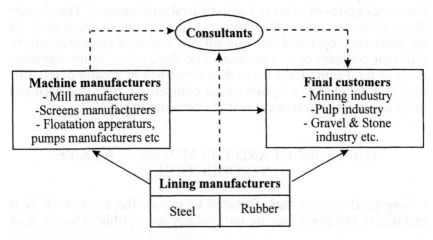

Figure 5.1   Actors in the Competitive Arena

screens, pumps, and other types of lining are also sold. As the process of refinement constitutes the most costly part of the entire manufacturing process, mining companies in general purchase lining products themselves, although for new mines or the introduction of alternative mining methods, companies often take advice from consultants, machine manufacturers, or from other mining companies. The Mining industry is international, but concentrated, which means that information is spread rapidly throughout the world. Mining companies are therefore well aware of the different suppliers to the industry, and possess considerable information on these suppliers and their products. This affects and eases the decision over which supplier to use.

The Gravel and Stone industry has been an important customer group for lining companies from the beginning of the 1970s. Products sold to the Gravel industry mainly comprise screens and protective rubber details. Entrepreneurial companies that operate regionally in different countries crush stone to produce gravel, for which demand increases at the same pace as investments increase in infrastructure (roads and airports). The biggest markets are in industrial countries, which makes Europe a growing market. The Gravel and Stone industry has developed and concentrated over time, and, through mergers, a small number of major corporations have established themselves in every country. The smaller units, however, still constitute an important part of the Gravel and Stone industry. Requirements on the finished product have increased at the same pace as the Gravel and Stone industry has developed. Gravel is sold in different sizes according to different uses. The demand for exactness, which has increased over time, means that increased requirements are placed on the screens that are used in the process of crushing stone.

The third customer category, the Pulp industry, is concentrated to a few actors using only rubber lining in their de-barking drums since the end of the 1970s. The wear that arises from the de-barking process can be reduced by lining de-barking drums with rubber. However, susceptibility to disruptions in the production process is considerable, and as disruptions to the process are costly, these customers were to begin with hesitant to use rubber lining.

Machine Manufacturers and Consultants

Machine manufacturers can be considered to be both competitors and customers. These companies deliver their machines complete with lining from other lining manufacturers, which means that they compete with Trellex and Skega, but they also purchase products from them. The machine manufacturers have concentrated to a small number of international companies, including Allis Mineral Systems, Marcy, Denver, and Nordberg. For the most part, machine manufacturers demand cheap products, which often gives foreign local manufacturers a competitive advantage over Swedish manufacturers. It is also more difficult to launch new products with machine manufacturers than it is with mining companies, as machine manufacturers are less willing to take the risks that are associated with new products.

Consultants are also important actors, as they develop suggestions for complete solutions to refining processes in mines and crushing processes for gravel companies. Consultants recommend different suppliers of mills, screens, pumps, and flotation apparatus, as well as designing and carrying out new investment projects. As with the machine manufacturers, there are a number of large international companies among the consultants. It is therefore important for the Swedish manufacturers to establish good contacts with these consultants, but perhaps more importantly to provide them with good information and knowledge about the advantages of rubber lining over steel lining, and subsequently the advantages of their products over those of their steel manufacturing competitors.

Competitors in the International Market

International competitors in rubber lining products sold to the Mining industry consist of a number of local foreign manufacturers, as well as the Swedish companies. The foreign competitors normally imitate the products manufactured by Skega and Trellex, often producing standard sizes, which reduces their costs for product development. As foreign manufacturers mainly sell their products to their own domestic markets, they do not incur as high transport costs or other costs associated with export. This means that Trellex and Skega compete with foreign companies that, due to a more advantageous costs structure, can offer products at lower prices.

The main competitors within the screen and lining product areas for the Gravel and Stone industry comprise a number of European, and mostly German, companies that are world leaders in this segment. Trellex, one of the two Swedish companies that operate primarily within this product area, considers these foreign companies as its major competitors, which makes the competition that takes place within the international market crucial. This segment of the market has grown during the last decade, and it is during this period of time that Trellex has begun to participate in international competition. Skega, the other Swedish competitor, relates its operations in this area primarily to Trellex.

In the de-barking drum product group, the major markets comprise the Nordic countries and Canada. It is primarily the Swedish manufacturers that compete in this product group. The table below presents a summary of the most important competitors in the Lining industry, illustrating that many of these operate within a number of different product groups, though in regional markets. A number of the companies, such as Gomy and Tip-Top, also sell their products to the rest of Europe. In the North American market, Rubber Engineering is perceived to be the most serious competitor, whereas in South America, this position is held by Vulco. Isenman, Mersten, Steinhaus and Küper differ from other companies by concentrating on manufacturing screens to the Gravel and Stone industry, and by operating internationally.

The Swedish Lining Companies

The Swedish lining companies comprise Skega's lining division and Trellex, which, until 1990, was part of the Trelleborg corporation. In 1990, this area of operation in Trelleborg was moved to Svedala Industries AB, which was 49% owned by Trelleborg. Trellex's operations have been organised in three divisions since 1991; screens and linings, conveyor belts, and fenders. It is primarily the screen and lining division that is of interest in this study.

Skega began its operations in 1932, being a family-owned company until 1969, when 50% of the company was acquired by Incentive. Skega was greatly influenced by the founder's son, Assar Svensson, until he retired in 1980. Assar Svensson considered product development to be central to the company's operations, consequently investing a great deal of resources into research and development. Svensson resigned in 1980, which gave rise to a number of organisational changes and shifts in leadership during the 1980s. Since 1990, the company has been organised into two divisions dealing with lining and industrial rubber. The lining products, dominated by mill lining products, constitute the major part of the company's operations.

Skega has a greater market-share than Trellex in linings for mills, de-barking drums, floatation apparatus, and pumps, whereas Trellex is a leader in screens and other types of linings. 63% of Skega's total turnover in 1990 was in exports. The lining division's share of

Table 5.1   The Main Competitors in the Lining Industry, Their Products and Markets

Competitors	Products				Markets
	Mill lining	Other linings	Screens	De-barking	
Skega	x	x	x	x	World-wide
Trellex	x	x	x	x	World-wide
Epton	x	x			N America
Rubber Enginering	x	x	x	x	N America
Gomy	x	x	x	x	Europe
Tip-Top	x	x	x	x	Europe
Fagum	x				ex-Yugoslavia
Vulco	x	x			Chile, Peru, Bolivia
Linatex		x	x	x	World-wide
Italgoma	x				Italy
Orion	x	x	x	x	Brazil
Pipsa	x				Mexico
Sodim	x				Morocco
Envirotech	x	x			Brazil
BBTR	x	x			UK, S Africa
Fraser Engineering					UK
Jobel Enginering					UK
Firestone	x				The Far East
Tera	x		x	x	France
Pirelli	x				Argentina
Deks-Thyer	x	x			Australia
Baker Technology	x				Australia
Vredestein					Holland
Isenman			x	x	World-wide
Mersten			x	x	World-wide
Steinhaus			x	x	World-wide
Küper			x	x	World-wide
Steel	x	x	x	x	Local, World-wide
Other material	x	x	x	x	Local, World-wide

Source: Summary of internal data from Skega and Trellex

export is considerably higher as the division for industrial rubber sells its products mostly to the domestic market. Trellex's share of export for the same year totalled 90%. The fact that the competing organisations are divisions in larger companies which also operate in other areas means that competition between the two companies is complex and conducted on several levels. Operations within some areas do not directly affect the competition that occurs in the lining area, but do provide the companies with internal pre-conditions and synergy effects through, for example, subsidiaries being able to sell several different product ranges. Trelleborg/Svedala Industries' operations in minerals and machine manufacturing does affect competition directly, however. Both these areas of operation are related to the Lining industry in that they include the companies' customers and/or competitors, as described earlier.

DIFFERENT CONTEXTS OF COMPETITION DURING THE HISTORY OF THE LINING INDUSTRY

From the description of the product and significant actors in the Lining industry, the chapter will continue with the identification of prevalent contexts of competition.

The history of the Lining industry can be said to comprise four phases, demarcated by three identifiable changes in the style of competition. Competition in this industry has always been very active, but the degree of symmetry between the two companies has changed at three specific points in time. The first change (separating phase two from phase one) took place when Trellex increased its area of operation within the screen product area, whilst Skega further developed its operation in international markets. The second change occurred when Trelleborg's acquisition of, amongst other companies, Skega's largest customer, Boliden, gave rise to different relative strengths between the competing companies. The third change was marked by Trellex's integration with machine suppliers and Skega's efforts to establish a position in the screen area.

This means that the first phase comprises the emergence of the industry. The second phase was characterised by the two competitors' differentiation from each other and the third phase by turbulence and by the transformation of the industry. In 1990s, the third phase moved towards its end and a new phase began to crystallise. However, the result of this particular change could not be ascertained at the time of the study, as the transition was so recent.

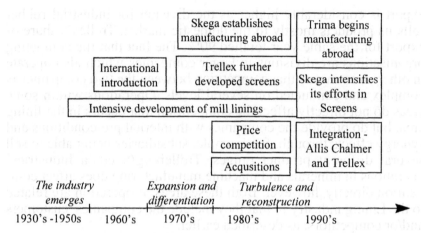

Figure 5.2 The Development of the Lining Industry Over Time

Figure 5.2 illustrates the major events that occurred during the history of the industry, separating the three main phases. These phases are presented in the next section.

Phase One — The Industry Emerges

The Lining industry emerged when Skega, a company in the north of Sweden, and Trellex, a company situated in the south of Sweden, developed lining for mills at the beginning of the 1960s. Prior to this, the founder of Skega attempted to create new areas of operations for products made out of rubber, such as rubber gloves. These attempts, and the perceptions and experiences that surrounded his meetings with other competitors in the rubber industry during this time, affected the perceptions of competition held by Skega during the first phase after the emergence of the industry. Therefore, before identifying the context of competition during the first phase of the industry, it is pertinent to describe the events that took place before the emergence of the industry.

Skega (or rather its founder) began to manufacture rubber gloves at the beginning of the 1930s, and thereby entered an industry comprising of many large companies producing rubber goods. Skega purchased rubber from these producers, including Trelleborg, a company that also manufactured gloves.

The founder of Skega perceived competition to have hardened significantly in 1939, as indicated by the following:

A number of difficulties began to arise due to the unwillingness of the rubber factories, where we bought our rubber, to accommodate the different grades of quality that we required. This can be seen from unmotivated increases in price, and slow deliveries, for example. We judged from the above and from our representative's visits to the companies that this was an 'attempt' to stop a prospective competitor from northern Sweden from establishing itself. This 'attempt' was particularly effective when the existence of this company lay completely in the hands of the rubber suppliers.[1]

Skega was forced to give up its production of rubber gloves in 1940, due to the ban on production of lined rubber gloves by the Swedish Trade and Industry Commission. At that time, Trelleborg manufactured unlined rubber gloves. One of Trelleborg's co-workers was a member of the commission, which is perceived by some of the interviewees at Skega to have affected this decision. The Trade and Industry Commission also introduced rationing of raw rubber due to World War Two. In 1945, Skega began its own production of rubber, as it was considered impossible to continue production under the conditions of the time. The company became self-sufficient in rubber, which improved the pre-conditions for the company's operations. After a period of difficulties brought about by the war, an expansion began at the end of the 1940s, which led to the emergence of the Lining industry. The 1950s and 1960s were characterised by growth in markets, turnover, number of employees, and number of premises.

The Development of Mill Linings and Screens

Towards the end of the 1950s, both Skega and Trellex came into contact with the difficulties associated with the use of steel in the refinement processes in mining, such as rapid wear and high levels of noise pollution. By the beginning of the 1960s, however, both companies had developed their first mill linings. In Skega's case, discussions took place as early as 1953 between the Managing Director of the time, Assar Svensson, and Boliden, a mining company situated in the same region, regarding the possibility of using rubber in its mills. Due to the scepticism against the new material, it was not until 1959 that Svensson gained a hearing for his ideas. Skega began an intensive period of development which resulted in

---

[1] Comments by the Managing Director, as appendixed in the company's yearly accounts.

the launch of the first mill lining in 1961. Boliden thus played an important role in Skega's development of its first mill lining, and the general opinion at Skega indicates that Boliden has always been positive to new products and to participating in developmental projects. Boliden has functioned as an external development laboratory for Skega since then.

As well as Boliden's role in the development of Skega's products, the development of the initial mill lining was greatly affected by Skega's co-operation with Bertil Brandt, who at the time was employed by Grängesberg (a Swedish mining company in the southern region of Sweden). Brandt saw the possibility of reducing wear and tear by using rubber lining in mills, and decided to leave Grängesberg for Skega. By combining Brandt's knowledge of mining and Svensson's knowledge of rubber, it was possible to develop the first mill lining in rubber. Boliden purchased the first product, which proved to be a success.

Trellex, the lining company situated in the south of Sweden, developed its idea for mill linings through the company's contacts with Swedish mines. Trellex's first lining product was developed in co-operation with Grängesberg. Both Skega and Trellex launched their mill lining products at approximately the same time, and it was this product that dominated their operations during the 1960s. A consequence of the launchings was that Skega and Trellex became active competitors, which lead to both companies keeping a close eye on the other. Patent applications were scrutinised, and both companies claimed that they were the first to launch mill linings. This was a particularly controversial issue, and was aired at presentations and other types of meetings with customers.

Apart from developing mill linings, Trellex also developed the idea to coat screens with rubber to reduce the wear and noise that arose from screening. A rubber screen called the Duenero was launched in 1962, which proved to be better than the traditional steel screen. Although the Duenero was sold to both the Gravel and Stone and the Mining industries, operations within the screen product area remained at a low level throughout the 1960s, and it was not until the end of the decade that other types of screen were developed at Trellex. In 1965 Skega developed its first screen in rubber and tested this product in Grängesberg's mines (where Trellex had tested its first mill linings). This proved successful, and resulted in the launch of the new screening sheet in 1967.

During the first phase, both organisations mainly manufactured lining for mills, which signifies that the symmetry in the companies' products was considerable. The first linings were installed in so-called secondary mills, to be followed by the development of linings for other mills and other types of milling equipment. In 1964, Trellex developed a new attachment system to fasten lining to mills, and the launching of this new system focused the discussion between Trellex and Skega on the advantages and disadvantages of the companies' two attachment systems. One of the managers at Trellex, however, is of the opinion that both systems functioned satisfactorily in the milling equipment and mills used in the 1960s, and that the differences between the two systems were more part of a sales pitch than actual advantages and disadvantages.

At the time of the emergence of the industry, Trelleborg's lining department, Trellex, was a very small part of the corporation. Trellex's business was considered to be an experimental operation, allowed to live its own life separate from Trelleborg's normal business. The developmental projects that Trellex instigated during the 1960s are seen to be an important explanation for the successful establishment of the company in the Lining industry. Although Trellex received support from Trelleborg for its developmental operations, the corporation had no other related operations within its total sphere. At that time, therefore, Skega and Trellex must be seen as two small but comparable organisations that, in competition with each other, established themselves in an emerging industry. The advantages that Trellex had by being part of a large corporation were of minor importance, as no crucial differences in resources between the companies are mentioned by the interviewees (this indicates a symmetry between the companies).

Opinions differ as to the companies' relative strengths in technical and/or market leadership. On the one hand, Skega is said to have been technical leader, as the majority of the interviewees in the industry as a whole held that opinion. On the other hand, the ongoing discussions regarding leadership suggest that the difference in leadership was not considerable, and that Trellex continuously endeavoured to become leader. The companies can therefore be described as being neither symmetrical nor asymmetrical in technical or market leadership. The issue of leadership seems to have been a matter of prestige, which can explain the fact that the companies participated actively in the struggle to assert leadership.

The National and International Development of the Market

During the 1960s, the mill lining market expanded both nationally and internationally. During the 1940s and 1950s, Skega had developed good relations with Boliden, and in this way had come to completely dominate sales to this company. Selling to Boliden was perceived by Trellex to be very difficult, which is why Trellex sold its products to LKAB, another mining company in northern Sweden, and to mines in the south. Skega also sold its products to LKAB and Grängesberg, although Boliden was its largest buyer. Thus, the two companies, Trellex and Skega, came into contact with each other in their penetrations of LKAB and Grängesberg.

The competition for individual installations was very hard. Descriptions of the competition of the time given at Trellex reveals that both companies tried to conceal from the other that they were approaching a specific customer. If the customer installed a lining manufactured by the competitor, the companies would offer to install their own linings in half of the mill to give the customer the opportunity to judge for themselves the quality of the competing companies' products. From the knowledge gained of which lining the competitor installed, it became possible to manufacture and install a lining with longer product durability.

Both companies also installed linings in mills used in the Cement industry. Skånska Cement, situated in southern Sweden, was the largest customer in this customer segment. At first, Skega dominated this segment, and one of the managers of the time describes the company's pride in having established a dominating position within Trellex's geographical home territory. One of Trellex's managers argues that the strong relationship that had developed between Skega and Skånska Cement's central market manager explains why Skega had developed such a strong position. Trellex then decided to approach the individual factories to try to gain market shares from Skega. This way of competing for individual installations led progressively to Trellex breaking Skega's domination of the cement market, and this type of competition between Trellex and Skega in the Swedish market continued during the 1960s and 1970s.

Parallel with the development of the Swedish market, a similar development also occurred in the international market, in that the two companies competed with each other to some extent at meetings with individual customers abroad. A certain amount of asymmetry can therefore be seen in the choice of distribution channel in the international market. However, international operations were minor, as they were at this stage still only just emerging. The companies' operations were therefore dominated by the domestic market, which involved sales representatives from both companies visiting Scandinavian mines, and the two competitors were symmetric in their domestic market operations.

In summary, symmetry between the actors during the first phase was considerable and competitive play was very active. The two Swedish companies competed actively in their product development and met each other in their contacts with almost every customer in common markets. The one company's actions were soon followed by similar actions by the other. Competitive plays were rapid and of great scope. Counter-moves were instigated as soon as the competitor obtained information about the other's actions.

Phase Two — The Differentiation of the Companies

During the 1970s, the two Swedish competitors began to differentiate from each other, which meant that competition in the Lining industry changed. Trellex further developed screens for the Gravel and Stone industry, and began to expand in this area. Skega, to a greater extent than Trellex, specialised in mill linings for the Mining industry, developing its international marketing organisation primarily in foreign markets. This, however, did not give rise to any difference in size between the two companies, and the symmetry in resources remained. Neither company as a whole developed technical or market leadership, even though there were differences in individual product and market segments.

Product Differentiation

The symmetry in the companies' product range decreased during Phase Two. Trellex initiated intensive efforts in the development of screens for the Gravel and Stone industry during the 1970s, and launched a new product family of screens called Trellcord. Trellcord proved to be successful in the market, and sales volumes of screen increased dramatically. Skega introduced a new screen, called the Skega-H, only a year or two later, and some of the interviewees at Trellex are of the opinion that Trellcord's success was the major reason for Skega to further develop its product range.

However, both competitors offered screens that differed from each other, in that Trellex produced punched screens, whereas Skega produced cast screens (in Skega's case, mainly for the Mining industry). Many at Trellex consider that the advantage of punching screens was that this could be done close to the customer, which in turn made it easier to provide appropriate customer service. Skega did not reach any high volumes with its product, which many interviewees at Trellex see as being due to the characteristics of the product; selling screens requires local establishment. As a result of the growth of the screen operations, which thus increased its share of the total operations within the industry, the symmetry in the companies' product offer decreased, despite mill lining still dominating both companies' operations.

Mills became larger, and milling techniques advanced. To cope with the new requirements that were placed on linings, Skega developed a new lining attachment system in 1977 that was both flexible and easy to assemble. Both companies improved the lifting capacity of the liners, using other compositions of rubber and other shapes so that the linings would work better in larger mills using other techniques. The two companies' product offer and product range within the mill lining area was still very similar.

International Expansion

A new era in Skega's history arose during the last few years of the 1960s. Skega had previously employed and trained agents in a number of foreign countries, and by 1964, the company had agents in Finland, Norway, Germany, Switzerland, Italy, Great Britain, Canada, the USA, and South Africa, as well as licensing in a number of other countries. However, international operations were still limited until the end of the 1960s, when Skega started to manufacture mill linings and other lining products in Chile. The company had delivered lining rubber to South America since 1964, mostly to Peru and Chile, and the South America Mining industry had been under expansion for a number of years. However, the protectionistic customs tariffs and the considerable geographic distance made it difficult to deliver spare parts quickly, which explains why it was deemed necessary to establish a subsidiary in the region.

When Skega had established their plant in Chile in 1969, Incentive AB acquired 50% of Skega. Skega gained increased goodwill, relative strength, and authority by becoming part of a larger corporation, which is considered by some to have eased the company's actions in foreign markets. Incentive's attitude that Skega's further internationalisation ought to take the form of establishing its own units abroad rather than through licensing also supported Skega's foreign establishments during the 1970s. Skega established another manufacturing subsidiary in Canada in 1974.

Trellex's internationalisation differed from Skega's in many respects. The international side of Trellex's operations were conducted within the framework of Trelleborg's international marketing organisation. The fact that Trelleborg was primarily established in the industrial countries of Europe and the USA, meant that Trellex also concentrated its international operations to these markets. European and American subsidiaries were organised with separate units for the sales of lining products.

Despite Trellex initiating internationalisation during the 1960s, it was not until the mid-1970s that the company gained a proper foothold in the European market, primarily in the British and French markets. It was not until the company intensified its efforts in the screens segment by opening so called 'workshops' for the finishing of the screens, that the company fully established itself internationally. During the 1970s, Trellex developed a strong market position in the European market, and towards the end of the phase, expanded its cultivation of more peripheral markets.

This means that symmetry in the companies' market choice decreased, partly as a result of the increase in importance of their international operations. The competitors chose different geographical areas, different forms of establishment and, to some extent, different customer segments. Despite this, the degree of symmetry between the two companies remained stable in the Scandinavian markets, markets that were still of great importance. Both companies developed and sold mill linings to the Mining industry.

Competitive plays in the main product and market area, mill linings for the Scandinavian market, remained active, as in the previous phase. In these segments, the two companies met and competed by direct move and counter-move. Competition was, however, relatively passive within both peripheral markets and within the screen product area. Competitive play also became less intense and of less scope as the development of mill lining was not as rapid as it had been previously. Trellex developed screens for the Gravel and Stone industry and Skega concentrated its efforts on further developing its lining product for the Mining industry, as well as internationalising its operations.

Phase Three — Turbulence and Reconstruction

Competition between the two companies sharpened and changed character during the 1980s. Company acquisitions and tough price competition were two new elements in the competition that was pursued. Although the activity in competitive play remained high, it changed character, in that relations between the two actors became highly conflictive. The degree of symmetry also changed, to becoming very asymmetrical.

The Trelleborg corporation as a whole began to operate extensively within a number of areas closely related to the Lining industry. Trelleborg grew through the acquisition of a number of mines such as Boliden, which at the time was Skega's biggest single customer, and the acquisition of a number of companies that were part of the Allis Chalmer group, a major American machine manufacturer active throughout the world. Trellex developed from a small experimental operation to become an important unit within the Trelleborg corporation, which in turn changed Trelleborg's commitment to Trellex's areas of operation. This gave rise to strong asymmetry in resources between Skega and Trellex, which meant that Trellex gained a strong position of power in relation to Skega. There was no change, however, in the perceptions of which company occupied the position as market and technical leader within the industry.

The product choice and market choice of both companies also became asymmetrical. Within the screen product area, both companies distinguished themselves markedly from each other, as they had done previously. Skega primarily produced cast screens for the Mining industry, whereas Trellex manufactured punched screens for the Gravel and Stone industry. Trellex also differed from Skega by offering a wider range of screens, which included fine, medium, and coarse screening. The importance of screens as a product area increased, and at the time of Trelleborg's acquisition of Boliden made up 50% of Trellex's business. As screens became progressively a more important part of Trellex's total business, whereas mill linings still dominated Skega's operations, the competing companies became asymmetrical in their product choice.

Asymmetry between the competing companies regarding the foreign market choice increased concurrently with the expanding international operations. Skega still maintained a stronger position in peripheral markets, whereas Trellex focused its operations to the European and American markets. The differences between the companies increased because of their choice of market establishments. Trellex kept to its strategy of manufacturing all of its products in Sweden, and only established sales companies abroad, whereas Skega started two new manufacturing companies during the 1980s. Trellex also began to develop a service organisation within the Swedish market (something which Skega did not do) as well as establishing service contracts with Swedish customers.

Asymmetry in the companies' choice of distribution channel therefore increased.

Competitive play became very active. Several competitive plays occurred simultaneously, though on different levels. Besides the direct competition between their lining divisions, competition occurred at a top level between Skega and Trelleborg. Measures within totally different areas of production had consequences for competition in their lining divisions. Skega's managers describe competition at the time as being two-fold, being partly between Skega's lining division and Trellex, and partly between Skega and Trelleborg on a higher level not directly connected to operations. Perceptions of competition on these levels influenced the direct interaction between Trellex and Skega and their attitudes towards each other.

Competitive play became conflicting and reactive. Action was complex and often charged with prestige; the company's own individual action is described as being either independent of their competitor, initiated by the entrepreneurs within the company, based on perceived customer needs, or as being reactive. Both companies consider that they have sometimes been forced to react to the competitor's conflicting action. The actions of the companies are described as conflicting or imitative in those instances when the competitor is considered to have copied products developed as a result of the company's independent action. The scope of competitive play increased due to a number of parallel and integrated competitive plays in product development, market penetration, and pricing. In that sense, competitive play was very active during this last phase.

The competitive play that took place during the third phase will be described in more detail in the next section of the chapter; this to exemplify the conflicting and reactive pattern of interaction that took place. However, before that description is given, the development and the changes of the contexts of competition in the history of the Lining industry will be summarised.

Contexts of Competition in the Lining Industry — a Summary

It can be stated that the symmetry between the companies and the activity in competitive play has varied over time. The two companies have found themselves in three different contexts of competition during the different phases of the history of the industry. When the Lining industry emerged, a very symmetrical and very active competition developed in the industry. During the second phase, both the activity in competitive play and the symmetry between the actors decreased, as the companies diversified in different directions. The asymmetry between the companies increased further during the third phase, and the degree of activity in competition play became active once again, partly as a result of Trelleborg's actions.

In Appendix 2, a presentation of the assessment of symmetry between the actors and activity in competitive play is given for the different phases in the history of the industry, which in turn is illustrated in the figure below. The points signify competition in the middle of a phase, whilst the arrowed line illustrate the change between these points in time.

COMPETITIVE PLAY DURING THE 1980S

During the most recent phase of the Lining industry, the context of competition has been active and asymmetrical. By analysing the

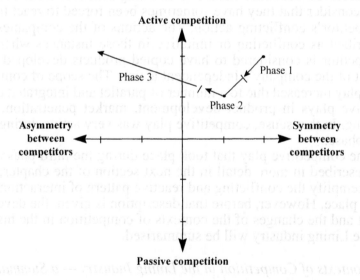

Figure 5.3   Changes in Contexts of Competition within the Lining Industry[2]

---

[2] The discussion in Chapter 8 explaining that Figure 8.1 gives a simplified illustration of competition and changes in competition, i.e. does not show variations and nuances, is also valid for Figure 8.2.

competitive play that has taken place during this phase, it is possible to attain knowledge of the nature and dynamics of asymmetric-active competition. The next section will present an in-depth description of the competitive play considered most important during this phase. Through this, a deeper understanding for the dynamics within an asymmetric-active context of competition should be gained.

Price Competition During the 1980s

The price competition driven between the two competitors during the 1980s became a new element in competitive play, and both Trellex and Skega describe the decade as a period of hardening price competition. Many interviewees at Skega describe Trellex as being inconsequential during the period up to 1986, offering at times very low prices, changing to much higher prices at other times. Trellex, on the other hand, describes Skega as always offering products at lower prices.

After Trelleborg's acquisition of Boliden, Trellex began to consistently compete through price at every business opportunity, according to many interviewees at Skega. The price competition that arose is assumed by some of Skega's interviewees to have developed as a result of Trelleborg's strategy of buying up companies and restructuring mature industries. Others question Trellex's actions as defensible business practice. In much the same way, many interviewees at Trellex question Skega's pricing policy, considering it to have been indefensible. Trellex wondered whether Skega considered it necessary to compete through price, following Trelleborg's acquisition of Boliden, to obstruct Trellex from entering new market segments. On the other hand, the fact that Skega offered lower prices to Boliden is considered to be understandable, as this meant that Skega could regain lost market shares.

According to many interviewees at Skega, the company participated in price competition that had been initiated by Trellex, offering prices at an unprofitable level, except where business was deemed to be of particular strategic importance. Low pricing in such situations was considered to be indefensible in the long run. Trellex also set prices that were unprofitable and it was considered to be acceptable in markets where Skega completely dominated the market. A change in the pricing of such markets would only affect Skega.

Both companies view the price competition of this phase to have been too severe, and are in agreement over the fact that both companies ought to set prices at a market level. The two parties also agreed that the price-war should be broken, but despite this, the price-war continued. Many interviewees at both Skega and Trellex stated that the companies had attempted to apply market prices, but that these attempts had been countered by the competitor, who offered prices at levels that were too low. One of the reasons for this, according to many of the interviewees, was the enmity and mistrust that existed between the two companies.

Company Acquisitions

The element of competition between Skega and Trellex most frequently discussed by the interviewees is Trelleborg's company acquisitions during the decade. Skega also acquired companies, though not in the same scope. These acquisition are described in this section, and are summarised in the figure below.

The Acquisition of Boliden

In 1986, Boliden was acquired by Trelleborg. Many interviewees at Trellex are of the opinion that the motive behind the acquisition was purely financial. Trellex itself was not involved in the decision to take over Boliden, in that the decision was taken at corporate

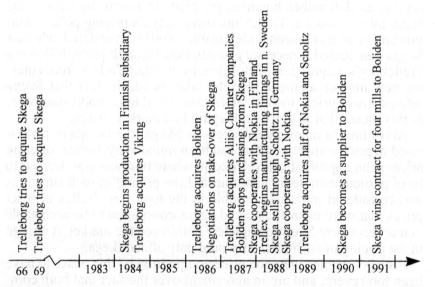

Figure 5.4   Company Acquisitions in the Lining Industry during the 1980s

level. Trellex's subsequent increase in sales of lining in the Swedish market is considered to be an effect of the acquisition rather than a reason behind it.

As a direct consequence of the acquisition, Skega terminated its co-operation in product development with Boliden. This meant that the project that was under development at the time between Skega and Boliden, the testing of a lining called the Poly-Met that combined both steel and rubber, was entirely transferred to the Canadian mine in which it was also being tested. Many interviewees at Skega mentioned that the acquisition of Boliden by Trelleborg led to the ideas behind the Poly-Met becoming known to Trellex, and that this in turn meant that it would have been difficult for Skega to patent the product in Sweden.

Though other managers at Trellex claim that they received very little knowledge of Skega's tests, one manager stated that the company already knew about the Poly-Met (i.e. before the acquisition), as Trellex had been testing the Steel-Cap, a similar product, in the same mine at Boliden at the same time as Skega had been testing its product. Some of the interviewees at Trellex also claim that it would not have been possible for Skega or Trellex to patent the product, as the ideas behind the product had been common knowledge for some time, and had already been tested in different ways. Skega did, however, patent the Poly-Met in a number of foreign countries, and as this is considered to have been wrong, Trellex attempted to have the patents annulled.

Since the 1950s, Boliden had functioned as Skega's main experimental laboratory. This was lost with the acquisition of the mine by Trelleborg. Skega considered it unsatisfactory to place the testing of new products completely in foreign mines as the main product development took place in Sweden, and therefore, to compensate for the major losses caused by the loss of Boliden, Skega increased its co-operation with LKAB, with developmental testing in a smaller mine. The fact that Trellex did not sell its products to this mine was considered to be a distinct advantage. During the latter part of the 1980s, co-operation in product development has also intensified with Skega's subsidiaries, and routines have been put into practice in Skega's management of its subsidiaries. The Canadian subsidiary, for example, was given responsibility for certain developmental projects, and this has helped to continue the co-operation with and flow of ideas from the subsidiary to Skega.

Skega's deliveries to Boliden also ceased after a short period of time. Directly after the acquisition, Skega received information that Boliden would continue to purchase its mill linings on business-like terms. At the time of the acquisition, Skega delivered approximately 90% of Boliden's mill linings, but after the acquisition, orders from Boliden did not materialise. Many interviewees at Skega believe that Trelleborg's corporate management expressly required that Boliden should now buy its linings from Trellex in order to shut Skega out from its previously biggest single customer. Although interviewees at Trellex admit being aware of the requirement that Boliden should buy from Trellex, a somewhat different picture is given of the motives and reasons behind these requirements. Many considered it wrong to make such demands, but nonetheless that it was necessary.

According to Trellex's managers, it soon became obvious that it was impossible for Boliden's purchases to be based on business-like terms. The previous links between Boliden and Skega, and the relations that developed between individuals in both companies, which were situated within the same region, made it impossible for Trellex to compete with Skega on equal terms. It was therefore deemed necessary to steer Boliden's purchases from Skega to Trellex. Trelleborg relaxed these requirements after a number of years, with the hope that the "pendulum would remain in 'normal' position", as it was expressed by some at Trellex, so that neither personal relations between Skega and Boliden, nor Trelleborg's purchase requirements would hinder purchasing on business-like terms.

In 1989, Skega came to an agreement with Boliden about the entire responsibility for mill lining at one of Boliden's smaller mines, the Enåsen gold-mine. When the company took over this responsibility from Trellex, Skega was able to state that Trellex had had considerable problems with stoppages. Some of the interviewees at Skega saw the fact of being able to supply Boliden again to be a major victory. Skega signed a service contract in 1991 for four mills in one of Boliden's mines, and sold linings for three mills at another mine owned by Boliden. Some of the interviewees at Skega see two explanations for this development; firstly that Trelleborg's influence over Boliden's choice of supplier decreased with the building of Svedala Industries AB, and secondly that Boliden had had problems in its relations with Trellex. Some of the interviewees at Skega consider that the company could deliver according to the demands set by Boliden better than Trellex.

Losing its biggest customer meant that Skega intensified its efforts on other products and markets. Sales to LKAB increased after the acquisition, and linings to the Ceramics industry were further developed in co-operation with Italian ceramics manufacturers. Smaller customers were cultivated to a greater extent than before, which gave rise to many smaller deliveries and shorter series. This led to the exposure of inflexibility and bottlenecks in the production process, which in turn led to the initiation of a thorough efficiency drive. New routines were introduced, the production process was made more efficient, and capital binding and costs linked to production were reduced.

Trelleborg's acquisition of Boliden also had consequences for Trellex. Sales to Boliden increased dramatically, which was considered to be positive by many at Trellex, but it also gave rise to a number of problems. For example, Trellex's production capacity was not enough to cope with the increase in orders, causing subsequent delays in delivery, and faulty products due to parts of the product not being completely finished. According to one of the managers, these problems arose from the fact that Trellex had not prepared itself in time for the enormous change brought about by the acquisition. However, the required capacity was built up over time, partly through measures that were taken at the factory at Trelleborg, and partly through the establishment of mill lining production at Gällivare, a town further north in Sweden, in 1988. Apart from the need for increased capacity, the investment at Gällivare is explained as being part of Trelleborg's willingness to show a greater regional responsibility by establishing another company in the region (following its acquisition of one of the largest companies in the region).

Some of the interviewees at Skega mention a further motive behind the Gällivare establishment. For a number of years, corporate management at Trelleborg had expressed an interest in acquiring Skega, and had discussed this possibility with Assar Svensson on a number of occasions, though the suggestion was turned down every time. Trelleborg made clear at these meetings that if the company could not acquire Skega, it would establish its own production in northern Sweden. Trelleborg's managing director, soon to be its Chairman of the Board, wrote in an article in the journal 'Rubbery' that "Skega will be in our hands within five years". The following year, in 1988, Trellex established its production at Gällivare (within Skega's 'traditional' territory), in much the same way as had been expressed at the negotiations between Trelleborg and Skega.

Some of the interviewees at Skega considered the fact that Trellex was part of the Trelleborg corporation to be threatening, as this meant that Trellex became to a certain extent relatively stronger that Skega. This fear can be explained by Trelleborg's repeated attempts to acquire Skega, as well as other measures aimed at

out-competing Skega. When Assar Svensson sold parts of Skega to
Incentive in 1969, he stipulated in the sales agreements that
Incentive must not sell Skega to Trelleborg.

The Viking (Norway) and Nokia (Finland) Acquisitions

Two company acquisitions affected competition in the industry indirectly; Viking, a Norwegian company, and Nokia, a Finnish company.
Trelleborg's acquisition of Viking in 1984 meant that Trelleborg came
to compete with Skega in the caterpillar carrier product area. This
event is not mentioned by Trellex as being part of the competition
between the two companies, but many of the interviewees at Skega
consider this to have been one of Trelleborg's competitive plays.
Those individuals that have been with Skega over a longer period of
time often discuss Skega relative to Trelleborg, whereas Trellex separates its actions from that of Trelleborg.

The second company acquisition that indirectly affected competition within the industry took place in 1989.

Skega and Nokia established a common sales company in 1988.
Nokia sold Skega's mill linings in Finland, and terminated its own
production, whilst Skega sold Nokia's products, such as conveyor
belts, piping, and punched screening sheets in Sweden. As a result
of this co-operation, Nokia's German company, Conrad Scholtz
GmbH, and its subsidiary also sold Skega's lining products. Many
of the interviewees at Trellex considered Skega's co-operation with
Nokia as an attempt to penetrate the punched screens market.
Trellex had previously expanded in this product area, whilst Skega
still only manufactured cast screens. The main argument for this
co-operation given by Skega, however, lay in the severe price competition in the Finnish mill lining market. Trelleborg's acquisition
of Nokia included Conrad Stoltz GmbH, which meant that Skega
was forced to terminate its co-operation with Stoltz. However, as
the co-operation between Skega and Stoltz had not really properly
begun in, the damage was not considerable.

The Acquisition of a Number of Allis Chalmer Companies

In 1987, Trelleborg acquired approximately twenty companies from
the Allis Chalmer corporation,[3] and thereby became owner to 50%

---

[3] The use of the term 'Allis Chalmer' in the rest of the text refers to those companies previously owned by the Allis Chalmer corporation that were acquired by Trelleborg.

of the world's machine manufacturers and almost 80% of the mill manufacturers. The Allis Chalmer companies continued to purchase mill linings from Skega after the acquisitions; one reason for this is that price plays an important part in the purchase decision in mill linings. Many interviewees at Skega state that deliveries to the Allis Chalmer companies decreased drastically, and some of them are of the opinion that Trelleborg tried to influence the machine manufacturers to do their purchasing within the corporation.

Sala International, a Swedish manufacturer of pumps, was also among the companies that Trelleborg acquired, and again, this company was one of Skega's regular pump lining customers. Many interviewees at Skega are of the opinion that Trelleborg initially decreed that Sala should purchase its pump linings from Trellex, but after a time, Sala began to purchase again from Skega, which is interpreted by Skega as indicating that Skega's linings met Sala's requirements better than Trellex. Skega's employees exhibit a certain amount of pride over having their company's superiority confirmed in this way. Many interviewees at Trellex, on the other hand, claim that the Allis Chalmer companies were not steered in their purchasing, as machine manufacturers buy their complementary products, such as linings, on business-like terms. However, during the past few years, deliveries from Trellex to Allis Chalmer have increased, and are expected to continue increasing in the future due to the increasing integration of Trellex with Allis Chalmer. The two companies' marketing organisations were integrated in the USA, which provided Trellex with a unique position relative to Skega, and Trellex also sold its products through Allis Chalmer's sales companies in other markets such as Chile.

Both competitors are of the opinion that Skega has gained an advantage in relation to the other machine manufacturers as a result of Trelleborg's acquisition of the Allis Chalmer companies. Those machine manufacturers not owned by Trelleborg purchase their mill linings from Skega, as Trellex is indirectly one of their competitors. For example, a number of French, German, and British machine manufacturers have contacted Skega to participate in co-operation.

Product Development — Race or Imitation?

It is primarily in the development of mill linings that Skega and Trellex have competed directly with each other. Skega considers itself as technical leader in the development of lining products, and many of the interviewees at Skega consider that it has been Trellex that has imitated Skega, rather than the reverse (although a number of examples are given where Skega has made use of developmental work done by Trellex as inspiration for its own product development). The view that Skega is a technologically intensive company that has invested considerable resources in product development and in high-risk projects is also held to be true by some of the interviewees at Trellex. Skega is also considered to be more persevering over time in its attempts to succeed with development projects. On the other hand, Skega is perceived to be narrower in its product development, due to its specialisation in lining products for the Mining industry. The measures that were taken in developing new products is summarised in the figure below.

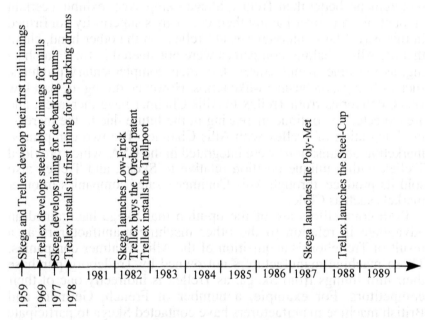

Figure 5.5   Product Development in the Lining Industry[4]

---

[4] Low-Frick and Trellpot are two similar products, which are used as protection against wear in the loading and unloading of caterpillar treads. These products are therefore partly outside the lining product area, which explains why their development is not treated in any detail in this book.

Many of the interviewees in this case-study believe that both competing companies have been stimulated in their development as companies by having a competitor that has applied itself intensively to product development, and this has given rise to increased risk-taking and perseverance in product development. Both companies talk of the importance of patenting, examining in detail the competitor's applications for patents, and through this being able to quickly gain information about the competitor's research. None of the foreign competitors are watched in the same way, partly because it is more difficult to gain access to their patent applications, and partly because the other competitors normally imitate Skega's and Trellex's products.

The Development of Mill Lining

Throughout the three phases in the industry, competition has been active in the development of mill linings. Both companies have therefore continually developed and improved the mill lining product range. During the 1980s, the Mining industry developed towards fewer and larger mills. The Poly-Met and the Steel-Cap linings, combining both rubber and steel, were developed for these larger mills. Although both Skega and Trellex had previously experimented with combining rubber and steel, no new mill linings were developed.

The initiative behind Skega's development of the Poly-Met was taken in Canada, where larger mills were markedly more in use. A product was therefore developed at Skega's Canadian subsidiary, which was subsequently patented in Canada. It was stated at Boliden that the capacity of the mills increased with lifts that had become somewhat worn down, which was why there was a demand by the company for lower lifts with the same durability as the higher lifts. Boliden therefore approached Skega, which then further developed the product that had been developed in Canada. As has been stated previously, the co-operation between Skega and Boliden was begun before Trelleborg acquired Boliden.

After Trelleborg's acquisition of Boliden, Trellex was given the opportunity of delivering the type of lining that Boliden requested. A Japanese company licensed by Trellex had previously developed a rubber and steel lining for large mills. When Boliden expressed a demand for this type of lining, Trellex made use of the knowledge gained from the developmental work done in Japan, resulting in the instalment in December 1986 of the Steel-Cap, a new lining with a lift topped with steel.

Many of the interviewees at Skega describe the development of the Poly-Met and the Steel-Cap, by stating that Trellex was able to make use of ideas developed by Skega at Boliden before the acquisition in its own developmental work, which later resulted in the Steel-Cap. According to one of the managers at Skega, Trellex developed a construction that included more steel, so that Trellex's product would not be identical to Skega's. This meant that the Steel-Cap became more expensive to manufacture, which was considered a disadvantage for Trellex. Some of the interviewees at Trellex, however, are of the opinion that Skega did not use enough steel in its product, and therefore consider the Steel-Cap to be a more substantial product.

The acquisition of Boliden is considered by Trellex to have been an important step in the development of the Steel-Cap, not because of the information on Skega's developmental work that was gained, but because Boliden gave Trellex the opportunity to develop the Steel-Cap. Many of the interviewees at both Skega and Trellex are of the opinion that Skega's product, the Poly-Met, was relatively more advanced when launched, and at Skega, this is considered to have been the result of the head-start that the company had in its developmental work. Trellex, on the other hand, sees Skega's low price to be the reason behind this.

The Development of Linings for De-barking Drums

During the 1970s, the floatation of timber decreased as a result of the increased transport of timber by land. Land transport resulted in gravel getting caught up in the timber, which in turn meant that de-barking caused greater wear and tear on the drums (which were normally lined with steel). When this problem attracted Assar Svensson's attention, he had the idea of lining the drums with rubber instead. Skega therefore instigated intensive developmental work in 1977, which resulted in the launching of rubber linings for de-barking drums and the patenting of an attachment system. Trellex installed its first lining in a de-barking drum in 1978. Many of the interviewees at Skega consider this lining in many respects to be similar to Skega's lining, and Trellex was not able to patent its product as the degree of new development in the product was very little. This led to the development and launching of a new type of lining a few years later, which Trellex patented.

The development of lining for de-barking drums was considered by Trellex to be a project with high risk and high costs, which meant that many were doubtful about putting a lot of effort into the product. The product would be sold in a market that Trellex had never penetrated before, and the technical performance of the lining in long-term operation had not yet been tested. Despite this, Trellex decided to develop the lining. Some of the managers state that the knowledge that similar developmental work was also being undertaken by Skega influenced Trellex's decision — if Skega had not been interested in developing linings for de-barking drums, it is doubtful whether Trellex would have taken that decision.

Both competitors consider Skega to have occupied a stronger position in the world market for linings for de-barking drums. Skega installed about 100 linings throughout the world in 1990, whereas Trellex only installed a few. This situation is explained by Trellex as being due to Skega's more intensive efforts in developmental work and market penetration. Many of the interviewees at Trellex further state that Trellex had a larger product range than Skega, which in turns requires a wider base of product and market development, whereas Skega specialised only in linings.

Skega perceived the price competition with Trellex in the de-barking drum area as being considerable, and this made launching products difficult. One of the individuals that actively participated in the developmental work states the following about Trellex's actions, "They tried more or less to buy their way into the market by cutting the price, which meant that we also cut our prices, ... the fact that they are now more or less out of the market doesn't mean that we can increase the price just like that". Trellex does not consider itself to be "out of the market", but views its linings for de-barking drums to be one product amongst others that they manufacture. The aim, however, is for Trellex to concentrate itself to core operations, and as linings for de-barking drums lie outside the company's core operations, this affects the way the company acts towards the products.

The Development of Other Products

Trellex offers screens for course, medium, and fine screening, whereas Skega operates within the course screening area mainly for the Mining industry. Skega and Trellex have not acted relative to each other in the development of screens in the same way as in the development of lining. Trellex developed and widened its range of screens at the end of the 1970s and during the 1980s, refining and further developing its screens and thereby gaining increased precision. Polyurethane (PU) began to be used in the screens, which gave them increased precision. As the material is relatively uncomplicated to produce, a number of local competitors established themselves in different countries. During the first half of the 1980s, Trellex developed a PU module system that increased flexibility, which made it easier to adapt the screening sheets to different types of screen.

Skega did not develop a similar module system, and this is interpreted by Trellex to mean that after a number of failed attempts to establish itself in the screen market, Skega had decided to prioritise the development of other products. Skega is therefore not considered as a serious competitor in this area. In 1991, however, Skega acquired Crigomsa, a Spanish company, which, amongst other products, manufactured screens. The acquisition is described by some of the interviewees at Skega as being a first move towards screens in order to broaden the company's operations.

A magnetic lining, the Orebed, is another product developed during 1980s. Two inventors developed a new mill lining with magnets vulcanised in rubber. They assumed that the magnets would attract stone containing iron-ore which would form a 'lining' of stone against which the rest of the ore could be grounded. The operative life-time of the magnetic lining would thus be 'eternal'. The inventors contacted Skega for help in developing the product and to sell the patent. Based on a market and financial analysis, Skega decided not to purchase the patent rights, but did participate for a while in developmental work, which the inventors then continued themselves.

The magnetic lining was installed in 1981 in two iron-ore mines, with good test results. The two inventors therefore approached Trellex to sell their patent rights, which Trellex bought and thereby became sole owner of the Orebed. The Orebed was first marketed as a lining with eternal life, but it became clear that Orebed had a more limited product life if the degree of iron-ore was not sufficient. This changed Trellex's marketing of the product, and the Orebed was re-launched in 1991 with a completely new marketing campaign based on other sales arguments.

Skega has followed this development and the results of the installation during the 1980s very closely. Many of the interviewees at Skega consider the Orebed to be a marginal product, and therefore do not count the product as a threat to their own products. Skega continues to follow the development of magnetic lining, in case its area of usefulness expands.

Competition in Marketing

During the 1980s, both Skega and Trellex have expanded their market organisations and measures taken by both companies during the 1980s is illustrated in the figure below.

International Market Investments

The 1980s began with a slight recession in Western European economies. As a recession in Europe was assumed to lead to a boom in America, Skega decided in 1980 to establish a manufacturing company in Mexico. Trellex had previously sold its products through its American sales company, but signals that Mexico was about to increase its customs tariffs led to a decision in 1980 to establish a joint venture with a Mexican company to sell rubber products to the Mining industry. A manufacturing licence was also attached to this joint venture.

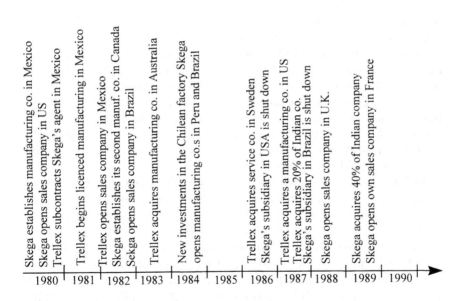

Figure 5.6   Action in the Competition for the Market in the Lining Industry

Many of the interviewees at Trellex are of the opinion that Skega countered this move by cutting its prices in competition with Trellex, which was possible because the company had established its own manufacturing operations in the country. This interpretation of the situation, however, is not shared by Skega, where many of the interviewees state that the competition from companies that manufacture steel lining is hard, and that price is therefore a crucial competitive variable in the Mexican market. Many of the interviewees at both Skega and Trellex state that Trellex had failed to develop a position in the market in Mexico, which was why Trellex decided to launch the Orebed in this market. One of the managers explains that this was to gain a foothold in the market. Skega has not instigated any counter-measures, partly because it does not believe in the product, and partly because Trellex's efforts have not yielded any obvious results.

Skega also established a sales company in the USA in 1980, and 1982 the company extended the old factory in Canada and built a new factory there. Some of the interviewees at Skega state that the most important reasons for investing in Canada were the expected increase in demand in the American market and the opportunity to compensate for the loss of a licensed manufacturer in the USA by increasing the share of the company's own manufacturing in the North American market. The expectancy of an expected boom in the market is also shared by many of the interviewees at Trellex as being a reason for these investments.

However, the expected boom in the American market did not materialise, which meant that the production capacity at Skega's newly built plants in Canada and Mexico could not be fully utilised. Skega was also confronted by harder price competition than it had expected. These setbacks led to a decision in 1986 to wind up the American sales company, and to co-ordinate manufacturing and marketing in the American and Canadian markets to the Canadian and Mexican companies.

In 1988, Trellex acquired a company in the USA, and planned to increase the manufacturing of the American company to include Trellex's entire product range. Skega did not instigate any counter-moves because, according to some of the interviewees at Skega, Trellex had previously had limited success in the States. Trellex, on the other hand, is of the opinion that its operations in the American market have developed positively, and in 1991, the company's commitment in the USA market was strengthened through the integration of the department of Trelleborg's sales company that dealt with lining products with the Allis Chalmer unit in the USA.

Both Trellex and Skega developed their positions in the South American market during the 1980s. In 1982, Skega established a sales company in Brazil, and manufactured its products under license in the country, which in turn led to the establishment in 1984 of a manufacturing company there (shut down in 1987 due to the high rate of inflation). New investments were injected into Skega's Chilean company the same year, as well as Skega acquiring 40% of a Peruvian company that manufactured lining (this share of ownership was increased at a later date). These investments were primarily aimed at consolidating Skega's position in the South American market, assessed to be a major market of the future. Operations in the Chilean and Peruvian companies functioned well, and through its investments there, Skega established a strong position in the South American market.

Trellex had mainly sold its products to South America directly from Sweden via Trelleborg's representatives, but in 1970 had established a manufacturing unit in Brazil, which was shut down in the 1980s. The rate of inflation in Brazil was perceived to be too high for it to be possible to operate efficiently in the country. Many of the interviewees at Skega are of the opinion that local manufacturing is needed if anyone is to succeed in the South American market. Some of the interviewees at Trellex state that the easing of customs tariffs in countries such as Peru has given them the opportunity to expand in South America, despite not having established a manufacturing plant there. At the end of the 1980s, Trellex began a co-operation with Allis Chalmer's sales company in Chile, and through this co-operation Trellex sees possibilities to further develop its penetration of the South American market.

The recession in Europe and America did not affect more peripheral markets, and both Skega and Trellex therefore increased their penetration of these markets during the decade. In 1975, Skega began to manufacture under licence in India, where in the period up to 1987 Trellex, according to Skega, was only marginally present in the market. In 1987, Trellex became joint owner of an Indian company, which began to manufacture and sell Trellex's products under licence. In 1989 Skega took over 40% ownership of the company that manufactured its products under licence in India. One of the managers is of the opinion that this was done to ensure that the licenced company would not be acquired by a competitor. Some of the interviewees at Trellex state that the potential of the Indian market is considerable, and that there is therefore room for both Trellex and Skega in this market.

Trellex also increased its commitments in Australia during the 1980s, a market in which Skega had been operative for a long time. Trellex's establishment was not considered to be a threat until 1991, when Trellex began manufacturing in the country. One of the managers at Skega stated that Skega, at the time of this study, was uncertain over Trellex's motives and ambitions with the establishment of this manufacturing company. Skega is therefore being cautious, seeking more information on the establishment.

At the end of the 1980s, Skega strengthened its marketing organisation in Europe, starting a sales company in Great Britain in 1988 to maintain the market leadership over mill linings that it had in Britain. In 1989, Skega also bought up its French agent, forming a subsidiary. Many of the interviewees at Skega are of the opinion that the company could strengthen its position within the E.U. region. One of Skega's employees commented on Trellex's presence in France, stating that "... they have a lot of people there, but nothing has happened yet". Many of the interviewees at Trellex do not consider Skega's actions as a threat, viewing Trellex's position as being stable. That Skega has "missed Europe" for some time, as one of Trellex's managers put it, means that Trellex has the advantage of already having established strong relations with the European customers, and these relationships are seen as a guarantee that Trellex will retain its position in Europe.

The Cultivation of the Swedish Market

The Swedish market has been of great importance to both Trellex and Skega as their major customers are situated in the home market, and the companies' knowledge of customer needs and new products has been developed in close co-operation with these customers. Different methods have been used to tie customers to the companies. For example, at the beginning of the 1980s. Skega offered service contracts to Boliden which entailed total responsibility for maintaining the mill linings against a charge per kilowatt-hour. Some of the interviewees at Skega are of the opinion that tight contacts with the customer are advantageous for the company in the long run. The offer was rejected by Boliden, which was afraid that by relinquishing responsibility, the company would lose interest in the further development of the products. In 1986, Skega did, however, manage to bring about a similar contract with LKAB.

Trellex Service, a new division within Trellex, was formed in 1986, comprising fifteen service units in Sweden, Norway, and Great

Britain. Through this service organisation, Trellex sold service contracts concerning total responsibility for the screen and conveyor belt
product groups, and also during the 1990s, for lining products. Many
of the interviewees consider that it is a competitive advantage to be
able to offer service for several product groups from one and the
same service organisation. Trellex's sales of screens have always
required regional units for the installation and punching of screens,
which has given the company considerable experience of adminis-
trating a geographically spread organisation. Many of the interviewees at Skega assess Trellex's efforts in this regard as being proper,
but Trellex is perceived as having had problems with developing
profitability in the individual units. One explanation for this is that
Trellex owns its service units, which can lead to a reduction in the
units' motivation to strive towards profitability. Skega therefore
decided that during 1989 and 1990, it would sign contracts of co-
operation with independent service units, that would result in a
similar service network, but with greater responsibility resting with
the individual units.

Competitive Play in the Asymmetric-Active
Context of Competition — A Summary

It is primarily in the product development of the companies and in
their cultivation of the market that competitive play has been most
evident, and this is illustrated in the figure below. In the continued
development of mill linings and in the development of lining for
de-barking drums, both companies have undertaken similar measures. Both Trellex and Skega surveyed the development of their
competitors very closely by examining the patent applications and
through the information they gained from their mutual customers.
Both companies point out that they were first, having created ideas
independently of their competitor, and that it was the competitor
that had imitated and undertaken similar developmental work. The
issue of which company that was actually first to develop, and
therefore stimulated the other, is full of prestige.

Three different competitive plays can be identified in Skega's
and Trellex's market development. Firstly, the companies competed in individual affairs at individual customers, which are not
included in the figure below.[5] Secondly, direct moves and counter-

---

[5] This is due to the companies not wanting such details to be published.

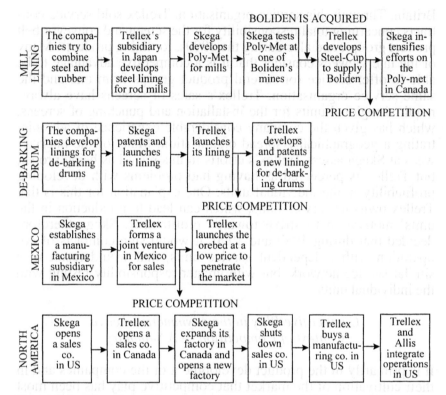

Figure 5.7   Examples of Competitive Play that Occurred Between Skega and Trellex in their Market and Product Development

moves can be identified, such as in the above description of the competition for the Mexican market. Similar competitive play has occurred in other markets, such as India and Australia. Thirdly, measures taken in one market are related to measures in other markets in the same region and between different regions, as in the North American market, where measures or the decisions not to implement counter-measures are related to the action of the competitor in the region as a whole.

Apart from the direct competitive plays between Skega's and Trellex's lining divisions, Trelleborg's and Skega's actions as a whole have directly affected competition between the lining divisions. It is primarily the company acquisitions of the 1980s that have brought about consequences for the competition in the Lining industry, as is illustrated in Figure 5.8 below. Despite, for example,

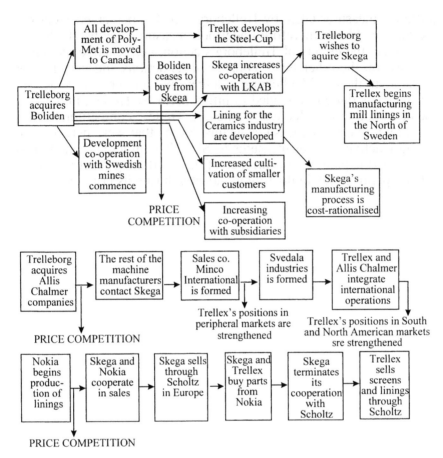

Figure 5.8   The Critical Company Acquisitions and their Effects on Competitive Play in the Lining Industry during the 1980s

Trelleborg's acquisition of Boliden being independent of both Skega and Trellex, the acquisition had direct consequence for the competition between them. The arrows in the figure illustrate which measures follow directly from others in time, though it must be pointed out that the measures have partly overlapped each other.

In summary, it can be stated that competition in the Lining industry, primarily during the 1980s, has been both complex and conflicting. The asymmetry that arose due to Trelleborg's company acquisitions within the Mining industry led to an increase in Trellex's strength relative to Skega. Skega constantly felt threatened by the different measures taken by Trelleborg, which it perceived Trellex to be part of. Skega therefore undertook measures against Trellex to counteract the effects of Trelleborg's action, i.e., reactive measures. Trellex, on the other hand, considered its actions and decisions as separate to those of Trelleborg, and therefore interpreted the actions of Skega as directly intended to inflict harm on Trellex, rather than being aimed at a collective 'Trelleborg-Trellex' competitor. Trellex therefore undertook measures against Skega that were perceived as being reactive counter-measures to Skega's conflicting action. This can in part explain the occurrence of the conflicting-reactive pattern of competitive play in the Lining industry during its last phase.

6. The Rack and Pinion Industry

The description of the Rack and Pinion industry in this chapter concludes the presentation of the three industries that are the focus of this book. The purpose of the chapter, as with the two previous chapters, is to determine which contexts of competition have emerged during the existence of the Rack and Pinion industry. The history of the industry reveals three phases, determinable by two distinct changes in the style of competition, which occurred during the first ten years in the industry's history. Since that time, which is now more than thirty years ago, the context of competition has been asymmetric and passive. Again, it is this last phase of the industry that is concentrated on in the descriptions of competitive play in the Rack and Pinion industry, though the conditions of the 1980s are emphasised. The analysis of this industry therefore provides important insight and knowledge about that context of competition, not exhibited by the previous two industries.

To be able to understand competition in this industry, a knowledge of the product concerned and its uses is required, though in this case it is more a question of the technology concerned rather than any specific product *per se*. This chapter therefore begins with a brief description of rack and pinion technology, its major areas of use, and the different categories of actor that constitute the industry and its environment. As in the previous two chapters, a chronological description of the history of the industry will then be given, with its different phases treated separately. Finally, the most recent phase of the Rack and Pinion industry is described in more detail, providing an in-depth presentation of the different competitive plays that were undertaken during this phase.

THE TECHNOLOGY/PRODUCT AND
THE ACTORS — A BRIEF INTRODUCTION

There are two principal ways of solving the problem of vertical transport in buildings and on building sites; either by using permanent cable or hydraulic lifts, or by using rack and pinion driven lifts. These two types of lifts differ mainly in the technology used for the drive system, but there are also differences in design (for example) between the two.

Line/cable driven lifts consist of a cage that is hoisted up and down the mast with the aid of a cable. A rack and pinion driven lift carries its own machinery either in the cage or on the roof of the cage. This machinery is fitted with pinions that climb a rack, which is bolted to a mast made out of a number of sections that can be easily assembled to the desired height.

Being driven by rack and pinion means that the products give rise to higher levels of noise and greater vibration, and the comfort that is associated with cable lifts manufactured for hotels and hospitals has not yet been achieved in rack and pinion driven products. However, these products are easy to assemble, and they do not require lift shafts or machine rooms. This gives rack and pinion driven products the advantage in the temporary vertical transport of people and material in difficult situations on building site and in industry, for example, in permanent installation in chimneys and towers.

The industry consists of operations within four rack and pinion driven product groups; raise climbers, construction hoists, special purpose and goods/passenger lifts (called permanent lifts), and Mast Climbing Work Platforms (MCWP).

Actors in the Industrial Environment

Among secondary actors, it is primarily the customer that affects the actions of the competing companies. Both construction hoists and work platforms are sold to the Construction industry, raise climbers are sold to the Mining and Plant industries, and permanent lifts are used in a number of different areas of application by industrial customers.

The Construction industry is concentrated to a few large actors, which means that the boundaries of the industry are relatively well defined. In Sweden, for example, there are approximately 25 key individuals that cover 80% of the sales channels. The Construction industry varies between different countries, however. In Sweden the process of building was rationalised and mechanised early in comparison with other countries. The labour laws and working environment legislation governing construction in Sweden are also extensive. The amount of lifts in use in the Swedish Construction industry is high, as it is normal to use lifts in the construction of buildings that are more than two floors high. The amount of lifts in use is also high in Australia and Britain. In the USA, however, it is not normal to install construction hoists unless the building is over ten floors in height, and in other countries, other modes of transport are made use of, such as cranes, and this reduces the use of lifts.

Work platforms are also sold to the Construction industry. The products were not launched seriously until the beginning of the 1980s, and as yet the market for work platforms comprises primarily the Nordic and European countries. Builders in the American market, in developing countries, and in the Far East, are assumed to develop a demand for the product when it has become more known. The future market potential is therefore assessed to be considerable.

Raise climbers for raising in mining and underground construction are sold primarily to mining companies, but are also used in the drilling of feeding pipes for hydro-electric power-stations. A description of the Mining industry can be found in the previous chapter, where it is stated that the industry is in recession in European and other industrialised countries. Canada and Australia, however, are two countries where the Mining industry is still important. Until the middle of the 1970s, the Mining industry expanded, which meant that the market for raise climbers increased. After the mid 1970s, there was a decrease in the market. From an international perspective, the Mining industry is concentrated, with a considerable transfer of information and competence between companies. For example, information about the advantages and disadvantages of a product is spread rapidly between actors.

In contrast to the Mining and Construction industries, the market for permanent lifts; i.e. special purpose and goods/passenger lifts, is very heterogeneous. Service and industrial lifts are permanently installed in various types of industry, and are sold to different types of customer, from farmers that use the lift to lift sacks a number of metres, to offshore service companies for oil platforms. In permanent installations of service and industrial lifts, cable lifts are normally installed, as it is only in a small area of use that the rack and pinion lift can provide the customer with advantages over other types of lift. For example, in cases where a decision is taken to install a lift in an existing industrial building without a lift shaft, the rack and pinion lift is a good alternative in cases where it is difficult to build a lift shaft, such as in chimneys and towers of different kinds.

The Swedish Rack and Pinion Competitors

The companies that manufacture and sell permanent cable and hydraulic lifts are mainly large manufacturers that operate internationally, whereas it is the smaller companies that manufacture rack and pinion driven lifts and work platforms. There are four companies in Sweden that manufacture rack and pinion driven products; Alimak AB, Tornborg AB, Tumac AB and Malmqvist AB. Alimak is the dominating actor in the industry, manufacturing all four products. Tornborg's and Tumac's main area of operations lie within other product areas. The lifts that these two companies manufacture and sell comprise only a few models that are sold mostly to the Construction industry. Malmqvist manufactures solely rack and pinion driven work platforms for the Construction industry.

The dominating company in the Swedish market, Alimak, is also world leader in the area for rack and pinion products. The company was founded in 1948 by Alvar Lindmark, but has been owned by the investment company Karolin Invest since 1987. In 1989/1990, Alimak employed a total of 506 employees, of which 307 were employed in Sweden. Alimak's turnover reached 425 million Swedish krona, of which approximately 10% came from Sweden, while the rest came from foreign markets. Alimak had approximately 65% of the total world market for rack and pinion driven construction hoists. Construction hoists constituted roughly half of the company's operations, permanent lifts answered for a quarter, and raise climbers for approximately one tenth of the company's turnover. The work platforms product group constituted only a few per cent of the turnover. Apart from offering these four product groups, the company also serves the after-sales market. Alimak has its own subsidiaries in Australia, Great Britain, Germany, France, Canada and the USA, as well as owning 60% of a manufacturing company in South Korea. Representative offices have been opened in Cairo in Egypt and in Singapore. Alimak also has distributors in a number of countries, and is represented in some form or another in more than 40 countries.

Alimak's two domestic competitors in the construction hoist segment are Tornborg and Tumac. Tornborg sells both lifts and cranes, concentrating until 1982 on the manufacture of lifts. In 1982, the company expanded its manufacturing of cranes, which subsequently became its largest area of operations. As far as lifts are concerned, Tornborg only manufactures a hydraulic lift. Tumac, the other competitor in the Swedish market, is smaller than Tornborg. The company changed owner at the end of the 1980s, and since then, Tumac's construction hoists have decreased in the Swedish market. In 1990, the company had a turnover of approximately 16 million Swedish krona, with 40 employees. Apart from construction hoists, the company also operates in a number of other product areas, such as pumps, machines, and accessories for the Stone, Glass, and Clay industries. Tumac and Tornborg manufacture special purpose and goods/passenger lifts, but these only comprise a very small part of their operations.

Alimak and Malmqvist are the two Swedish companies that operate in the segment for rack and pinion driven work platforms. During the latter part of the 1980s, Alimak intensified its efforts in this product area, whereas Malmqvist had begun manufacturing work platforms at the beginning of the 1980s. Malmqvist was acquired by a Dutch company, Hek, in 1989, but despite this acquisition, continued to manufacture and sell work platforms. This meant that both Malmqvist's and Hek's work platforms were sold in the Swedish market. In 1991, Hek placed Malmqvist into bankruptcy, and the receiver sold the company.

Competitors in the International Market

The international market comprises companies that manufacture rack and pinion driven products, though manufacturers of cable lifts must also indirectly be considered as competitors. The competitors that manufacture rack and pinion driven products consist mainly of a large number of local manufacturers of rack and pinion driven products in a number of different countries. Many of these have imitated Alimak's lifts, and every company builds on the rack and pinion technology originally developed by Alimak. Of the companies in the industry, only Alimak and Hek operate globally. Hek dominates the world market in work platforms, and is represented in the Swedish market through its agent, Hünebeck, which is a sales organisation that also operates in other countries. The rest of the competitors in all of the product segments operate locally or regionally in a small number of countries.

Competition from cable lift manufacturers is especially noticeable in the segment for special purpose and goods/passenger lifts. The cable lift manufacturers primarily consist of large global companies, such as Kone in Finland, Otis in the USA, and Schnidler in Austria. The entire world market is assessed to sales of approximately 120,000 permanent lifts per year, and only a few thousand of these are rack and pinion driven.

Cable lifts and rack and pinion driven lifts do not compete directly with each other, but are considered to complement each other. Cable lifts are used in the Construction industry at lower heights, whereas rack and pinion driven lifts can be more suitable for higher heights. The table below presents the most important customers in the three product areas described above.

The product group not referred to in the table below is the raise climber. Alimak is the only manufacturer to produce this lift in the Swedish domestic market. Foreign competitors are primarily domestic manufacturers that in many cases have imitated Alimak's raise climber, and these domestic manufacturers, with few exceptions, operate only within their national markets. However, an alternative method of mining to raise driving has been developed; full-face drilling. Alimak therefore competes with companies such as Atlas Copco and Tamrock in the mines' choice of mining method. This competition ceases when the mines have made their decision over which method to use, as there is no competition regarding product.

DIFFERENT CONTEXTS OF COMPETITION DURING THE HISTORY OF THE RACK AND PINION INDUSTRY

The description of the industry, its companies and the industrial actors involved has been based on the situation as it appears today (or rather at the time of the study). However, the present state of the industry is the result of a developmental process that has emerged over a longer period of time. Alimak's present dominating position must be related to and understood in the light of the competition that has prevailed during the first phases of the industry.

The first phase comprised the relatively independent development of new product and market areas by the companies involved, but came to an end when the domination of the industry that Alimak had developed, through being the first manufacturer of line driven construction hoists and raise climbers, was broken. The emerging second phase was characterised by intensive competition between the competing companies in the construction hoist product area. The second transition from one climate to another came about when Alimak launched its rack and pinion driven hoist, resulting in the company regaining its dominating position in the industry. The third phase, still prevalent today, is characterised by Alimak's dom-

Table 6.1   The Competitors in the Three Product Areas of the Rack and Pinion Industry and Their Markets

Products / Competitors	Construction hoists Personal/ material	Goods/ material	Permanent lifts	Working platforms
Alimak	World-wide	World-wide	World-wide	World-wide
Champion	USA, C		USA	
Hilleröd	DK	DK		
Hishino	Japan		Japan	
Wickham	UK, HKG		UK, DK	
Hek	NL, F, UK	NL, F, B, UK		World-wide
Ponteggi Dalmine	I, N Afr, UK			I
SAFI	I	A, CH		I
Ebbs & Radinger	A, CH			
Tornborg	Sv, UK			
Torgar	ES			
Torboiber	ES			
AZO	FRG			
Tumac	Sv			
Oh Dae	S Korea			

Table 6.1   *continued*

Products Competitors	Construction hoists Personal/ material	Goods/ material	Permanent lifts	Working platforms
Il Kwang	S Korea			
Chung Gu	S Korea			
Koshihara	Japan			
A Elmentti		SF		
PKZ		FRG		
Steinweg		FRG, UK		
Maber		I, B, UK		
Cadillon		F		
Condecta		CH		
RUX		FRG		
ACE			UK	
PD			I	
Electruk			Aus	
Malmqvist Products				S, N, SF
ORT				I

Table 6.1   *continued*

Products Competitors	Construction hoists Personal/ material	Goods/ material	Permanent lifts	Working platforms
Tractel				F, B
Select Etem				F
Piat				I, F, UK
VAE				I, F

Source: Internal material at Alimark[1]

[1] The above summary has been put together from the information provided by Alimark about its competitors in the different product groups. This information has been based on analyses of competition that have been carried out by the company.

inating position in the industry and by the other competitors developing their own niches. The three phases of the Rack and Pinion industry and their related contexts of competition are illustrated in the figure below.

Phase One — The Industry Emerges

Alvar Lindmark constructed the first rope driven construction hoist in 1952 in order to ease work on building sites. Other companies saw the possibilities of selling hoists to the Construction industry, and during the second half of the 1950s, two other manufacturers appeared on the scene, Tornborg and Amaco. A new sub-industry thus emerged for hoists used to facilitate different kinds of work. The larger companies that manufactured cable-driven lifts for hotels and hospitals chose not to enter this market.

The newly emerged industry consisted of three relatively small companies, but Alimak took a leading position regarding both the market and the technology. This can be explained by the fact that the company was the first to develop a construction hoist. Although the company manufactured only construction hoists at the beginning, it concurrently attempted to develop new products for vertical transport within other areas. In 1956, Alimak launched the 'Jacob's Ladder', a forerunner to today's work platform. It was a work platform based

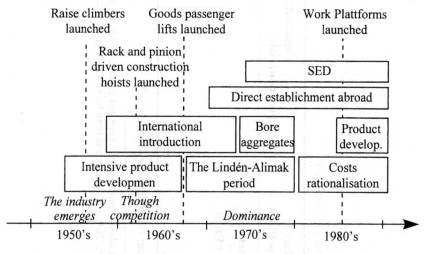

Figure 6.1   The Development of the Industry for Rack and Pinion Driven Products

on rack and pinion technology, and was used to put up neon signs, to wash windows, and other similar work. This new technology came to the attention of two Swedish mines, LKAB and Boliden, and a product development co-operation was entered into in 1957 to develop a raise climber. The first prototype was tested by LKAB, and was re-tested after a certain amount of re-construction by Boliden. This second prototype functioned well, which was certified by Boliden in writing. With this written testimony as part of its marketing, Alimak began to sell the raise climber to Swedish mines.

Some forty mines in central Sweden showed interest in the product, and sales increased both domestically and internationally. Alimak grew as a result of the launching of the raise climber and become bigger than the rest of the competing companies. Thus differences between the companies regarding products and resources were minor. Alimak, as well as Tornborg and Amaco, primarily manufactured and sold cable-driven lifts, and raise climbers were only a very small part of Alimak's, and thereby also the industry's, total operations.

The companies primarily served the Swedish construction industry and even though only Alimak marketed one product to the Mining industry, this area of operation was very small. Alimak had also began to expand internationally, though its international operations were still in their infancy.

Competitive play was very passive. The competing companies acted, to a great extent, independently of each other. The action that occurred during this phase focused mainly on finding new marketing opportunities; the potential market for lifts was perceived as large. Alimak concentrated on the development of raise climbers and on the company's internationalisation, which meant that it had neither the time nor the resources to actively compete in its main product segment, construction hoists. Amaco and Tornborg developed similar products, which indicates that they competed to some extent and inspired each other. However, the market was expanding, and the two companies therefore did not actively compete for the same customers. This indicates that the context of competition during this phase was symmetric and passive.

Phase Two — The Competition Hardens

During the first few years of the 1960s, five different models of the raise climber were developed. The product development of the raise climber has been limited ever since then, and the original models were still being sold during the 1980s. The co-operation with Swedish mining companies played a great role in the development of the raise climber. One of the managers states that it has been an clear advantage to have been able to co-operate with Swedish companies.

The 1960s saw an expansion in Alimak's international markets whilst the other companies mainly concentrated on the domestic market. During the 1950s, a certain amount of rope driven construction hoists had been exported, but it was only after the launch of the raise climb that an international breakthrough came. When Alimak introduced the raise climber at Swedish trade fairs, these were visited by representatives from other countries, which resulted in enquiries and orders from abroad. The raise climber became a major success, and expanded quickly in the international market, rapidly being sold to most of the larger mining countries. The product gained such a hold in the Mining industry that the driving method soon became known as 'The Alimak Method'. Alimak was the first company in the world to launch its climbs, and has practically remained alone in the world market. A certain amount of competition has occurred, though this has taken the form of competition with local manufacturers that have exported their products during limited periods of time, then returning to operating only in their domestic markets. Product competition is therefore perceived as being limited.

Competition between the Swedish manufacturers of construction hoists increased successively during the last years of the 1950s to become razor-sharp at the beginning of the 1960s. Alimak's efforts in developing and launching the raise climber internationally meant that the company did not participate in the cultivation of the market for construction hoists. Tornborg and Amaco developed new market segments and new cheaper products with lower installation costs while Alimak expanded internationally with raise climbers. As a result, Alimak lost its dominant position within the construction hoist product area, though no other company stood out as a clear leader, and the differences between the companies in resources were as previously not considerable.

One of Alimak's managers explains that at the beginning of the 1960s, the company was assumed to be the largest supplier of construction hoists in Sweden, but, despite this, Alimak only delivered spare parts during 1962. A phase of intense competition between Alimak and the other manufacturers commenced, and at Alimak, it was stated that drastic measures were needed if the company was to regain a leading position in the market. The positive experiences that Alimak had had with the raise climber led to a decision in 1962 to develop a rack and pinion driven lift. The implementation of this decision is commented by one of the managers, and the following quotation illustrates the intensity of the competition that prevailed during this phase.

> Why did we begin to develop the rack and pinion lift when we could have continued to manufacture rope lifts and raise climbs with its rack and pinion? It was because competition was so fierce, and if you look at the product specifications on our quotations of the time, you can see that we specify a net lining in our cages of 3 millimetres of wire-mesh compared to our competitors, who could only boast 2.5 millimetres. It is almost embarrassing to admit to having written quotations like that, but it just shows you how hard the competition was between Tornborg, Amaco and us.

By developing a hoist that was built on rack and pinion technology previously used in Alimak's raise climbers (but further developed), Alimak distinguished itself from its competitors, in order to avoid the hard competition that characterised the industry. The end of 1962 saw the launch of the first rack and pinion driven construction hoist. This rack and pinion hoist was exhibited at a Swedish trade fair in 1962, and reactions from Alimak's competitors were strong and very negative, because, according to them, the rack and pinion technology was impossible to use on a building site. Alimak's efforts in this area were strongly questioned, which can be illustrated by this quotation; "We have never had so much ridicule thrown at us before in our lives. I've never been to a trade fair before where our competitors have bitten our heads off so much. 'You can't believe in this?', and, 'This won't work!'.

At the same time as the launch of the rack and pinion lift, a committee was formed at *Ingengörsvetenskapsakademin* (The Academy of Civil Engineers), the I.V.A.'s crane and lift section, consisting of the technical managers at Tornborg and Amaco, and one of Alimak's managers. The representative from Alimak at the time states that Alimak's competitors did not believe in the new technique, and that he had tried to tone down the advantages of the new rack and pinion driven lift so that it would not be imitated by the others. The technology was known, which made it impossible for Alimak to patent the rack and pinion technology. It wasn't until three years later that Alimak's competitors began to manufacture rack and pinion driven lifts, and these years are seen as being very important for Alimak, and for the dominant position that the company managed to develop and maintain during the third phase.

Thus, despite the scepticism of competitors, sales of rack and pinion hoists went very well. From not having sold a single construction hoist in 1962, Alimak sold 80 rack and pinion driven hoists in 1963. *Sveriges byggnads- och entreprenörförening* (The Swedish Building Contractors' Association) carried out a test to compare rope driven hoists with hoists driven by the rack and pinion technique, which came to the conclusion that rack and pinion hoists were a cheaper and better alternative for the Construction industry. The results of this test became an important marketing weapon for Alimak in its continued sales, and contributed to convincing Alimak's competitors that the rack and pinion driven lift had come to stay.

By the mid 1960s, Alimak's competitors began to manufacture rack and pinion driven construction hoists. One of Alimak's constructors that had been involved in the first failed attempts to develop rack and pinion driven construction hoists moved over to Amaco in 1963, and he is assumed to lie behind Amaco's decision to begin manufacturing rack and pinion hoists. Another of Alimak's employees was placed to the company's offices in Stockholm when the sales of rack and pinion lifts expanded. This person quit Alimak after a while, and started his own company, Tumac, which began to manufacture rack and pinion driven hoists. Tornborg also decided to manufacture rack and pinion driven hoists, which meant that by the mid 1960s, there were four competitors in Sweden.

In summary, the context of competition in the Rack and Pinion industry became more asymmetric and active during the second phase. Alimak's sales of raise climbers and rack and pinion construction hoists increased, and as their competitors developed their own niches within the construction hoist product area, the symmetry in the companies' product range decreased. The symmetry in the companies' choice of market segment also decreased as a result of Alimak's international expansion and its penetration of the mining industry. These product and market segments were still minor, but should not be ignored. The loss of its leading position resulted in that Alimak strove to regain its dominating position, which meant active competition. From being very passive, competitive play became active as described above. However, the scope of the competitive play was not considerable, as it was primarily in the meeting with the customer that the companies actively competed against each other.

Phase Three — Alimak Dominates the Industry

As a result of the headstart gained by being the first to launch rack and pinion hoists, Alimak progressively developed a dominating position in the industry. Competition between the Swedish manufacturers was hard during the first half of the 1960s, but during the second half of the 1960s and the entire 1970s, competitors are not mentioned in the descriptions of action undertaken during that period. The only event discussed by some of the interviewees at Alimak is the acquisition by Alimak of one of the competitors, Amaco, in 1976. The motive given behind this acquisition is that Amaco had destroyed the pricing levels in the market and had shown some measure of success in the Swedish market. Some of the interviewees at Alimak state that a certain amount of competition can be healthy, but that it is important not to allow competitors to grow strong and achieve high volumes and high levels of profitability. Alimak's domination of the industry increased therefore from the second half of the 1960s to 1990 by continued product and especially market development. Organisational changes, changes in the economy, and external events affected Alimak's development rather than its competitors, but because the development of Alimak was affected, the development of the industry was also affected.

Alimak's Continued Product and Market Development

Alimak broadened its product range in 1968 by starting to manufacture rack and pinion driven special purpose and goods/passenger lifts. The fact that the manufacture of industrial lifts was not affected by changes in the economy in the same way as the manufacture of construction hoists, was considered an advantage by many at Alimak. Alimak expanded rapidly by internationalising its operations, and by producing permanent service and industry lifts. These lifts also began to be manufactured by the competitors, but on a small scale. The internationalisation of Alimak gave the company better internal pre-conditions for competition than its competitors. Turnover increased, which gave the company better financial opportunities.

During the 1970s, the development of permanent lifts consisted for the most part of modifying construction hoists so that they could be used for other purposes. Permanent lifts were therefore often adapted to fit specific customers' needs. It took a long time before these permanent lifts were considered to be a product area in its own right with its own product development plans. The two major areas of use for permanent lifts comprised lifts for towers of different kinds, masts and the like, and lifts for offshore industries, such as oil platforms. A module system was also developed in the mid 1970s, which could be used for both permanent lifts and construction hoists. Masts and cages were built in modules which could then be assembled and combined according to the needs of the individual customer.

In 1965, Robbins Inc. in the USA launched a new product called the 'Raise Borer', which was based on the idea of drilling/boring through mountain rock with large drilling heads. Within a few years, seven companies had taken up the manufacture of Raise Borers, and with this product, a new method of raise driving called full-face drilling began to be used. This meant that a certain degree of competition between methods of boring developed alongside the slight competition in product in the world market. The opinion at Alimak was that there was a demand for both methods, a demand which would continue into the future. Alimak decided to concentrate solely on the manufacture of raise climbers, and many therefore did not consider the companies that manufactured products for full-face drilling as direct competitors, even though the two methods competed with each other to a certain extent.

Although Alimak further developed its international operations, it was not until the mid 1960s that the export of rack and pinion driven construction hoists, which were sold mainly to the Nordic countries, took off. Alimak established a subsidiary in Denmark in 1964, and the agent employed in Norway also sold the product to the USA. Shortly afterwards sales were started in Germany, France, and Great Britain. As the expansion of sales of construction hoists gained momentum, Alimak had also develop an international sales network for raise climbers. Even though construction hoists were aimed at other markets, the company was able to use the knowledge and contacts gained by the sales of raise climbers in the introduction of construction hoists in the international market. To begin with, both construction hoists and raise climbers were sold via the same marketing organisation.

When Alimak began to manufacture rack and pinion driven service- and industry lifts for permanent installation in 1968, it seemed natural to also sell these lifts abroad, which led Alimak to strengthen its international commitments at the end of the 1960s and the during entire 1970s by establishing subsidiaries abroad. By the end of the 1970s, Alimak had established subsidiaries in Great Britain, France, Germany, Australia, and Canada.

Alimak's managers provide a number of reasons for the internationalisation of the company, one of which is the considerable interest internationally in Alimak's products. Sweden was a pioneering or leading country in building technology, and Sweden was therefore looked to by Europeans and then by Americans to find new building solutions. When foreign building contractors came into contact with the Swedish Construction industry, they also found out about Alimak's construction hoists. Another reason for the internationalisation of the company is seen by many interviewees at Alimak to lie in the personality of Alvar Lindmark, the owner of the company. Lindmark was greatly interested in expanding into international markets, and was not afraid to do so. He considered Alimak's products to be the best in the world, which should make it possible to sell them internationally. Therefore, he and his colleagues spent a few intensive years travelling around the world launching Alimak's products.

Organisational Changes Bring About Internal Competition

During the 1960s, Alimak had expanded both with raise climbers and with construction hoists. The expansion occurred rapidly, which meant that it was difficult for the small company to cope financially. Alvar Lindmark therefore considered that it was necessary to sell the company, and in 1965, the company was acquired by Promotion, which had also acquired Lindén AB, a crane manufacturer. Promotion decided to merge the companies, and in 1968, integration was complete and the new company was given the name Lindén-Alimak AB. Synergy effects were obtained through the merger, as both cranes and lifts were sold to the same customers, and it was also possible to co-ordinate parts of the manufacturing process of both product groups.

Two completely different opinions are expressed in descriptions of the merger between Alimak and Lindén given by individuals employed in the company at the time. The employees, and the sales force in particular, were accepting and positive to the fact that the company's product range would now include construction cranes. This positive attitude changed to irritation, however, and the latter part of the 1970s was characterised by a more negative attitude towards selling construction cranes. This was because the domestic market matured, which led to severe profitability problems for the product.

Those individuals in leading positions in the company expressed a somewhat negative attitude to the merger from the start. The

Head Office and the manufacture of cranes were situated at Lindén's, and it was felt by Alimak that Promotion was primarily interested in the development of construction cranes and that hoists were considered to only be a complementary product. There was a feeling of fear over the possibility that Alimak's operations would be moved, and the struggle for survival was expressed in many ways. One of the managers states that the personnel wore clothing bearing the Alimak logo to a greater extent than before, and that at meetings where Lindén or Promotion were represented, note paper and pens with Alimak's name printed on them were used in an attempt to promote the company.

It can therefore be stated that internal competition took place, in which Alimak's management aimed to claim a right of existence for the company. This struggle cemented the personnel together, and many claim that the 'Alimak spirit' ("We have always been biggest, best, and most beautiful!") grew stronger. The struggle for where Lindén-Alimak AB should be located resulted in the transfer of the company's top management to Alimak's buildings in Skellefteå, where the local manager at the time became managing director of the new company. In 1988 Promotion sold Alimak to Karolin Invest, a company also situated in Skellefteå.

Operations Diversified, then Consolidated

The 1970s were characterised by an ambition to diversify. The building boom that had contributed to the expansion of building-related operations slackened off at the beginning of the 1970s, and changes in the economy of the Construction industry made their presence known. To deal with the declines in fortune that followed and to replace the receding demand for cranes, Lindén-Alimak decided that a diversification of the company's operations was necessary.

In the mid 1970s, Lindén-Alimak began to manufacture fully hydraulic bore machines for mining. Interviewees at Alimak provide two reasons for this. Firstly, due to its international position in the raise climber product segment, the company had good knowledge of, and good contacts with, the Mining industry, and this was assumed to aid the launching of the fully hydraulic bore machine. The company's product development was also considered to be an effect of the reduction in the raise climber market due to the stagnation in the market and to the replacement in some part of the industry of raise driving by full-face drilling. The other reason was that the company had so far only manufactured products involving a relatively low level of technology. By taking up the manufacture of an advanced product, the level of technology in use in the company was expected to be raised throughout the company's entire production.

The decision to invest time and effort into the development of bore machines and bore aggregates was taken in 1974, and after a period of intensive developmental work, the first prototypes were finished by the end of 1975. This was followed by work on a complete range of products, on building up a stock of spare parts, and a service organisation. The sole purpose of this was to cultivate a small niche in the mining drill market area, and the hope was that the company's competitors would not react to its establishment. At the time of the establishment in the market, Atlas Copco had an approximate 60% market share, and the Finnish company Tamrock had 30% of the Swedish market. These two competitors reacted sharply and rapidly to Lindén-Alimak's attempts at establishment. Competition within the industry was shown to require a high rate of product development, and this rapid pace of development made it difficult for Alimak to bear the costs of product development. The other two competitors, however, were larger and had better financial resources available to deal with the intensive competition with a fast rate of product development and direct counter-moves.

As mentioned earlier Alimak started the service and industrial lifts for permanent installation, which compensated for the losses incurred by the recession in the Construction industry. Offshore operations became an important part of the company's operations linked with special purpose and goods/passenger lifts during the whole of the 1970s. The needs of offshore industry for soft-ware with instructions and for service increased successively, and after a time, a requirement that the company became 'pre-qualified' to tender quotations on offshore projects arose. Alimak received a certificate to that effect, which provided the company with a good reputation around the world, and which was also made use of in tendering quotations for other complex projects. Alimak has purposefully specialised in large and referential projects which could subsequently be used in external advertising.

The further diversification of construction-related operations occurred primarily through company acquisitions, co-operation with foreign companies, and by buying patents for new products. By the beginning of the 1980s Lindén-Alimak had become a diversified company, but it confronted a number of problems mainly linked to the recession, difficulties with the crane operations, and hardening competition from other manufacturers of bore aggregates.

External circumstances, such as recessions, caused problems for the competitors' profitability, which made the concentration and consolidation of their operations necessary. During the first years of the 1980s, a number of areas of operation that had not shown any real profitability were liquidated, and Alimak concentrated its operations to the company's core operation, rack and pinion driven products. During the second half of the 1980s, this core operation was further developed and strengthened. The concentration of operations meant that the competitors actually became more distant relative to each other. Tornborg chose to focus its operations on the manufacture of building cranes, whereas Alimak focused on rack and pinion products.

Contexts of Competition in the Rack and
Pinion Industry — a Summary

Before the competitive play of the 1980s is described in depth, a summary will be given of the competition during the three phases described above. The assessments of competition, and changes to competition, in the rack and pinion industry are summarised in Appendix 3, and illustrated in the following figure. In the same

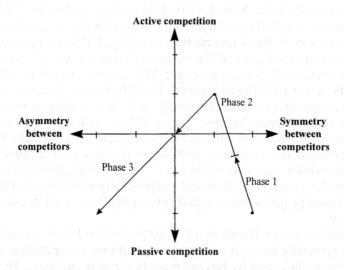

Figure 6.2   Changes in Contexts of Competition Within the Rack and Pinion Industry[2]

---

[2]   Figure 6.2 gives a simplified illustration of competition and changes in competition, i.e. does not show variations and nuances.

way as for the other industries, the points mark the assessment of competition in the middle of each phase, whilst the lines symbolise the change during each phase.

During the first phase, competition was very passive and very symmetrical. Competition changed progressively during the second phase, towards becoming symmetric-active. Due to the lead that Alimak had gained in developing rack and pinion driven lifts, competition changed during the phases and a development towards asymmetrical and passive competition emerged. Since then, during the third phase, competition has been characterised by Alimak's domination of the industry. Alimak was able to develop a relative strength in resources during this phase, as well as leading positions in the industry regarding technology and market.

During the last phase, three companies operated within the construction hoist and permanent service and industry lift product areas. The competing companies developed products for demarcated purposes and areas of use, which gave rise to asymmetry in product offer. Asymmetry was also high with regards to the choice of market segment. Alimak developed its image of service and quality, and established large number of subsidiaries throughout the world, to an extent which was not matched by its competitors. Alimak developed a leading position in the world market. Concurrently with Alimak's expansion and its increasing domination of the industry, the competitors developed their own niches in the home market. Alimak chose more or less to leave the niches where its competitors operated. This gave rise to a high degree of asymmetry in the companies' choice of customer segment.

Competitive play became very passive, characterised by competitors acting independently of each other. In 1965, a new method for the mining of ore, full-face drilling was developed, which grew over time, and partly replaced raise driving. The two methods competed against each other, though Alimak did not consider the producers of full-face drill aggregates as competitors. This explains why the company acted independently, and why no real development of raise climbs occurred during this phase.

COMPETITIVE PLAYS DURING THE 1980s

This industry differs from the other two under study, in that no real competitive plays were undertaken by the domestic competitors during the 1980s. Alimak has continued to dominate the industry for the most part, which means that the development of the industry can be described based on the development of Alimak. The next section will present a discussion of a number of measures that were undertaken during the 1980s, to illustrate the limited scope that the national competitive situation affected action, and what other motives lay behind the company's actions during the 1980s.

The Concentration of Operations

Many of the areas of operations that had appeared during the period of diversification of the 1970s caused considerable problems, which led to a period during the 1980s where Alimak decided to concentrate on its core operations. The sales of cranes had gone badly for a number of years, and Promotion chose to dispose of this area of operations in 1982. This took some time, due to the integration of the marketing and sales organisation during the 1970s. The manufacture of fully hydraulic bore machines was also shut down. Despite the fact that Alimak had developed a bore aggregate that many considered to be very good, competition was too considerable for a successful establishment to be possible, and this area of operations was disposed of as well. The process of concentration also resulted in leaving other areas of operations that Alimak had entered earlier.

The only product area that in itself was a result of the diversification of the 1970s to survive this period of concentration was the special purpose and goods/passenger lifts and related products for offshore industry. The offshore industry slackened off during the 1980s, which led to a decrease in volume in the market. Today, the offshore segment is considered to be one amongst other market segments for permanent lifts, and has therefore lost the particular position in the company that Alimak had during the 1970s.

The product groups that remained after the period of consolidation were raise climbers, construction hoists, and special purpose and goods/passenger lifts. When this concentration of operations to rack and pinion driven products was complete, product development was intensified in order to expand in this area.

The Raise Climber — New Efforts

From the mid 1960s, when five models were developed, to the 1980s, only minor changes of the raise climber had been made. By the mid 1980s, the Mining industry found itself in a recession, and less than twenty raise climbers were sold per year, compared to the hundred per year sold during the 1960s and 1970s. The ambition to expand in the mining-related area of operations remained, which resulted in a new developmental project with the aim of modernising the raise climber and incorporating new customer requirements, developed over time. With the new product, Alimak wanted to improve the working environment of operator of the raise climber, by designing an ergonomically correct work position and ensuring a low accident risk. The company also wanted to standardise the lift's components.

The first, newly re-designed, raise climbers were delivered in 1989 to a consortium of Japan's largest building contractors. Another raise climber was sold to a Swedish mining company. These first deliveries were perceived by the personnel of the company's mining division to be part of the continued developmental work. By installing these prototypes in authentic environments, valuable knowledge could be gained for further development.

The new type of raise climber met competition mainly from the manufacturers of machines for raise boring. The advantages and disadvantages, and the future prospective of the two methods became more and more important in the assessment of future development of the raise climber. One of the managers is of the opinion that raise boring can replace the Alimak method in many situations. Raise borers are, however, approximately five times more expensive than raise climbers. If the rock is porous, the raise climbing method provides for greater flexibility, as it allows more consideration to be taken to the condition of the rock. The raise climbing method has clear advantages in cases where precision is particularly required, but the current raise climber does not fully meet the requirements placed on the working environment in many countries.

Opinions over the future of the raise climber are split. On the one hand, the raise climber should remain in production without further development, thereby functioning as a cash cow with good profitability. On the other hand, it is felt by some that there are possibilities of strengthening the mining-related operations, but that this would require proper investment in product development to produce a product that would completely replace the present raise climber. There is a general agreement that Alimak should not develop products for raise boring.

Development of Construction Hoists to Meet New Customer Requirements

Although the development of the construction hoist has mainly consisted of continual modifications to existing products, a few new product types have been developed in response to specific customer needs, and a new product programme has also taken form as a response to more general needs. The product development of construction hoists during the 1980s has also been characterised by an increased emphasis on safety, which can be explained in part by Alimak's response to the safety requirements demanded by the offshore industry (which in turn has led to increased knowledge and competence in this area).

An example of the modifications to the original product is that the machinery and electricity box have been moved to increase the space in the lift's cage, in line with customer needs. The Scando 9.20, an example of a lift that was developed to meet a specific customer need, was designed for peripheral markets, where transportation costs were considered high. Another product, the diesel driven construction hoist, developed in 1984, is another example of product development in response to a specific customer need (a prospective customer in Cairo required a diesel driven lift, because the electricity in Egypt was not always reliable). 1987 saw the introduction of the C-door, another such example. This lift was developed to take into consideration the wishes of customers from a number of countries, regarding a lift which could lift a large amount of palleted goods.

In 1988, Alimak launched a completely new product programme, with modernised lift capacity, lift speed, shape of the cage, and assembly method. The development of the early 1980s was integrated into the new product programme, which also included improvements to the product resulting from demands from retailers and subsidiaries around the world. Routines for the collection of information on market needs and new customer requirements were designed and implemented. A certain amount of stimulation for the product development did originate from Alimak's competitors, but it is Alimak's many customers and the feedback from the market that are considered to have been the primary sources of inspiration.

Alimak Draws Closer to 'The Big Boys'

At the beginning, the differences between the two product areas, construction hoists and permanent lifts, were somewhat diffuse, as permanent lifts were often construction hoists that were rebuilt. During 1981, Alimak attempted to create a natural place for permanent lifts in the company's product range, which in turn affected product development. The second half of the decade saw the development of a completely new permanent lift, the Alilift, and through this development, Alimak expected to move towards the manufacturing of a standard product in greater volumes.

The Alilift is a person and material lift which approached the performance of the cable lift, due to its lower levels of noise and greater comfort compared to earlier lifts. In the mid 1980s, the Swedish state gave grants for repairs, rebuilding, and extensions to older buildings. The opportunities provided by the interest in the property market, together with the demands of customers, led in 1985 to the commencement of development on the Alilift. Older buildings in which lifts were now meant to be installed often lacked lift shafts. Many interviewees at Alimak were of the opinion that rack and pinion lifts were more appropriate in such cases, as they did not require lifts shafts to be built. Space could also be saved in new buildings by installing the lift on the outside of the building. Alimak therefore developed a modulated system for installations in the property market. In its contacts with industrial buyers, Alimak's sales force had also noticed that Alimak's lifts did not completely meet customer's needs for comfort, a softer start, acceleration, etc. The Alilift was therefore developed to meet such needs, with a lower level of noise, better comfort, and with softer starts and stops than other lift types.

The Alilift was first launched in the American market. The market manager of the American subsidiary had previously worked for Otis, a company that sold cable lifts. The company employed sales personnel from the cable lift industry, with long experience in selling permanent lifts. Some of the interviewees at Alimak meant that their knowledge about the market would facilitate the introduction of the Alilift.

The new product meant that Alimak came to compete with large international companies that sold cable lifts. Many interviewees at Alimak saw the necessity of learning more about the lift accessories sold by these companies, such as doors and cages, as well as the need for better training of the sales forces to meet the demands of the new market. The company did consider the threat of a reaction from the larger manufacturers as serious, as shown by the following quotations:

> The 'Big Boys' did not react because the segment we entered was so small. They manufacture standard products in large series and are not interested in specially manufactured products.

> They see us as being small. If we occupy a small niche which pre-
> cludes larger series, they ought to think that that would be good.
> We're not a threat to them. If a customer approached them with a
> need better suited to Alimak's products, they could employ us.
> They always meet those kinds of customer needs.

Almost every interviewee considered the risk of counter-measures
from the cable lift manufacturers to be minimal. However, at the
time of the recession, some of them had noticed that some of the
companies were offering lifts in the smaller markets that Alimak
had gone into. Many were aware of the fact that the larger manufacturers could react, which led to attempts to establish good contacts with the competitors in order to bring about co-operation
rather than competition. In 1989, therefore, Alimak participated in
a trade fair that catered to the cable lift market. The Alilift was presented there, together with rack and pinion driven lifts, as a complement in special situations to the cable lifts.

Climbs — A New Product Area

Alimak's climb, the 'Jacob's Ladder', was developed by Alimak in
1954, but did not become its own product area until the 1980s,
when Malmqvist, a competitor, began production. Malmqvist's
founder had previously worked at Lindén-Alimak at their unit in
Västerås, and therefore knew about Alimak's attempts in developing the climb. He saw the opportunity to create his own niche, and
therefore decided to start manufacturing himself. At that time,
Alimak was at the height of its period of concentration, and was
therefore not interested in developing climbs itself.

Having gained a foothold in the Swedish market, Malmqvist
decided to expand its operations internationally. The company therefore contacted Alimak, which resulted in a co-operation in sales that
involved Alimak selling Malmqvist's climbs in the international
market. A sales co-operation was assessed to be possible due to
Alimak's well-developed market organisation. Malmqvist's climbs
were also assessed to be good products with high market potential.

In 1987, Alimak appointed a new managing director, who did not
agree with the policy of selling climbs without having manufactured
them. The climbs that were sold in the market were constructed on
the rack and pinion technique that Alimak had developed, were
designed to ease vertical transport, and were sold to the Construction industry. The only difference between a construction hoist and a

climb is the work space — in the one case a lift cage was raised and lowered by rack and pinion technology, and in the other a work platform. In the eyes of the new managing director, climbs were therefore within Alimak's area of competence. Climbs could also made a part of Alimak's modulated system, and customers could therefore make use of masts and other parts of the system they had already bought. Another positive effect of incorporating the climb into Alimak's production was assumed to be an increased volume in the manufacture of the parts of the modulated system, resulting in a decrease in costs per unit produced.

The market of climbs followed the same booms and recessions as the Construction industry. This was seen by many to be a disadvantage, but others considered it to be only a minor problem, as illustrated by the following quotation;

> Climbs follow the same peaks and valleys as construction hoists, but are at the same time virgin territory, and if you look at the product life-cycle, the market is expanding, which counters the effects of swings in the economy.

The sales contract with Malmqvist's was terminated, and Alimak began to manufacture its own climbs. This was considered by all to have been a good decision. Developmental work began which after a time resulted in a climb that met all the requirements demanded by Alimak.

For the first time, through Alimak's commencement of climb manufacture, the company came to compete with a company that had achieved prominent international positions with rack and pinion driven products, Hek Ltd. The consequences of this became evident when Hek acquired Malmqvist in 1989. Many interviewees at Alimak felt that the acquisition involved more disadvantages than advantages for Hek — Hek and Malmqvist would have to co-ordinate their market organisations and modulated systems to achieve an acceptable level of their total economy. This was assumed to cost a lot of time and money.

The same year, Alimak began to co-operate with an Italian company called Cimar Ponteggi. Through this agreement, Cimar would sell Alimak's entire lift programme in Italy, and Alimak would sell Cimar's series of lighter climbs internationally. Alimak aimed to continue its production of heavier climbs, and by including lighter climbs manufactured by Cimar, could offer a complete product range. Hek manufactured and sold both heavy and light climbs both through Hek and through Malmqvist.

Some interviewees at Alimak are of the opinion that Alimak's establishment in the climb market led to Hek intensifying its efforts on the construction hoists. Hek had sold construction hoists for a number of years, though only marginally. Some interviewees at Alimak are of the opinion that Hek's increased interest in construction hoists was a response to the direct challenge posed by Alimak's investments in climbs. Alimak was a major manufacturer of construction hoists and Hek was a major manufacturer of climbs, but both companies attempted to establish themselves in each other's markets at the beginning of the 1990s.

Establishment in Peripheral Markets Strengthened

By the beginning of the 1980s, Alimak had developed an international market organisation that was further developed during the following decade to strengthen the company's position in peripheral markets, but also to concentrate its original market organisation. In 1979, Alimak had opened a representative office in Singapore, and although no direct sales occurred through this office, its main function was to act as a point of contact between Alimak and its distributors in the Far East. The geographical and cultural distance made it impossible to contribute with the sales support the market demanded. Support was therefore given in terms of overseeing offers, product-related training, and market research and analysis. The establishment of a representative office in Singapore led to an increase in the level of knowledge and in the degree of service of the sales force in the Far East. Despite the fact that the building boom began to level out, leading to a reduction in the amount of building in the Far East by the mid 1980s, Alimak managed to retain a relatively high level of sales, serving approximately 90 per cent of the market for rack and pinion driven lifts, which many at Alimak relate to the establishment of the representative office.

1985 saw the establishment of another representative office, this time in Cairo. Egypt was the single largest market in the Middle East, and the reason behind establishing an office there was the same as with the office in Singapore. Despite Alimak being able to solve some of the problems related to distance with the help of these representative offices, a number of problems still remained. The lifts were still manufactured in Sweden, which due to the high levels of transport costs meant that Alimak had difficulties in keeping to a low enough price. The levelling out of the building boom in the mid 1980s meant that customer price sensitivity increased. Moreover, a number of competitors began operations, especially in South Korea. Competition also increased from domestic manufacturers during the second half of the 1980s. This led Alimak to sell customer adapted lifts to a greater extent than before, motivating a higher price. Towards the end of the 1980s, building work expanded in South Korea, and although market potential was assessed to be considerable, Alimak experienced difficulties in increasing its share of the market.

In order not to lose the South Korean market and other markets in neighbouring countries, Alimak decided in 1990 to establish a manufacturing company in South Korea. Alimak owned 60% of the new company, with the remaining 40% owned by Alimak's former distributor, U-Young. Alimak planned to increase its percentage in the ownership of the new company progressively. The new company manufactured only one standard model of lift, but it was assessed to meet the needs of the market. Other models were to be manufactured as and when the market demands increased.

Competitive play in the Rack and Pinion Industry — A Summary

In summary, no 'real' competitive play has occurred between the Swedish competitors (i.e. no real national competition), but three separate patterns of change linked to the international competition can be distinguished. However, the 'competitive plays' on the international level cannot really be described to be competitive plays in themselves (with the exception of the competition between Alimak and Hek), rather, they are general trends or tendencies that can be discerned in the action of the group of actors in the international market. These tendencies, or patterns of change, are illustrated in the figure below.

As shown by the figure, the first course of events leading to change implies that two previously separate industries, the Rack and Pinion industry and the Cable Lift industry, can integrate. Alimak will then meet its international counterparts to a greater extent than it did earlier, due to the fact the companies manufacturing cable lifts are international. Secondly, a similar development is implied in the Climb industry, where Alimak, by launching its climbs, now compete with not only its domestic competitors but also with Hek, a company that acts in the international market. The third course of events illustrates how competition in different countries, especially in minimum-wage countries, gives rise to general trend in competition, where price is used as a means of competition between competitors.

THE ACTORS

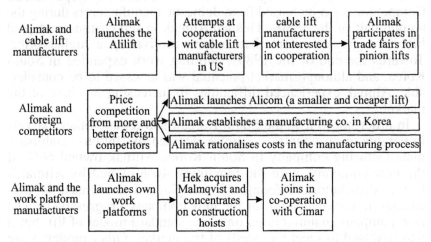

Figure 6.3   Three Tendencies or Patterns of Competition in the Rack and Pinion Industry during the 1980s

This book, however, focuses on the effects of national conditions for competition on the dynamics of industries, rather than international conditions. Even if no 'real' competitive plays have occurred between the Swedish actors, due to the fact that they have mostly acted independently of, and passive relative to each other (i.e. independent moves), competition still exists. This competition is potential rather than actual, which means that it is not the actual competitive moves and counter-moves that occupy the minds of the competitors, but rather the constant *risk* of moves and counter-moves. However, the asymmetry arising from the extensive domination of the industry by Alimak, has led to a stability in the latest context of competition arising from Alimak's power to respond to the attempts of the other competitors to expand in the market (as was the case with Amaco). Alimak is therefore able to maintain the status quo between the actors in the industry. The threat from potential competition is therefore minor.

****

Through this study, the description of three industries, where four different contexts of competition have been discerned and described, is completed. These four contexts of competition are based on the two dimensions that were determined in Chapter Two to be of importance in the study of the nature and dynamics of competition; namely, the degree of symmetry between competitors and the degree of activity in competitive play.

In the first industry, the Front-loader industry, a symmetric-passive context of competition was shown to have prevailed during the first years of the 1980s to then become symmetric-active. The context of competition in the Lining industry was assessed to be asymmetric-active, and, finally, the study of the Rack and Pinion industry has revealed a context of competition that was asymmetric-passive. The studies of these three industries therefore exemplify four contexts of competition that exhibit diametrically opposing characteristics of the two dimensions. This can then be used in the further development of knowledge about the nature and dynamics of different climates of competition, as will be shown in the following three chapters.

7. Four Climates of Competition

In the previous three chapters, different contexts of competition in the industries of this study were determined, based on structural characteristics in terms of symmetry between actors, and on behavioural characteristics in terms of activity in competitive play. This chapter will discuss the *climates of competition* that develop under different structural and behavioural conditions. Four separate climates of competition can be distinguished. Beginning with a discussion of the concept *climate of competition*, the chapter continues with a presentation of the four climates, which are the climates of *revolutionary*, *evolutionary*, *co-existing*, and *rivalling* competition. The dimensions used to describe these four climates are then introduced, to be followed by a description of the distinctive characteristics of each climate.

THE CONCEPT 'CLIMATE OF COMPETITION'

The concept *climate of competition* will be used to analyse and describe the nature of competition. The concept is based on both structural and behavioural aspects of competition, which are by nature interrelated (and therefore in reality not possible to separate). The concept climate of competition expresses the simultaneous perception of symmetry and activity in an industry. A climate of competition develops through the ongoing processes of interaction between competing companies. In organisation theories, the concept 'climate' is used to express or describe the internal climate in an organisation.[1] Culture is described as being underlying values and attitudes in an organisation, whereas climate is considered to be the reflection of culture that has consequences for the actions of an individual. Climate can therefore be directly connected to action in an organisation. In the same way, a climate of competition can be described as the internal climate of an industry that develops in and through the interaction of competing actors. A climate of competition is an expression of the strategic thinking and action of individual companies. The action of competing companies can be understood through their interpretations of current conditions, and of the expectations that are the basis of organisational action. The climate concept thus includes perceptions and interpretations of competition in an industry.

Chapter Two presented a discussion of perception and its importance for a company's actions and interaction with competitors, based on concepts such as atmosphere, cognitive groups and industry recipes. Atmosphere was described, in much the same way as climates of competition, as a result of interwoven variables. The environment, the companies, and interaction were described as important factors in the atmosphere that develops between actors. Overall atmosphere was described from aspects such as conditions of power-dependency, the state of conflict or co-operation, closeness or distance between actors, and the mutual expectations of actors concerned (cf. Håkansson, 1982). In a comparison of the three industries, the dimensions that appear to be important for the description of climates of competition are to a great extent comparable with, or conform to, the dimensions with which atmosphere in a network is described.

However, certain central differences can be found between the two concepts. Network theory can be said to apply a perspective of harmony, as the mutual interest of the actors in participating in interaction is taken as a point of departure. The atmosphere that develops as a result of interaction, and the relationships between actors in a network, are described in terms of the network's atmosphere of co-operation. However, competing actors are opponents, which is a fact that must be central for analysis if interaction between competing

---

[1] The concepts *culture* and *climate* have both been defined in many different ways, and no one uniform and valid definition prevails (cf. Lindfors, 1989 and Smirch, 1983, amongst others).

actors is to be understood. The climate that develops between competitors differs therefore from the atmosphere that develops between actors in buyer/seller relationships.

If the concept *climate of competition* is compared to Spender's (1989) discussion of industry recipes, a climate of competition similarly expresses the logic of action or the shared pattern of beliefs that develop in an industry. Climate of competition is, however, a narrower concept as it is only the pattern of beliefs related to competition that are included in the concept. Industry recipes are also said to reflect the common beliefs of actors. The basis of competition, the state of being opponents, means, however, that actors can develop different mental models about, and perceptions of the interaction that takes place, and of the competitors that are involved (cf. Porac et al., 1989). A climate of competition can therefore express contrasting as well as common conceptions.

Despite certain similarities, the concepts that were discussed in Chapter Two in the 'Conceptions of Competition' section cannot be completely carried over to the concept *climate of competition*, which is why the term climates of competition is used in this study to describe conceptions of competition and the ways that competitors interrelate. In order to discuss different climates of competition and to identify the different dimensions that distinguish these climates, empirical studies must be used as points of departure. By analysing the processes of competition that are present in different types of competition, an understanding of the nature of the different climates of competition can be gained.

Table 7.1   Context of Competition in the Three Industries During Different Phases

Context of Competition	Front-Loader Industry	Lining Industry	Rack and Pinion Industry
Symmetric/active	**Phase 4**	Phase 1 Phase 2	Phase 2
Symmetric/passive	**Phase 3** Phase 1		Phase 1
Asymmetric/active	Phase 1 Phase 2		**Phase 3**
Symmetric/passive		**Phase 3**	

Table 7.1 illustrates the contexts of competition that have been most prominent during the different phases of the three industries. The phases marked specifically in bold print indicate the 1980s, and it is primarily these phases that are the foundations for discussing the climates of competition and their different natures in this chapter. By analysing the ongoing processes of competition that were prevalent during these phases, four climates of competition have been possible to identify. These four climates are illustrated in the figure below.

As it is difficult to obtain information on interpretations made in the relatively distant past, the analysis presented in this chapter is based primarily on the climates of competition that prevailed during the 1980s. During this decade, the Front-loader industry was dominated by climates of rivalling and evolutionary competition, whereas the climate of revolutionary competition prevailed in the Lining industry, and the climate of co-existing competition describes the competition in the Rack and Pinion industry. The climates that prevailed in previous phases are primary used as support for, or further examples of, the different natures of the climates of competition. Later in this chapter, the designations of the climates of competition

	Asymmetry between competitors	Symmetry between competitors
Active competition	REVOLUTION	RIVALRY
Passive competition	CO-EXISTENSE	EVOLUTION

Figure 7.1 Four Climates of Competition

will be explained and the nature of the different climates described. First, however, the dimensions that have been used to distinguish the different climates from each other will be described.

DIMENSIONS THAT DISTINGUISH THE CLIMATES OF COMPETITION

Three dimensions have been identified that describe the climates of competition during different phases in the histories of the studied industries. These dimensions are thereby generated empirically. A number of common attributes for each climate of competition have been listed from the interviewees' description of the processes of competition presented in Chapters Four, Five, and Six. 'Good competition', 'information via market signals', and 'sales through the same distributor' are examples of attributes that have been identified. These attributes have been compared and brought together in three general dimensions of climates of competition, which are listed below.

– Distance between actors
– Surveillability of competition
– Acceptance of current conditions for competition

By discussing differences between differing contexts of competition with regard to the above dimensions, four climates of competition can be identified, and their natures described. Descriptions taken from observations of these dimensions in the three industries will, in the following section, be related to theories dealing with similar phenomena. This discussion will then serve as a point of departure for the section describing the climates of competition.

The Distance Between Competing Companies

The distance between competing companies varies, and has both a functional and a psychological aspect. Functional distance is connected to the companies' operations. If the companies act relative to each other within the same product and market areas, and if they resemble each other regarding choice of product and market, a functional proximity develops between them. This proximity can develop, for example, as a result of the competing companies cultivating the market in the same way, or as a result of the companies operating in the same customer segment. Examples of functional proximity are provided by the Lining industry, within which the companies cultivated the same customers, and the Front-loader industry, where each company sold its products through SLR, and where companies' product development resulted in products which to a great extent resembled each other. Functional distance, however, can arise when companies choose to sell their products to different market niches.

Functional proximity develops from functional interaction between the competing companies. Functional interaction occurs by different functions of the competing companies engaging in competition, making move and counter-move. Interaction between companies is often connected to the commercial exchange between actors (this can be compared to Johannisson's and Gustavsson's (1984) discussion on functional networks). Economic exchange, as described by Johansson and Mattson (1987), does not occur between competitors in any real meaning, but functional inter-action can develop through companies competing against other actors for the economic exchange.

Functional interaction is based on the direct resources (company controlled) and indirect resources (not under the control of the company) used in competition (cf. Håkansson, 1987). A company gains indirect resources through its interaction with others, as exemplified by Trima's access to Nordwin's hydraulic valves, whereas companies have control over direct resources, such as patents and, for example, Skega's own machine for producing lining products. Companies compete in order to receive better direct and indirect resources than their competitors. The above can be related to Porter's (1991) discussion on a company's strategic base, where he states that a company places its strategic base in those areas that can best obtain necessary resources, and that it is for these resources that companies compete. In the studies of the industries that have been carried out, there are a number of instances where companies have tried to obtain the same or similar resources as a competitor, or to obtain resources from other actors which competitors have no access to. Competing companies therefore keep a close eye on each others' patent applications, examine each others' products and materials, offer discounts to competitors' customers, and so on. These are examples of functional interaction, and expressions of functional proximity.

Psychological proximity between competing companies can also vary, which is evident in that attitudes toward competitors differ between different phases. The importance or intensity of the values and attitudes that develop can also vary. In those cases that conceptions of and attitudes to competitors heavily colour the descriptions of interaction between actors, psychological proximity can be said to exist between them. Psychological proximity and attitudes to competitors develop in and through interaction, and it can be assumed that the social interaction that occurs has particular importance for the attitudes that develop.

When competing companies meet each other, for example in contact with customers and at trade fairs, social interaction develops between individuals in the competing companies. This can be compared with that which Johanisson and Gustavsson (1984) describe as the interactive network, which is made up of personal and social contacts that develop between the interacting individuals. Through social interaction, relationships among competitors develop that are affected by the opposing positions that they as competitors occupy. This gives rise to attitudes of a more psychological or emotional nature, which can be described in terms of prestige, pride, and self-assertion, or in terms of loyalty and respect.

Company pride and prestige are expressed in, for example, the discussions between the lining companies about which company produces the best attachments, and in the description of how the one company took customers from the other. Respect and loyalty between competitors can be exemplified by the descriptions of each other relative to foreign competitors of front-loader companies, even though conflict has occurred between these companies. This indicates that there is a psychological proximity between the front-loader companies, as opposed to the psychological distance which is expressed in Alimak's neutral descriptions of its national competitors. Earlier experiences of competitors and their behaviour, and the perceived threat from them, can give rise to psychological tension between the competitors. If, for example, they operate in the same product and market area, and if the threat from competitors is perceived as being serious, the tension between actors increases.

Surveillability of Competitive Play

The different contexts of competition also differ, due to the actors' overall grasp of the competitive play that occurs. In certain types of competition, actors have great insight into the competitive plays that occur, giving them the ability to predict to a great extent the competitors' next moves. For example, the front-loader manufacturers can predict that their competitors will release a new series of loader a few years after they themselves have launched one. In other types of competition, there is great uncertainty about what really goes on in competitive play. Surveillability of competitive play can be connected to the competing companies' awareness of each other, to information available, to the ways that companies watch and spread disinformation to each other, and to the nature of competitive play.

Processes of communicative interaction occur between competitors through the increased surveillability that arises from companies watching and analysing each other. At the same time, measures are taken to mislead and to conceal important information, which in turn reduces surveillability. In the Rack and Pinion industry, Alimak attempted to tone down the advantages of the rack and pinion technology to hinder its competitors from imitating Alimak's products. In the Front-loader industry, Ålö tried to conceal its plans for initiating co-operation with Stoll, which was possible even though Trima had established contact with Stoll. However, a form of trust can also develop in the relations between competitors, which means that an informal exchange of information is accepted. This is exemplified by the lining companies' co-operation in the development of rubber materials.

The degree of complexity, or alternatively the degree of simplicity, in competitive play is variable, affecting communicative interaction and surveillability. Competitive play is complex if competitors take measures relative to each other in many different areas and if competition occurs on several levels, which is the case in the Lining industry. The entire organisation and individuals in different areas of the organisation are in this way integrated, and at the same time take part in different competitive plays.[2] This makes the competitive play complex. Simple competitive play occurs mostly within a limited area, and a certain continuity exists in the ways that competing companies act relative to each other. Surveillability also varies, depending on whether competitive play is direct or indirect. Competitive play can be described as being indirect if counter-measures are taken as a reply to signals from the market, and as being direct if counter-measures are taken as a direct reply to competitors' action. There are examples of both direct and indirect competitive play during the first two phases in the history of the Front-loader industry.

Acceptance of Roles, Rules-of-Play, and Positions

A distribution of roles between actors can develop over time, which can be described in terms of power and dependency rela-

---

[2] Cf. Lawrence and Lorch's (1969) discussion on relationships between the organisation and its environment.

tions between the actors. The roles and positions of competitors can be either clear and unambiguous, or uncertain and ambiguous. Clarity in the distribution of roles between competitors can be connected to both the complexity of competition, and the surveillability of competitive play.

If competitive play is complex and the surveillability of competitive play is low, uncertainty can arise about the current distribution of roles between competitors, and vice versa. If there is great turbulence in the industry, uncertainty about how the actors' positions will be changed can be considerable. The Lining industry has been characterised by this kind of uncertainty during the 1980s. It was perceived to be difficult to predict a competitor's price for a specific business deal, for example. The perception of a considerable threat from competitors can also give rise to uncertainty about positions and roles, which can be exemplified by the threat of acquisition in the Lining industry.

The different climates of competition vary regarding the acceptance that actors have of the current distribution of roles. In certain climates of competition, the actors accept the distribution, whereas in others they strive to change it. Ålö, for example, did not accept Trima taking a leading position in the Swedish market during the 1970s. Skega also did not accept that Trellex had gained a strong position in the European market, which was why counter-measures were planned. Ålö and Trima, on the other hand, accepted the relationship of equality that had developed between the companies in the latter half of the 1980s. Acceptance of the distribution of roles in the Rack and Pinion industry is another example. The above can be linked with Kock's (1991) description of the relations between actors in a network and the commitment that develops through interaction. Companies accept the current relationships, and are willing to engage in interaction within the given framework.

In all the climates of competition, mention is made directly or indirectly of how competition ought to be undertaken, i.e. what norms and rules-of-play ought to apply. Rules-of-play define how one should behave towards one's competitors, and which methods are most appropriate in competition. Trust develops between actors as a consequence of the existence of norms, and the distribution of power, norms, and trust all affect the continuing interaction in the network. According to Macaulay (1963), norms replace and fill the same function as contracts between actors.

The differences that exist between the four climates of competition lie primarily in the way that actors keep to the rules-of-play.

These rules-of-play are not followed in exactly the same way during every phase. Differences between phases also occur in the opinions of how one's competitors play the game. Forsgren and Olofsson (1989) comment on the relationship between the uncertainty and the commitment or acceptance that develops in a relationship. One way to deal with uncertainty is to become engaged in a relationship. Uncertainty can also, however, lead to the break-up of the balance of power and the acceptance of the current distribution of roles, which can lead to rules-of-play not being followed.

Håkansson (1987) suggests that the main aim of action by actors is to increase their control over the network. Actors make use of their experience and competence to strengthen their positions in the network. In the same way, the main purpose of interaction between actors can be said to be in order to maintain or strengthen individual positions against the competitors. How this is done depends on the relationships that have developed between the competing companies and on the climate of competition that has subsequently arisen. Competing companies can maintain or strengthen their own positions either by goal-oriented action, or by object-oriented action (cf. Easton, 1987). Goal-oriented action occurs primarily when acceptance of current rules-of-play and the current distribution of roles is great. Object-oriented action can be equated with low acceptance for current rules-of-play and roles or positions.

From the above discussion, it is apparent that the dimensions are related to each other. They describe different sides of the same phenomenon, and therefore affect and strengthen or weaken each other. No one dimension can describe a climate of competition. To gain an increased understanding for the climates of competition and their natures, a comprehensive description of all of the dimensions needs to be given. A description of the climates of competition and their natures will therefore be given in the following section.

THE NATURES OF THE FOUR
CLIMATES OF COMPETITION

The Climate of Rivalling Competition

Symmetric-active competition is characterised by the rivalry that exists between companies despite competitors acting in a form of concord or harmony with each other. The term *rivalling competition* has therefore been chosen to describe this climate of competition.

The climate of rivalling competition can be compared to IO-theory descriptions of oligopolistic action in homogenous oligopolies or strategic groups (cf. Knickerbocker, 1973 and Porter, 1979). Competition in this climate can also be compared to Easton's (1987) concept of competition in his description of relationships between competitors. The companies involved do not take action purposing to damage their competitors, but in order to fulfil their own goals. Despite this, competitors must be observant of each other, and constantly instigate innovative measures so as not to lag behind.

Functional interaction is greatest in the climate of rivalling competition. The climate of competition is characterised by the functional proximity that follows from the symmetry between competitors and the activity in competitive play. The competing companies operate in the same product and market areas, and therefore they interact functionally with each other. Links of time, technology, and knowledge develop between the competing companies. Move and counter-move are rapidly instigated, one after the other. Considerable similarity occurs in product development, and knowledge develops about the other competitors and about their style of action.

In more peripheral markets where companies only act indirectly, via retailers, functional distance can arise between competing companies, for example in the front-loader penetration of the Japanese market. This counters the thesis on international relations, and factors that support the distinct national competition are eroded as a result of the globalisation of business (cf. amongst others, Leontiades, 1989).

A collegial mentality develops in the relationships between competitors. They relate to each other and interact in meeting with customers, at trade fairs, etc, which gives rise to psychological proximity. Social relationships are characterised by a certain amount of harmony. In the same way that disharmony and conflict can be found in co-operation between competitors, a form of harmony develops between competing companies in this climate. Collegial mentality is, however, partly a facade, as disharmony both exists and constantly threatens. In that the competing actors are similar, the companies meet comparable opponents, which is why they have to continuously compare themselves with each other.

Great awareness, the spreading of information, and keeping watch on each other gives surveillability in this climate. The awareness of and information on competitors is considerable. Functional and psychological proximity makes it possible to keep watch on the actions of competitors. Both lining companies often met each other at their customers, and thereby were able to collect information about each other. The front-loader companies sold their products via the same market channels, which meant that they could gather information on each other in similar ways. This was complemented where possible with statistics on market shares.

Competitive play is both simple and direct, which contributes to surveillability. Competitive play is simple in the sense that moves are followed by counter-moves that are easy to predict regardless of whether they occur in the same product or market area, or whether they take the form of multiple moves taken in other areas. Awareness, information, and simplicity in competition lead to good surveillability of competition in the climate of rivalling competition.

Activity in competition and proximity between actors leads, on the other hand, to an increased caution regarding the spreading of information to competitors. The competing actors deliberately hinder the spreading of information, which in turn means that possible counter-moves are not initiated because of a lack of awareness of the other's actions. For example, Trima did not react to Ålö's co-operation with Stoll in the German market, where there was considerable proximity between actors. Despite this proximity, Ålö was careful to withhold information about their co-operation with Stoll for as long as possible. Trima visited Stoll, via Baas, and in this way tried to keep itself informed about, for example, Stoll's product development. Trima therefore assumed that it had access to necessary information, which was not the case. However, it is only in a few areas that this type of informational black-out is possible, and this the actors are aware of.

A certain amount of unawareness is also present as a result of the distance between companies in certain areas. In the more peripheral markets, companies have not replied to the measures taken by competitors to the same extent as in markets closer to home. This is partly because of unawareness of the actions of competitors, and partly because these actions are assessed as not being threatening to the company's own position and development. This can be exemplified by Ålö and Trima's action in the Japanese market. The psychological proximity was considerable on the other hand, as is shown by the stormy emotions that were a result of the 'clash' between Ålö and Trima in Japan.

Role distribution and rules-of-play are clear and accepted, and the symmetry in the companies' relative strength is considerable. No one actor dominates the industry; companies are instead considered to be comparable. According to Scherer (1980), symmetry and dependence between actors in homogenous oligopolies lead either to competitors acting based on mutuality, or to defensive adaptation, in order not to break the equilibrium. This is explained by actors knowing that conflicting action will worsen the situation for every company involved. However, companies in the climate of rivalling competition do not act defensively, but actively instigate measures to maintain their positions in the market. They accept the current distribution of roles, and therefore expect active moves and counter-moves from their competitors. In spite of the clarity and acceptance of the distribution of roles, competitors are still a potential threat. The individual actors are aware that an advantage that they have gained, or a lead that has not yet been discovered by their competitors, can result in that the equality in the competitive relationship may change and that one company can develop a dominant position. This awareness can explain the activity in competition.

Acceptance can, however, give rise to a form of harmony which makes goal-oriented action possible despite the companies being opponents. This is exemplified by statements that are made by the interviewees in the Front-loader industry that they would rather that the companies were active in the same markets, and that they should help each other to spread information about the advantages of the advanced loader. In that way both companies could receive stronger positions internationally. Action is not usually undertaken with the primary purpose of inflicting damage on or weakening the position of any competitors. Neither is action interpreted in that way. The purpose of action is rather to maintain individual positions, and to further develop the companies' own operations, but as this occurs in continual competition with a comparable opponent, action does affect the competitors (cf. Easton, 1987). Competitors' goals are therefore conflicting, which is why counter-moves are undertaken.

Competitors in this climate of competition are called colleagues, and good ethics in competition is said to exist. The understanding is that each and every competing company acts to a great extent in concordance with this morale. It is because of this understanding that actors can call each other colleagues. This indicates that certain norms and power relationships are accepted as prevailing pre-conditions for interaction. Acceptance of rules-of-play and the norms that develop give rise to an increased certainty in relations between competitors (cf. Håkansson, 1987).

However, in a number of instances, company action has led to direct conflict, where, for example, a competitor is considered to have acted contrary to the current rules-of-play. This type of action has either occurred in peripheral markets, or as a reply to a perceived threat from the competitor. Despite these examples, the rules-of-play are described as being clear and for the most part accepted.

The Climate of Revolutionary Competition

In asymmetric-active competition, a climate of revolutionary competition develops, where the action of competing companies is characterised by companies acting in concord with each other. The contrasts between competing companies give rise to action that directly worsens the situation for competitors. The climate of revolutionary competition can therefore be compared to that which Easton (1987) calls conflicting competition, and that which is considered as intending to inflict damage. This is illustrated by the following quote:

> The first and perhaps most important distinction between competition and conflict lies in the objective ... conflictful behaviour is that which is largely or mainly governed by the objective of destroying or seriously weakening an opponent. Similarly competitive behaviour may, indeed often will, hurt competitors but such is not the prime objective of that behaviour.
>
> (G. Easton, University of Lancaster, Feb 1987, s 7)

The term *revolutionary competition* is used, as the clear intent to inflict damage can not be identified in the included case-studies. However, the actions of competing companies are interpreted as attempts to exclude or eliminate competitors. The interpretations of the actions of competitors lead to actors revolting against the current forms of relationships. Competitive play is therefore characterised as action giving rise in the short term to destructive consequences for every company involved.

A *functional distance* exists between the companies in this climate of competition. Functional interaction in the climate of revolutionary competition is limited by asymmetry in the companies' product and market choices. This can be explained by the uncertainty, and the insufficient surveillability that will be discussed below. Attitudes regarding competitors are characterised by affection. It is primarily *psychological proximity* and affected relationships that are expressed in this climate. Affections can principally be related to asymmetry in the relative strengths of competitors, and to the fact that competitors' actions are perceived as being threatening. The descriptions given of competitors' express uncertainty about, or the suspicion that, the competitor aims to strengthen his own position to the cost of the own company's position.

Competitors are considered to be enemies that continuously try to destroy or weaken the other's operations, which can be related to the companies' earlier experiences of competition. Earlier experiences are important for the way that the actions of competitors are interpreted, and for the way that psychological proximity develops between actors. From the beginning of the Lining industry, it was perceived that Trelleborg actively tried to reduce Skega's possibilities to establish itself in the industry. Earlier experiences of Trelleborg's actions affects the way that Trellex acts in the industry, as well as the interpretations of the intentions that lie behind the actions of Trellex's competitors.

Psychological proximity is expressed in the prestige and pride that characterise the ways that actors describe themselves and their competitors. This can be exemplified by the opposing perceptions in both of the lining companies as to which company held the leading position in a number of areas. What is seen as misguided investments by competitors or disadvantages relative to the own company, are often mentioned, as well as the own company's advantages.

The complexity and uncertainty of this climate makes information difficult to access, easy to conceal, and easy to misunderstand, which decreases *surveillability*. The uncertainty that pervades the climate signifies that information is ambiguous. Suspicion of, and insufficient trust between, competitors can be described as disturbances in the communication between them. The climate of revolutionary competition is also the most complex of the four climates. One company can hold strong positions in certain areas or within certain product groups where the competitors are weak, and vice versa. Actors can exploit their own positions and strengths in certain areas, and thereby weaken the positions of competitors in totally different areas. Complex competitive play in such situations becomes usual. A move in one area is countered by a move in other areas. If the companies are also diversified, complexity may increase in that measures taken in entirely different arenas of competition can function as complex multiple moves. Consequently, the effects of, and the links between individual measures are many and difficult to grasp.

The climate of revolutionary competition can be compared to heterogeneous oligopolies. The asymmetry that characterises these forms of market are assumed to give rise to uncertainty, and to actions that are not concordant with that of the competitor. This is explained by the fact that the companies cannot identify in which areas concordant action is required, nor which negative consequences may follow from conflicting action (cf. Scherer, 1980).

This study shows, however, that other factors that are linked to the nature of the climate of competition can help to explain conflicting action.

Considerable affection and psychological proximity between competitors mean that the actors gather information on each other and continuously watch each other. As in the climate of rivalling competition, information is gathered on a company's competitors through, for example, the contacts that are made with common customers or through inspecting patent documentation. At the same time, the interpretation of such information is made more difficult by the uncertainty, complexity, and antagonism between the companies. Motives behind the actions of competitors can often be difficult to understand, which means that the intentions behind action can be interpreted as conflicting. On the other hand, a company's own individual action is described as being independent, i.e. motivated by the customer situation or the company's own goals, or as reactive, i.e. a necessary reaction to the actions of competitors. Trellex, for example, describes its establishment in Aitik as an independent act caused by partly exogenous events, whereas Skega perceived this action as conflicting.

The *distribution of roles* is not accepted, and the *rules-of-play* are not followed. The climate of revolutionary competition is characterised more by conflict about the current distribution of roles between competitors, than by acceptance. It is primarily the distribution of power in relationships that is not accepted. Action in the climate of revolutionary competition is characterised by uncertainty and by the companies' object-orientation. The ways of relating action to competitors varies, however, as the actions of competitors are interpreted as conflicting whereas the company's own actions are described as reactive. The non-acceptance of the distribution of roles means that a change in the relative positions of the competing companies is seen as an important goal for company action, which thus becomes object-oriented.

Turbulence in the climate of competition gives rise to changes in the rules-of-play. Trellex and Skega faced new rules-of-play as a result of the actions of the Trelleborg group, in spite of the fact that the actions were not primarily intended to change the competitive situation in the industry. As acceptance for new distributions of roles is low, no new rules-of-play for interaction develop when the position of competitors change. In the Lining industry where the climate of competition was rivalling before it became revolutionary, good competition is spoken of as an ideal. Earlier norms for good competition remain as ideals, but in practice the companies act against the rules-of-play. The companies take measures that they themselves consider indefensible as they act contrary to good competitive morals. However, the companies hold that such action is necessary as a defence against the actions of competitors, which are considered as being taken in order to inflict damage.

The Climate of Co-existing Competition

In asymmetric-passive competition, a climate of co-existing competition pervades. Competing companies do not confront each other directly, but adapt to each other or act independently within their own individual market areas. Unlike the climate of revolutionary competition, there are no real contrasts between the competing companies; they exist in a kind of symbiosis with each other, they co-exist. Competition in the climate of co-existing competition can be compared to Easton's (1987; 1992) description of co-existent competitive relations. Easton considers that companies can come to co-exist as a result of one company dominating a industry, or as a result of companies being unaware of each other. As both known and unknown co-existence can be identified in the asymmetric-passive climate of competition, Easton's concept has given this climate its name.

Functional distance is considerable. The competition that is pursued in this climate is of a completely different character than competition in the other climates. The intensity of competition is very low, and in those instances that the competing companies act relative to each other, their purpose is primarily to adapt to each other, or to further distance themselves from each other. The positions that have been obtained in the market as a whole, or within delimited market segments, are thereby maintained. By distinguishing themselves in all aspects that are considered important, and by not competing actively with each other, a functional distance is created between the companies. The two small competitors in the Rack and Pinion industry operated mostly in the domestic market, whereas Alimak focused mainly on international operations. Moreover, the companies distinguished themselves from each other in their products. This gave rise to functional distance.

In the climate of co-existing competition, the actions of the competing companies are not considered to be relative to each other. Even so, actors do occupy opposing positions, and, in this sense, their positions can be said to be relative, which means that actors can be said to interact indirectly. Easton (1992) means that competitors are relative if they as a result of their positions are related. Consequently, a potential for interaction develops among them. Easton's reasoning means that the companies' relative positions, and the consequential indirect interaction that occurs between them, gives rise to a development of relationships even for those companies that only co-exist.

Neutral attitudes of consent develop in the relations among competitors. In the Rack and Pinion industry, an elder/younger brother mentality characterised relationships between the companies. Alimak was relatively indulgent towards the smaller companies, whose actions within the same areas of operation as Alimak were accepted by Alimak and not seen as threatening. In the same way, these smaller companies accepted Alimak's position as leader. This gives rise to harmony between the competing companies, and their actions are considered to be harmless. Alimak does not dominate the relationship with manufacturers of products for raise climbers, but the companies do co-exist by operating within well-delimited product segments. Attitudes towards these competing actors can be described as neutral.

The *surveillability* of competition is limited by distance and the insufficient spreading of information. Competing actors gather and analyse data on each other to a very limited extent. The exchange of information is of a different character in this climate than in the other climates. The information that is exchanged regards the relative strengths of the companies, rather than their operations. Actors are primarily interested in obtaining an acknowledgement of the own company's position in the industry or in product or market segments. The actions that characterise this climate of competition, and that to a great extent can be seen as a result of co-existence, can be described as independent moves. These independent moves are instigated by innovators and entrepreneurs in the companies and from the customers' demands which the companies come in contact with in their markets. If any one company instigates an independent move which has consequences for its competitors, no countermeasures will appear, despite the increase in the real threat from the competitor. This is primarily because companies are unaware that their actions can, in the long run, become a serious threat.

Role distribution and *rules-of-play* are clear and are accepted. In the climate of co-existing competition, the power structure that develops is accepted, which is why a company's successes within one area can be accepted and seen as being action within individual territories. This can be exemplified by Alimak's decisions to partly leave the niches that its competitors had cultivated. The clear distribution of roles among competing companies explains the passivity of this climate of competition. Goal-oriented action is possible, due to the distance and the lack of direct interaction between them. Independent action is not seen as relative to competitors. The motivation for action does not stem from a company's competitors, nor is it interpreted by competitors as intending to inflict damage or to challenge. Action can be described as potential competition or general competition for the needs of the customer.

In this climate of competition, rules-of-play are not discussed between companies, nor is that which ought to be considered good competitive morale. Rules-of-play can be considered superfluous, or so obvious and natural that they do not need to be mentioned in the descriptions of competitors. The companies allow each other to act undisturbed in their individual areas. If one company shows tendencies of expanding outside that which is generally perceived to be its 'territory', rules-of-play or the accepted distribution of roles can be said to be questioned. The opinions voiced at Alimak exemplify this, in that a certain amount of competition is seen to be useful but that it is important to hinder one's competitors from growing too strong (i.e. from developing relatively high volumes and high profitability). As long as the competing companies remain within their own individual territories, no real measures are taken, even though the companies to some extent inspire each other in their actions.

The Climate of Evolutionary Competition

In symmetric-passive competition, the climate of competition is *evolutionary*. The climate is characterised by ongoing change in the industry, in much the same away as the climate of revolutionary competition. However, the change that takes place in this climate is not as dramatic an upheaval as in the climate of revolutionary competition. Here change occurs gradually through companies becoming increasingly proximate to each other. Companies become more aware of the threat of increasingly active competition at the same time as they become aware of increasing symmetry between the competing companies. It is this mental evolution that characterises this climate of competition. The conditions for competition in the climate of evolutionary competition has not been discussed or been given in economic theory or in studies of competitive relations.

Functional distance is considerable. There is a functional proximity between actors as a result of the symmetry between them, but this proximity is limited as they do not actively compete against each other. Symmetry in product and market does not automatically lead to considerable functional proximity between actors, and no links in technology, time, or knowledge develop between them in spite of the symmetry. This can be explained by their passive action. As in the climate of co-existing competition, the competing companies act independently.

There is an increase in the awareness of and vigilance over other competitors in this climate, which means an increase in *psychological proximity*. In agreement with Easton's (1992) discussion that relations develop between competitors as a result of their positions being relative to each other, relations also develop in the climate of evolutionary competition, in spite of the fact that companies do not engage in direct interaction. It is through these relationships that companies develop an awareness of and a vigilance over other competitors in the climate of evolutionary competition.

Surveillability is limited, but increases progressively. The limited exchange of information between actors can be said to be due to the insufficiency of information channels. An effective communication between the competitors is hindered because of the indirect nature of competition, and because of the delays that indirect competition involves. The climate of evolutionary competition is characterised by the increasing mental proximity of the competing companies. This leads to an increased surveillability in competition, an increase that occurs over a long period of time. The time delay is due to the deep-rootedness of memories, and the fact that these memories are difficult to change. It is only when change is obvious that awareness of the new competitive situation begins to grow. Ålö considered itself to be both a national leader and an international leader. This pre-supposition changed progressively, almost unnoticed. It was only when Trima had taken over leadership of certain areas that Ålö changed its opinion of its own strength and dominance. At the same time, Trima became aware of their own strength, and of the possibilities that this gave the company in future competition.

The second explanation is that signals from the market which provide information on change are indirect, in that competing companies do not compete directly against each other. The independent action of the competitors gives rise to market signals regarding the symmetry between competitors. Information is indirect in that it is structure and not action in itself that brings the actors together. Structural change in the Front-loader industry gave rise to a series of signals from the market, which were only noticed after a while. Official acknowledgement of Trima's products, the different customer views of Trima's products as being advanced, and the fact that Trima's loader could be found at foreign retailers are examples of such market signals. In the same way, Alimak became aware of the strength of its competitors during the second phase in the industry history, when the company, previously market leader, only sold reserve parts whilst its competitors had developed their own niches.

The *distribution of roles* between competitors and the *rules-of-play* are unclear and are not accepted. Awareness of the threat that the competitors pose, and the opportunities that develop as a result of the comparability of the competing companies, means that the companies question the current distribution of roles in the industry. Contrasts increase progressively, but do not achieve the same conflicting characteristics as in the climate of revolutionary competition. Those companies that have previously dominated the industry will regain their dominating position. Those companies that have succeeded in growing to become opponents of equal strengths will continue to develop, thereby gaining a leading position in the industry. The companies do not have the same perception of, and do not accept, current power relations in the industry. No direct measures are taken to change the distribution of roles; any reaction can instead be described as silent protest through internal mobilisation against the pre-conditions for competition or against the opportunities that these pre-conditions provide.

In much the same way as the conflicting and reactive action of the climate of revolutionary competition, evolutionary action is described as being relative to competitors' actions, though primarily focusing on the motives behind the company's own action. The main motive is considered to be preparation for active competition. As mobilisation occurs internally, it is difficult for competitors to gather information on and analyse this action. This explains why it is primarily the company's individual motives that are described relative to the company's competitors.

There are no clear rules-of-play. Existing rules-of-play are followed at the same time as new rules-of-play progressively develop. The companies of the Front-loader industry competed in a climate of co-existing competition when competition gradually became evolutionary. The existing rules-of-play (i.e. that each company kept to its own area) lived on, despite incremental change. As symmetry between the competing companies increased, the existing rules-of-play were abandoned successively, as the companies began to compete (if only to a minor extent) in each other's areas. Consequently, the rules-of-play became more diffuse and uncertain.

FOUR CLIMATES OF COMPETITION — A SUMMARY

Four climates of competition have been identified and described in the description of interaction and relations between actors. The similarities and differences between these four climates of competition are given with regard to three dimensions in the table below. These three dimensions are both woven together and relative to each other; together, they provide an illustration of the nature of the four climates of competition.

Through a comparison of the climates of competition that have been identified in this study and the structural descriptions of competition that were presented in Chapter Two, a number of similarities can be identified. The same type of behavioural patterns that are discussed within theories of competitive strategies can be found in the studied industries. A company's relative strength and position has emerged as being of fundamental importance to that company's actions. Rational action as a result of the assessment of individual relative strength and position has not, however, been identified.

The findings of this study are also consistent to some extent with descriptions of action in different oligopolistic situations, and with descriptions of competition in and between strategic groups. That symmetrical competing companies act in similar ways, whereas asymmetrical companies adapt to each other, is explained by economic theory as being due to uncertainty and power or dependency relations between the companies. Economic theory thereby takes into consideration imperfections in the market, and their significance for action. However, the effects of uncertainty and dependence on interaction are not analysed to any great depth.

Porter (1979) means that strategic asymmetry increases rivalry within a strategic group while symmetry brings about tacit coordination among competitors. Cool and Derrickx (1993) raise a slightly different discussion in arguing that symmetry can give rise to active competition, in that no company has any specific competence that is difficult to copy. This discussion is consistent with the conditions that arise in the climate of rivalling competition. Functional proximity and the opportunity to contest each other's

Table 7.2 The Characteristics of the Four Climates of Competition

Character	Rivalry	Revolution	Co-existence	Evolution
Proximity/ distance	Great functional proximity Collegial mentality Psychological Proximity	Limited functional proximity due to asymmetry Affected relationship	Functional distance, 'Big brother' mentality or attitudes of neutral acceptance	Limited functional proximity due to passivity, competitors are perceived as threatening and carefully watched
Surveillability	Direct and clear information is communicated Great Surveillability	Information that is difficult to interpret. Complexity and uncertainty make surveillability difficult	Distance, lack of awareness and lack of information reduces surveillability	Indirect communication and the process of improving awareness takes time means that surveillability is gained, but with a time-lapse
Distribution of roles and Rules-of-play	Role distribution and rules-of-play are clear, accepted and followed. Action is goal-oriented	Distribution of roles is not accepted. The actors revolt Rules-of-play change and existing norms are not followed Action is object-oriented	Distribution of roles and rules-of-play are clear, accepted, and followed. Action is goal-oriented	Distribution of roles is not accepted and actors mobilise for potential competition. Rules-of-play are unclear Action is object-oriented

market position, can provide in part an explanation for the rivalry that develops between companies.

The difference between active and passive competition can, however, be explained by the nature of the climate of competition, rather than the degree of symmetry between actors or by strategic diversity. A number of aspects to do with the actors' conceptions and interpretations are missed if discussions of symmetry and strategic diversity only consider functional interaction. An increased understanding of company action can arise through including the process of interaction and conceptions of competition as points of departure.

8. Climates of Competition and Dynamics

Chapter Seven presented four climates of competition. This chapter will discuss the dynamics of competition in those climates, where dynamics are expressed partly within the individual climates of competition, and partly in the transition from one climate to another. The durability of the climates of competition and the continuous processes of change in the industry need to be analysed, in order to gain an increased understanding of both the dynamics within each climate of competition and the dynamics that are expressed in the transition between climates. The point of departure for the above is discussed in the first part of this chapter, and the second part presents an analysis of the dynamics of competition in each of the climates of competition. The third part of the chapter deals with long term change in the climates, where one climate transforms into a second climate, and then into a third, and so on. The chapter finishes with a theoretical discussion on the dynamic processes that have been identified in the three studied industries.

THE DURABILITY AND CHANGEABILITY
OF CLIMATES OF COMPETITION

Chapters Four to Six described competition in the different phases of, and change over time in, the three studied industries, as is illustrated in the figure below. Certain similarities and differences can be observed regarding both the durability of the climates, and the direction of change. A comparison of the durability of the climates of competition shows that the climate of co-existing competition lasts

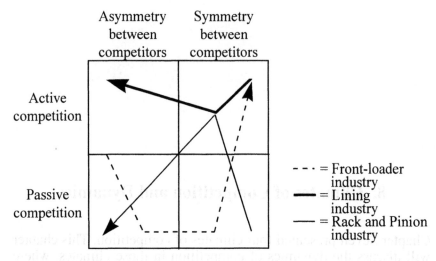

Asymmetry   Symmetry
between   between
competitors competitors

Active
competition

Passive
competition

- - - · = Front-loader
       industry
━━━ = Lining
       industry
──── = Rack and Pinion
       industry

Figure 8.1   Change Over Time in the Climates of Competition

the longest and is the most stable. In both the Front-loader industry and the Rack and Pinion industry, the climates of co-existing competition lasted almost thirty years (see Appendix 1-3). The climates of evolutionary and of revolutionary competition lasted for five and nine years, respectively. Both climates can, therefore, be described as lasting for a shorter time than the climates of co-existing competition. They are unstable in that change occurs continuously in one form or another (this is discussed later on in this chapter). That these two climates lasted several years can be explained by the fact that change takes time.

The climate of rivalling competition lasted only three years in the Rack and Pinion industry, whereas it lasted over twenty years in the Lining industry, and has characterised the Front-loader industry since 1983. Due to its nature, this climate must be described as being more stable than the climates of evolutionary and revolutionary competition, but less stable than the climate of co-existing competition. However, the stability of the climate of rivalling competition is dependent on the ability of the competing companies to maintain the symmetry and balance between the actors.

A comparison of the direction of change in the four climates of competition reveals an number of patterns. A superficial examination of the figure above gives the impression that the climates change in many different directions. A closer analysis, however, shows that it is possible to distinguish and discuss a small number of tentative patterns of change. The patterns of change that can be observed show the direction of change towards what can be called the positive and negative poles of competition, either directly, or via one of the two climates that are called climates of transition (see Figure 8.2 below). The climate of rivalling competition is named *the positive pole of competition*, and the climate of co-existing competition is given the term *the negative pole of competition*. These terms have been chosen partly to emphasise the fact that competition tends to develop in one or the other direction, and partly in order to distinguish between the two poles in terms of the dynamics that develop in the climate of competition. Phases with climates of revolutionary or evolutionary competition are more temporary by nature, and can therefore be described as climates of transition. The figure below provides a more refined illustration of the patterns of change.

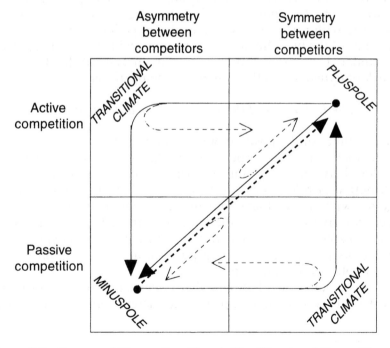

Figure 8.2 Patterns of Change Over Time in The Climates of Competition

The described patterns of change appear as the most probable from the studies of the industries included in this study, and are marked with continuous lines. Other patterns may be possible,[1] where, for example, the direction of development can be broken and the climate of competition restored to its former nature. A development directly from a climate of co-existing competition to a climate of rivalling competition is also possible. These patterns of change have been marked with broken lines as they have not been observed in the cases included in this study. The following text presents an analysis of the dynamics of the climates of competition, together with a discussion on the above tentative patterns of change. This will be based upon the analysis of the different natures of the climates of competition of the previous chapter.

DYNAMIC PROCESSES WITHIN
THE CLIMATES OF COMPETITION

Dynamic processes developed in three of the climates of competition, while in the fourth (exemplifying the negative pole of competition), a very low degree of dynamics develops. The dynamic processes within the positive pole of competition differ from the dynamics of the two climates of transitions, which in many respects are similar. The next section presents an analysis of the dynamics, or lack of dynamics, in the climates of competition.

The Dynamics of the Positive Pole of Competition

The dynamics of the positive poles of competition are expressed in the interactive learning processes and the pressure to compete that develops between competing companies. Acceptance of the current distribution of roles found in the climate of rivalling competition, together with the fact that companies can alternately dominate over time, can give rise to stability and a form of harmony between actors, in spite of the rivalry. If companies are able to expand, and continuously re-conquer leading position in alternating processes, this climate will remain in force.

In the product development that occurred in the Front-loader industry, the competing companies alternately launched new series

---

[1] General patterns of change cannot be determined from this study due to the limited number of case studies involved in this study.

of loader, incorporating improvements of the loaders launched by competitors. A continuous process of learning developed in that the products were continually improved despite the lack of direct pressure for such change from customers. These learning processes can be explained by both the fact that the exchange of information and the proximity between the competing companies is considerable, and by the previous experiences of the companies.

The Lining industry showed that the competing companies learnt from each other through the information that was gathered through their customers, through the inspection of patent applications, and through the analyses of material in competitors' products. Customers played a very important role in the development of applicable knowledge, as well as the contribution gained from competitors. The development of this type of knowledge has been stimulated through the contest over customers, and the meetings at customers' offices.

The study of the companies' action regarding the market shows that previous experience of the actions of competitors play an important part in the companies' learning processes. Trima's experience of Ålö's successful establishment abroad became one of the reasons behind the argument that even Trima should be able to establish strong positions in international markets. Trima also presumed that Ålö, in the same way that the company 'forgot' the domestic market during the 1970s due to its internationalisation efforts, would 'forget' the European market due to its efforts to establish a position in the American market. Trima did therefore not expect countermoves when it decided to expand in Europe.

The empirical findings of this study also indicate that the companies' risk-taking is stimulated in the climate of rivalling competition. Risky and uncertain decisions are sometimes taken because competitors have taken similar decision in the same areas, rather than through strategic consideration. Competition is thereby stimulated towards increased risk-taking. When it was apparent within Trellex that Skega had developed de-barking drums, Trellex also decided to develop and launch a similar product, in spite of the fact that it was considered to be risky, and that it was a product that was peripheral to their core business operations.

Lack of Dynamics in the Negative Pole of Competition

Of the four climates, the climate of co-existing competition is the most stable, as competing companies operate within clearly defined and delimited areas, and they also accept the current distribution of roles. The companies' goals do not conflict with each other, as they do in the climate of rivalling competition. Competitive play therefore becomes passive, which can be compared to Porter's (1979) reasoning about the dependency between competitors' market segments that is presupposed for the occurrence of rivalling action. Stability in the climate of co-existing competition can be explained by the absence of this dependency.

Competitive blindness arises in the climate of co-existing competition. Competitive blindness means that companies are not aware of threats from potential product substitutes, or opportunities for development within areas where customer requirements and demand is unclear. Alimak, for example, did not consider raise boring as a competitive method, and did not take advantage of the developmental potential that raise boring gave. Älö did not appreciate to any great extent the demand for development that Swedish customers voiced. Competitive blindness leads to a low degree of readiness to meet unforeseen changes within the industry.

A company dominating an industry, or a product or market area, provides experience of success and strength relative to its competitors — one's own position is perceived as being certain. Älö had both product and market leadership before the internationalisation of the company. The company considered itself as dominating, whereas its competitors were seen as being small and not dangerous. Alimak has considered itself throughout the history of the industry as being "biggest and best". The company still dominates the industry and considers its domestic competitors as unimportant. The competitive blindness described above, and the lack of dynamics in the climate of co-existing competition can be explained by the perception and experience of being dominant and being secure.

Another explanation of competitive blindness and lack of dynamics is that distance between the actors, which is a consequence of asymmetry and passivity in competition, reduces the spreading of information. In delegating to a considerable extent the cultivation of the domestic market to SLR, Älö increased the distance between itself and customers and competitors. This can explain that the changed demands of the Swedish market and Trima's expansion were not given the same due attention that would have been given if Älö had itself actively participated in the cultivation of the market.

The lack of competition may have paralysed Alimak's innovative ability. Within the raise climber product group, a number of models were developed between 1957 and 1964 to meet customer requirements. Thereafter, product development became very limited, until the middle of the 1980s. During the 1960s, raise climbers were a considerable part of Alimak's total operations, but its importance has decreased since then, which means that Alimak has lost market shares relative to other raising methods. The lack of competition, or the conception that raise boring could not be considered as a competitive method, means that an important driving force behind product development was not present.

The same pattern can be discerned in the development of the work platform. The first platform was developed as early as 1954. A new attempt to resume development of the product occurred in 1963, but this development was not successful. It was not until the 1980s that a substantial attempt to develop the product group was made. It can be assumed that if a competitor had begun development and production of platforms during the 1950s, Alimak would have been stimulated to continue its developmental efforts. The lack of this type of stimulus led to the cessation of product development.

The Dynamics of Transitional Climates

Both transitional climates can be described as dynamic, in that they are characterised by the transformation that occurs in the industry. Change in the climate of revolutionary competition is turbulent, whereas change in the climate of evolutionary competition occurs more progressively. That the climate of evolutionary competition endures over a longer period of time can be explained by the time delay that exists from the point in time that the climate comes into being to the time that actors become aware of the situation and undertake measures to change the situation.

In both of these climates of competition, the companies relative positions are uncertain, and the current distribution of roles is not accepted. A pressure to compete develops between the competing companies which can be related to the fact that the companies are in conflict with each other. In the climate of evolutionary competition, this conflict is only expressed indirectly, in the form of internal mobilisation. In the climate of revolutionary competition, however, the competing companies act in direct conflict with each other, taking measures that can be destructive for every company. Conflict in the transitional climates can be related to the object-orientation of the companies; they act with the intention of affecting their relations with competitors, which affects the psychological proximity that exist between them (as discussed in the previous chapter).

In the climate of evolutionary competition, knowledge about the comparability of the competing actors increases the companies' watchfulness and mobilisation. The companies no longer consider themselves to be superior or inferior, but become aware of the real threat that their competitors have become. Such an awareness developed within Ålö, due to signals from the market about the threat that Trima had become, which gave rise to the development of plans to actively engage in competition with Trima. At Trima, awareness of its comparability in relative strength with Ålö resulted in plans to expand internationally. Trima and Ålö were the largest actors in the domestic market, and Trima realised that a continued expansion would mean that it must either compete with Ålö for SLR's customers, or that it would have to expand internationally. Personnel were recruited, and the international ambitions for the continued expansion of the company were set down. This type of action can be described as an internal mobilisation, mental as well as actual, to meet the future.

In the climate of revolutionary competition, companies are forced to be aggressive and creative. The conflicting action of competitors forces the companies to instigate measures that may not otherwise have been taken. Skega, for example, was forced to react against Trelleborg's acquisitions of other companies, as this led to the loss of important customers. Skega reacted by taking different kinds of measures to compensate for the decrease in customers, and to find other partners in product development. If Skega had been able to keep its major customer and partner, Boliden, the company would not have been forced to seek new market opportunities or new forms of product development. Trellex was also forced to react to Trelleborg's acquisition of Boliden and the opportunities that this presented. The competing companies become more aggressive in their actions, in the sense that they are continuously on the watch and continuously prepared to instigate counter-measures. Experience of the state of opposition between the companies leads to an expectation of conflicting action from competitors.

CHANGE IN THE CLIMATES OF COMPETITION

If competition is analysed over a longer period of time, the dynamics of competition can also be expressed in the form of movement and change which give rise to shifts in climate. An analysis of the shifts in climate and of the different natures that these shifts take on in the different phases in the histories of the industries, can also include a discussion of the importance of competition for development in the individual industries. The case-studies included here indicate that the different climates of competition fulfil different functions over a longer period of time, and that these climates together stimulate the development of both companies and industries. This statement is supported by Porter's (1990) claim that competition between proximate actors stimulates development in competitive international industries and that the history of an industry is of importance in the understanding of why this is so.

In this study, however, it is the nature and dynamics of competition that are focused upon, not the importance of competition for industrial development, which would require the analysis of other factors important for the development of companies and industries. The knowledge that has been attained about the nature and dynamics of competition makes possible a hypothetical discussion on how competition between proximate actors can contribute to the development within an industry. In the following discussion of the dynamics in shifts in climate, hypothetical consequences to industry development of such shifts are also discussed.

Why and How Do the Climates of Competition Change?

The strong rivalry in the positive pole of competition is demanding, and requires considerable efforts from the competing companies. These companies must be constantly alert, and should develop at the same rate as each other. This can be considered by the companies to be negative, and can lead to the companies striving to escape the tough competition. If the equality between the actors is broken, the climate of rivalling competition ceases to exist. This can occur, for example, as a result of external events, or because a company succeeds in developing an advantage in one area that the competitors cannot regain.

Competition can be avoided by fusion or through acquisition of competitors, for example. In the Front-loader industry, the desire to avoid competition was expressed in Ålö's plans to buy Trima. The Front-loader companies operated in a saturated market during the 1980s. Despite this, the companies could expand in a parallel manner, which is explained by the fact that the Swedish companies offered advanced loaders and the agricultural industry developed towards an increased degree of mechanisation. As a result of the international expansion of the companies, market potential became more difficult to exploit. This led to their actions becoming more relative to each other, and the rivalry between the companies hardening. A fusion between the companies would have meant that the rivalry would have ceased. The climate of competition would thereby have become a climate of co-existing competition, with one dominant actor and a number of smaller actors operating within partly demarcated niches.

The development towards a climate of co-existence can also arise through competing companies creating sufficient asymmetry between themselves. In the Rack and Pinion industry, the companies moved from a climate of rivalling competition to one of co-existence. The companies did not maintain the balance and symmetry that had characterised the industry for a number of years. Alimak launched a new product, and consequently could take a leading position in the industry.

However, the three industries show that the development towards the negative pole of competition can be obstructed by a number of causes. Trellex developed an advantage in the screen product area at the same time that this segment underwent expansion, which resulted in that the climate of competition developed directly towards a climate of co-existence. In the Lining industry, the balance between the companies in the mill lining product area was maintained, and the development towards a climate of co-existing competition was thereby interrupted during the 1980s. Instead, the climate of competition became revolutionary. The explanation for this development is that the intensity of the competition in the mill lining product area increased. The climate of revolutionary competition was also strengthened by Trelleborg's company acquisitions.

It was primarily the asymmetry in relative strength that brought about the climate of revolutionary competition. In this climate, the stronger actor has more resources and is better equipped, which can also lead to the climate ceasing to exist. If the strongest actor can increase his dominance, or distinguish himself in some other way from his competitors, a climate of co-existing competition is likely to develop. The competitors are then forced to seek out their own niches to be able to exist in the same industry as the dominant actor, which means the climate of competition is characterised by co-existence. Such a development would mean that the dynamics of competition would decrease.

If competing companies find themselves in the negative pole of competition, a change can occur if one competitor is able to develop its operations unnoticed. The competitive blindness that develops in the climate of co-existing competition can mean that progressive change towards symmetry between the actors is left unnoticed. During the 1970s, for example, the Front-loader industry underwent concentration partly as a result of Trima/Bergsjöverken's decision to expand through fusions and company acquisitions. The consequences of this progressive chain of events was not noticed until symmetry had developed between the competing companies.

When competing companies are aware that they exist in a climate of evolutionary competition, they undertake measures to either compete actively, or to again distance themselves from their competitors. The dynamics that are a result of the increased symmetry between the Front-loader companies during the 1970s led to the transition of the climate of competition from evolutionary to rivalling competition. The fact that Ålö became aware of the threat that Trima posed, and that Trima became aware of the opportunities for the company to continue its expansion, lead to the development of active competition between them.

The positions of relative strength between companies change when the companies find themselves in a climate of evolutionary competition. Ålö enjoyed a dominating position during the first and second phases of the history of the industry, but this changed, and the symmetry in the industry became greater during the third phase. As a result of the time delay which has been discussed previously, Trima could take over the leadership in some areas, even if only to a limited extent, before Ålö reacted. Awareness of the increasing symmetry between companies did not arise during the time when the symmetry developed; it was only when the "pendulum was about to swing in the other direction" that countermeasures were taken, which led to the development of a climate of rivalling competition.

The Different Functions Over Time of the Climates of Competition

The development of a climate from being stable, to being changeable, to becoming stable again, stimulates an industry's long term development. Both stability and changeability are necessary for long term development, as the different states fill different functions.

Stability and harmony in the positive pole of competition stimulate a continued development within existing areas of operation. Harmony in the climate of rivalling competition contributes to company and industry development as long as it is of a temporary nature. If, through fusions or the building of different types of cartels, harmony becomes permanent, the climate of rivalling competition will cease to exist, and the previous relationship as colleagues will become negative for the development of the industry. The fruitful combination of a collegial mentality, which makes reciprocal learning possible, and the threat of conflict and disharmony disappears if the comity between companies becomes permanent.

If the climate of competition becomes revolutionary, development and innovativeness in new product and market areas is stimulated. To ensure that the destructive nature of competition does not lead to the companies "competing to the death", a development towards the positive or negative poles of competition is necessary. The stability and lack of active competition in the negative pole of competition provides companies with the opportunity to further develop the product and market areas identified as being of interest during the period of revolutionary competition. Through goal-oriented action, companies can develop their areas of operation.

The transformation of the climate to being a climate of co-existing competition can also be contributed to the development in the industry, but if the climate becomes permanent, competing companies become paralysed, as does the industry's continued development. The climate does not provide any motivation for continued development and change. Acceptance of the current distribution of roles means that the companies become passive, but nonetheless, change can occur. The competitive blindness that characterises this climate makes it possible for the competing companies to grow unnoticed, and this increases the symmetry in the industry. In that the climate of competition becomes evolutionary, companies mobilise their resources and their state of readiness for active competition. The continued company and industry development as a whole is thereby stimulated.

SIMULTANEOUS DYNAMIC PROCESSES

The dynamics that develop in, and between, the different climates of competition are expressed in different ways, and the different factors that explain dynamics vary. However, the dynamics of the climates of competition can be described as two slightly different, but simultaneous, forces or movements. Firstly, competition gives rise to different types of learning processes, and secondly, a pressure to compete develops. This forces the companies to constantly undertake new measures or competitive moves, thus, in the long run, the innovative action of the companies is stimulated. The two processes or forces which are expressed in competition, can be explained by the degree of stability, harmony, dependency in the competitors' relationships, and the companies' relative strengths. This is discussed further in the next section.

Learning Through Competition

The dynamics in the different climates of competition can be partly understood through knowledge of how learning is stimulated. In his discussion of the development of business strategies, Mintzberg (1989) describes this as being a continual learning process. Learning processes arise in the organisation when organisations and individuals interact with their environments. Individual awareness about, and understanding of, what occurs in the environment increases through observing and experiencing one's own action and that of others. These experiences are subsequently built into the strategic action of their companies.

March and Olsen (1976) describe organisational learning as a cyclical process; a line of thinking that can be found in most literature dealing with organisational learning.[2] March and Olsen's point of departure lies in that an individual's set of beliefs is the foundation for his action. An individual's action is, in turn, the basis for organisational action. This action leads to responsive measures for actors in the environment, and these responses affect, in their turn, the individual's set of beliefs. The external environment, in this case the climate of competition, is thereby crucial for the learning process.

In discussions about learning processes, it is the changeability and the opportunity to give the environment a meaning, that is decisive for which learning processes take place. Hedberg (1981) distinguishes between stable and turbulent environments, and means that the learning process in stable environments are cumulative. New knowledge is added to previous knowledge in much the same way as pieces in a puzzle are put together. The multiplicity and rapidity of change makes it impossible to try out new solutions to problems, and to develop the creativity that is needed to bring about company and industry development. A certain degree of stability is needed to be able to build up a image of the environment, and to be able to act relative to the environment.

---

[2] Cf. Weick (1979); Hedberg (1981); Björkegren (1989), and Söderholm (1991).

The dynamics that exist in the climate of rivalling competition —
the positive pole of competition — are expressed in the cumulative,
reciprocal learning processes that develop through interaction
between competing companies. The climate of rivalling competition
has been described as being relatively stable and harmonious, but not
for that reason as being paralytical. The acceptance that develops for
the current rules-of-play and the distribution of roles between competing companies makes the climate relatively stable and predictable.
Reciprocal cumulative learning processes can thereby develop,
despite the companies' fundamental rivalling positions. The extensive interaction and proximity between competing companies makes
it easy to interpret competition, and to develop an understanding for
the effects of one's own actions and the actions of competitors.

The stability and harmony in the climate of competition makes
possible the development of understanding of the competitive situation. Newell and Simon (1972) argue that earlier stimuli and experiences are stored over time and are included in the interpretations
that develop in the individual and within the organisation.[3] The
stability of the climate of rivalling competition means, therefore, that
earlier experiences of interaction with one's competitors strengthens
the conception of the competitive situation, and contributes to learning. The structure of knowledge is given new nuances and complexity for the individuals in the organisation. The stimuli arising from
the actions of the competing companies can thus be countered by
multiple competitive moves (cf. Feigenbaum, 1970).

The cumulative learning described above cannot be found in the
other climates of competition. The climate of co-existing competition is characterised by stability and harmony in much the same
way as the climate of rivalling competition. Despite this, the learning processes that arise out of the interaction between competing
companies can be described as one-way learning (cf. Hedberg,
1981). Individuals learn behaviour without necessarily being aware
of cause and effect. Companies adapt to each other or act within
their own individual areas without being aware of either the
reasons behind, or the consequences of, competitors' actions.

Stability and harmony are needed for learning processes to
develop, but they must not become overpowering. Hedberg (1981)
states that situations that are too stable produce little information,

---

[3] Cf. Argyris and Schön (1978).

and therefore few opportunities for learning. This can be compared to the situation in the climate of co-existing competition, where the communicative processes between the competitors are practically non-existent, and the distance between the competing companies is considerable. A competitive blindness to the actions of competitors develops in the climate of co-existing competition; competitors have not developed a perception of possible cause and effect in the actions of competitors relative to each other. Therefore, companies act independently of each other to a greater degree, and the actions of the companies do not bring about counter-measures from competitors.

Imitative action can develop in this climate. The companies can imitate each other in the expectation of gaining the same results by studying the competing companies and concluding that their action is successful. This type of action has been linked by Hedberg (1981) to stable environments where dependency between actors is of no great importance, as is the case in the climate of co-existing competition.

The dynamics of the climates of revolutionary and evolutionary competition, the transitional climates of competition, can be explained by the changes in the current perceptions of competition, and by the non-acceptance of the new situation. These dynamics are expressed in the accommodative learning processes that develop in these two climates. Argyris (1976) distinguishes between 'single-loop' learning and 'double-loop' learning, and Björkegren (1989) links two types of learning to the two loops. The first is assimilation, which involves the incorporation of experiences into existing structures (Björkegren, 1989; p. 45). This type of learning is linked to single-loop learning, and leads to the confirmation and strengthening of current interpretations. The second type of learning, accommodation, involves the reconstruction of, or change to, existing knowledge structures (Björkegren, 1989; p. 45). This type of learning is built from observations of gaps and contradictions in the existing set of interpretations. These gaps and contradictions can be perceived as being threatening, which leads individuals, at least in the beginning, to try to fill in the gaps and rework the contradictions. However, if contradictions are particularly explicit, the current set of interpretations can change, and a double-loop learning process can commence. Changes in interpretations lead to changes in action.

In the two climates of transition, learning can be primarily described as accommodation, or double-loop learning, which is explained by the fact that the earlier perceptions of the competition no longer correspond to the information that arises as a result of the actions of competitors. Before the occurrence of change, the studied actors in the climate of revolutionary competition found themselves in the climate of rivalling competition, where the relative strength of the companies was symmetrical. The climate of evolutionary competition was previously a climate of co-existence. When the climates became evolutionary, or alternatively revolutionary, the actors' earlier perceptions of competition no longer corresponded with the information and experiences gained. This gave rise to change in the frameworks of interpretation and in the conceptions of competition.

The relationships among the competitors were also characterised by conflict. Uncertainty was brought about by asymmetry between the companies in the climate of revolutionary competition, and by the indirect competition in the climate of evolutionary competition. The communicative processes were made more difficult as a result of companies no longer integrating functionally or technically with each other (or if they did, only in limited areas). The difference between the two climates can be linked to the way that information about competitors is gathered. In the climate of revolutionary competition, information is gathered directly through interaction between the competing companies. In the climate of evolutionary competition, however, information is gathered indirectly.

Changes in the climate of revolutionary competition are more rapid. When a competitor undertakes measures that do not correspond to the expectations of the other companies, these measures are interpreted as being conflicting, and reactive counter-measures are undertaken relatively quickly. Partly exogenous events, or what has previously been described as competition at several levels, strengthens the diversity of the climate, which increases the dynamics. It is easier to conceal information or market signals that contradict current conceptions of competition in the climate of evolutionary competition. This can be explained by the fact that market signals do not involve direct consequences for the companies. It therefore takes a longer time before contradictions become strong enough to lead to what Björkegren (1989) calls a double learning loop.

The Pressure to Compete

The dynamics of competition cannot be understood solely from an understanding of the learning processes that arise from interaction between companies. It was stated earlier that the dynamics that develop in the climates of competition are constituted by two slightly different, but simultaneous, forces or movements. These two forces are pre-requisites for each other. The above discussion has dealt with one of these forces, learning processes. In order for these learning processes to come about, the second force, the pressure to compete which competitors exert on each other, must also be present. The companies in the positive poles of competition are forced to participate in the reciprocal learning processes that occur in order to avoid sliding into an inferior position, and to develop a dominating position. In the transitional climates of competition, companies are forced to rethink their accommodative learning processes if they are to gain/regain a dominating position.

The dependency between companies in the climate of rivalling competition, and their comparable position, means that the companies must constantly compare themselves with each other. This gives rise to a situation of intense rivalry, where move and counter-move occur frequently. This presses the companies to more creative and innovative action, and to taking greater risks. The goal-orientation that characterises the climate of rivalling competition, however, means that action is motivated by factors other than the competing companies action, at the same time as their goals are related to each others'. This stimulates risk-taking. The companies develop new solutions and ideas from their knowledge of customer needs, materials, and processes of production. The fact that their competitors also develop similar solutions also stimulates the companies' continued development and risk-taking, which leads to high risk projects being carried through.

However, the fact that companies in the climate of co-existing competition are goal-oriented in their action does not bring about increased risk-taking, as the goals are not relative to those of the competitors. That these goals are not confronted can be explained by the limited dependency between companies. Stability, harmony, dependency, and comparable positions are therefore important characteristics which must be present simultaneously for the cumulative learning processes and an increased risk-taking to arise in an industry. If, however, stability and harmony is too great, at the same time as the companies' positions are distanced and it is possible for them to act independently, no pressure to compete arises. A form of competitive blindness develops instead, which explains the absence of dynamic learning processes in the interaction between competitors.

The two transitional climates emerge as a result of the discontinuation of stability in the positive and negative poles of competition.

These contexts of competition are dynamic as a result of the dependency between the competitors' actions. That the pre-conditions for the companies' actions change means that their relative positions are uncertain. Uncertainty and dependency give rise to the pressure to compete, which forces companies to mobilise themselves in preparation for future competition. The companies in the climate of revolutionary competition have conflicting perceptions of current conditions, and relations among the competitors are affected. Competitive moves are therefore instigated to change the situation and to improve the companies' own positions. In the climate of evolutionary competition, the lack of acceptance for the current situations lead, however, to internal mobilisation and to watchfulness of each other.

A simultaneous effort to gain/maintain a dominating position, and to gain/maintain equal positions can be observed in the two transitional climates. In the climate of revolutionary competition, the one company strives to effect a development returning to the positive pole of competition, whereas the other tries to gain a dominating position. In the same way, the one company in the climate of evolutionary competition attempts to regain its dominating position, while the other company tries to effect a development towards the positive pole of competition. The pressure to compete that is a result of the companies' efforts to avoid competition without losing their positions in the industry, can be compared to the actors' efforts to gain control in a network (cf. Håkansson, 1992). The processes described above aim to bring about stability in competition through increased control of the established relations among competitors. This stability and control can be achieved both through domination, and through equal relationships between competing companies.

THE DYNAMICS OF THE CLIMATES OF COMPETITION — A SUMMARY

The understanding that can be attained of the dynamics within the climates of competition is summarised in the table below. The natures of the climates of competition provide different pre-conditions for the development of dynamic processes within each and every climate. There are primarily four pre-conditions for the occurrence of dynamism that can be emphasised and related to the natures of the climates of competition. Stability and harmony are necessary in order to bring about cumulative learning processes. If stability and harmony are too

Table 8.1   Dynamics in the Four Climates of Competition

Climate of Competition	Characteristics	Preconditions for Competition	Dynamic Processes
Rivalrous Competition	– Proximity – Acceptance and goal-orientation – Surveillability	– Stability – Harmony – Dependency – Equal positions	– Reciprocal cumulative learning processes – Pressure to compete that stimulates risk-taking
Co-existent Competition	– Distance – Acceptance and goal-orientation – Limited spread of information	– Great stability – Strong harmony – Little dependency – Separated positions	– Weak dynamics – Paralysis – Competitive blindness
Revolutionary Competition	– Psychological proximity – No acceptance and object-orientation – Uncertain information	– Rapid change – Direct conflict – Dependency – Uncertain positions	– Re-orientation and new thinking – Pressure to compete that stimulates external mobilisation
Evolutionary Competition	– Psychological proximity – No acceptance and object-orientation – Indirect information	– Successive change – Indirect conflict – Dependency – Uncertain positions	– Re-orientation and new thinking – Pressure to compete that stimulates internal mobilisation

great, the dynamic processes in the climates are paralysed. If, however, the climates of competition are characterised by the conflict and change, companies are forced to rethink and re-orient themselves. A prerequisite for learning, rethinking, and reorientation to occur is the existence of a pressure to compete in the industry. A pressure to compete develops if the companies are dependent on each other, and if their positions are comparable or uncertain.

Two parallel forces or movements have been identified within the climates of competition; learning and the pressure to compete. In the positive pole of competition, cumulative learning processes develop, and through the competitors' struggle for supremacy in the industry, a pressure to compete develops which stimulates risk-taking and learning. This stimulates the further development of the industry. In the two transitional climates, accommodative learning processes are brought about, and in the one competitor's efforts to gain dominance of the industry combined with the other competitor's efforts to maintain or develop a comparable position, a pressure to compete develops which leads to a mobilisation in the companies. In the climate of co-existing competition, however, learning as a result of competition is limited, and the pressure to compete is low.

The dynamics of competition are also expressed in the processes of change through which the climates replace each other. The dynamics in the one climate bring about change to that climate of competition. The efforts to avoid competition stimulate change towards the negative pole of competition, either directly or indirectly via the climate of revolutionary competition. The competitive blindness that develops in the negative pole of competition also makes possible a development towards the positive pole of competition via the climate of evolutionary competition. In the long term, the different climates of competition can be assumed to fulfil different functions, and to contribute to company and industry development. Consequently, the negative pole of competition can also be positive for development within the industry.

9. Conclusions and Implications

This chapter provides a summary and discussion of the findings of this study. The understanding that has been attained of the nature of the climates of competition is summarised in the first part of the chapter. The nature of the climates of competition can contribute to an understanding of the dynamics generated through competition, and this is discussed in the second part of the chapter. The two sub-purposes of this book have therefore been fulfilled, as has the main purpose, which is *to analyse the process of competition in industries where the actors have considerable geographical proximity to each other, in order to increase understanding for the nature and dynamics of competition*. The book has answered a number of questions, has illustrated others, and has also provided a number of new areas for research within the framework for this research area. The chapter will therefore finish with a discussion of the practical implications of the book and a discussion of the necessity for continued research.

THE FOUR CLIMATES OF COMPETITION DESCRIBE THE NATURE OF COMPETITION

By analysing the process of competition (cf. Figure 1.1) in the three industries, a partly new approach to competition has been attained. The book has thereby contributed to an increased understanding of the nature of the climates and dynamics of competition in the industries that have been studied. The industries are similar in three respects. Geographical proximity exists between the actors (as their strategic bases are located in Sweden), the companies' degree of internationalisation is high, and the industries have concentrated to become, as they are today, oligopolistic industries. Despite this, competition differs between the three industries.

The nature of competition could be described through a comparative analysis of the process of competition during different phases in the history of the three industries studied. The concept *climate of competition* was introduced to help provide a comprehensive description of the nature of competition. Four climates of competition were described from the functional and psychological distance between the actors, their possibilities to survey the competition, and from the acceptance of the current rules-of-play. These climates were the climates of *rivalling, revolutionary, co-existing*, and *evolutionary* competition. A summarised description of the natures of these climates of competition is given in the following.

From the natures of the four climates of competition, two opposing poles of competition and two transitional climates can be described. The climate of rivalling competition, named the *positive* pole of competition, is a dynamic climate of competition that stimulates further development in an industry. The climate of co-existing competition has been described as the *negative* pole of competition, as it paralyses competition by nature. The two transitional climates of competition, the climates of evolutionary and revolutionary competition, are dynamic, but differ from the positive pole of competition, in that they are more temporaneous by nature, and stimulate transformation and new approaches to competition. Table 9.1 below summarises the characteristics of the four climates of competition.

Co-existence and Rivalry — Two Opposite Poles

The climates of rivalling and co-existing competition have a number of common characteristics, but are still described as each other's opposite poles. In both climates, the current distribution of roles and the current rules-of-play are accepted by the competing actors, and relationships are characterised by harmony. This can be related to the goal-orientation that is expressed in the companies' actions. In the climate of co-existing competition, however, company goals are not described as being relative to the goals of competitors, and therefore neither is the achievement of goals, as is the case in the climate of rivalling competition. Another difference between the two climates is that surveillability is sought after and obtained in the climate of rivalling competition but not in the climate of co-existing

Table 9.1 The Four Climates of Competition

	Asymmetrical Actors	**Symmetrical Actors**
	Revolutionary Competition	Rivalling Competition
Active Competitive Play	DISTANCE – Limited functional proximity – Psychological proximity with affected relationships SURVEILLABILITY – Information that is difficult to interpret – Complexity and uncertainty make surveillability difficult ACCEPTANCE – Distribution of roles is not accepted – Rules-of-play change and existing norms are not followed – Action is object-oriented	DISTANCE – Functional proximity – Psychological proximity with colleagial mentality SURVEILLABILITY – Direct and clear information is communicated – Considerable surveillability ACCEPTANCE – Distribution of roles and rules-of-play are clear, accepted, and followed – Action is goal-oriented

Table 9.1 *continued*

	Asymmetrical Actors	**Symmetrical Actors**
Passive Competitive Play	Co-existent Competition DISTANCE – Functional distance – 'Big brother' mentality or attitudes of neutral acceptance SURVEILLABILITY – Lack of awareness and lack of – information reduces surveillability ACCEPTANCE – Distribution of roles and rules-of-play are clear, accepted, and followed – Action is goal-oriented	Evolutionary Competition DISTANCE – Limited functional proximity – Considerable psychological proximity with watchful relationships SURVEILLABILITY – Indirect communication and the process of improving awareness takes time means that surveillability is gained, but with a time-lapse ACCEPTANCE – Distribution of roles is not accepted – Rules-of-play are unclear – Action is object-oriented

competition. Functional and psychological distance differs between the two climates. In a comparison of all four climates, direct inter-action and proximity is greatest in the climate of rivalling com-petition, whereas the lack of proximity and the absence of direct interaction is greatest in the climate of co-existing competition.

That the symmetric-active climate is rivalrous can be explained by the fact that company achievement of goals is dependent on the actions of competitors. Through functional and social inter-action, links between the actors develop, which in turn strengthen the dependency between competing actors. However, the compan-ies can maintain their positions and develop at the same time. A type of collegial mentality and harmony therefore develops between them. That the climate is rivalrous means that the competi-tion is active, and that companies continuously measure and compare their relative strengths. A constant struggle goes on over which company is 'king of the castle'.

In the climate of co-existing competition, the companies ignore each other, and can therefore co-exist in harmony. The fact that the companies do not interact, and do not seek information about each other, means that links between the actors are few and far between. A sibling mentality develops in this climate. Interaction is indirect, and it is not deemed necessary to talk about the rules-of-play that exist, nor is it necessary to control that they are followed.

Revolution and Evolution — Two Transitional Climates

The common characteristics of the climates of rivalling and co-existing competition described above are not found in the climates of evolutionary and revolutionary competition. However, object-oriented action, psychological proximity, and insufficient accep-tance for current distribution of roles can be found in both climates. The major difference between the climates is that direct competi-tion characterises the climate of revolutionary competition, whereas competition in the climate of evolutionary competition is indirect.

The fact that competition is indirect in the climate of *evolutionary* competition can be related to the fact that it is structural symmetry and not action that gives rise to proximity in this climate. The fact that the companies are symmetrical in relative strengths and their product and market choice is not sufficient for direct functional interaction to develop. Actual symmetry must also correspond to perceived symmetry. Therefore, functional activity is indirect in the climate of evolutionary competition. The information that is obtained primarily concerns market signals that are indirect by nature. Moreover, the actors do not absorb the information that is available, as this would break with the conceptions of competition that exist in the companies. However, the actors do become progressively aware of changes to the competitive situation. The changing situation is not accepted, which leads to internal processes arising to change the situation. The companies find themselves in this climate of competition for the time that it takes them to become aware of such change, and to instigate internal mobilisation.

The difference between the climate of revolutionary competition and the climate of evolutionary competition, is the direct nature of competition. Functional interaction and proximity are limited because of asymmetry, whereas psychological proximity and activity in competition are considerable. Asymmetry and competition in several areas gives rise to complexity and uncertainty, and the information that is obtained is very difficult to interpret. The actions of competitors are therefore interpreted as intending to inflict harm, which leads to the development of emotional tension between companies, and thereby considerable psychological proximity. The competing companies are aware that counter-moves will be undertaken, but it is difficult to predict how and within which areas. This reduces surveillability, and increases suspicion between the competitors. The non-acceptance of the current distribution of roles and the perception of being threatened leads to the current rules-of-play being broken, which is considered to be unfortunate, but necessary for the defence of the companies' own positions.

Direct Relations Among Competitors

In the analysis that has been presented, it has been pointed out that an interactive perspective is necessary for the study. In order to describe the climate of competition that develops in an industry, consideration must be given to the fact that individuals and organisations act relative to each other, and to the fact that they act within a historical context. The research approach that has been chosen corresponds to a great extent with the network theory approach which has also dealt to a certain extent with relations among competitors. However, network theory deals mainly with indirect relations among competitors. This study emphasises that competitors also interact directly with each other (cf. Easton, 1987; Easton and Arajou, 1992).

Competing companies attempt to avoid interaction, i.e. companies ultimately attempt to avoid competition. They do not chose to interact with each other, as for example buyers and sellers do, but are forced to do so because their positions are relative to each other. If an understanding is to be gained for the direct relations among competitors, a point of departure must be based in their fundamental positions as opponents. Despite the fact that competitors do not have a mutual interest in taking part in interaction, a kind of harmony and mutual understanding can be found among them. This is of a different nature, however, than the harmony that can be found in relations between vertical actors in a network (buyers and sellers). The fact that the competing companies in the climate of rivalling competition are in fundamentally opposing positions, despite the description of the climate as being harmonious, presses the companies to an increased risk-taking, which is an example of this.

Co-operation and/or collaboration between competitors are examples of relations that can be found to a certain extent in the studied industries. This type of interaction does, however, occur in other industries. The theories that describe co-operative and collaborative relations between competitors are based on the actors' mutual desire to participate in interaction. Through co-operation, two competitors can compete in a better way against a third (cf. Leontiades, 1989). This is partly why networks develop between competitors where the actors' interests in participating in interaction are mutual. However, the competitors' fundamental opposing positions affect relations among them, even in these types of relations.

The interaction and the relations that have been studied here can not be considered to be a result of the actors' mutual interests and advantages of participating in interaction, nor as solely being indirect via interaction with other actors in a network. Competitors interact directly with each other, and direct relations therefore develop among them. In the climates of revolutionary and evolutionary competition, the competing companies meet each other at mutual customers, and interact directly with each other in order to meet the customers' needs better. New products are developed in order to gain an advantage over the competitors rather than in order to meet the needs of the customers, which signifies that the relations cannot be solely described as being indirect.

In relations among competitors another form of indirect interaction can be identified, however. In both of the passive climates of competition, the climates of co-existing and, perhaps primarily, evolutionary competition, interaction can be described as being indirect. The competing companies' relative positions and the threat of potentially active competition between them is expressed through market signals. In the climate of co-existing competition, functional proximity is limited, which is why such market signals are unusual and why indirect interaction occurs primarily due to the actors' awareness of the possibility that their positions can be relative to each other.

THE DYNAMICS OF COMPETITION

By using the natures of the climates of competition, their durability, and the direction of change in the climates of competition as points of departure, an increased understanding for the dynamics of competition has been gained. Different types of learning processes and a pressure to compete developed in three of the climates of competition, which led to the development of dynamism in these three climates. The nature of the fourth climate, however, is described as being paralytical. Apart from the dynamics that are inherent in the climates, a dynamism also developed in the industries as a result of the transition from one climate to another. The understanding that has been gained of the dynamics of competition is summarised in the following.

The Dynamics of the Four Climates of Competition

Traditionally, dynamics in an oligopoly are assumed to be less than with perfect competition, which in itself is described as being idealistic because market forces can function without imperfections hindering that which is considered by society as optimal action. This study shows, however, that oligopolistic industries can also be dynamic, and that factors other than the number of competitors, customers, and products, are important for dynamics to develop. The dynamics of the climates of competition can be described as two slightly different, but simultaneous, forces or movements. Competition partly gives rise to learning processes of different kinds, and partly presses companies to take innovative and creative measures. The figure below illustrates tentative connections between the natures of the climates, their dynamics, and the stimulus or paralysis that arises within the different climates.

In the climate of rivalling competition, named the positive pole of competition, action is stimulated in existing areas of operation. The nature of the climate of competition gives rise to stability and harmony that makes cumulative learning processes possible. Earlier

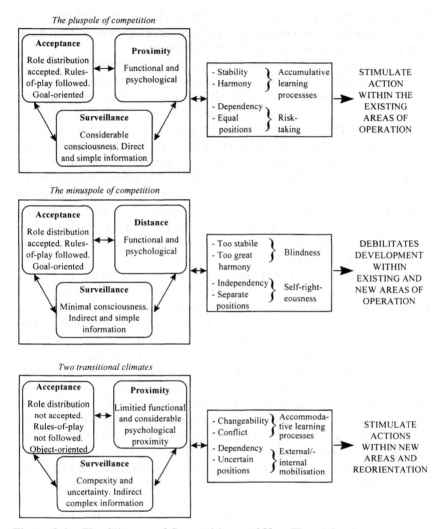

Figure 9.1 The Climates of Competition, and How They Stimulate and Paralyse Development and Change

experiences and the progress of competitors are taken advantage of in the continual development. However, stability and harmony are not sufficient for the occurrence of further development. The dependency that exists between actors, and the threat that the balancing act the companies find themselves in can be broken, presses the companies to daring and risk-taking. The learning processes that occur within the climates and the daring or risk-taking of the actors stimulates the companies' further development within existing areas of operation, as shown in the figure.

The positive pole of competition can be compared to homogenous oligopolies, though in descriptions of homogenous oligopolies, the dynamic processes illustrated by this study are not given due attention. Action is instead described as being defensive adaptation between competing companies in order not to break the existing equilibrium (cf. Scherer, 1980). Action is described as a "zero-sum game" where no one can engage in action without both parties losing. The findings of this study prove, however, that even homogenous oligopolies include inherent dynamics that are expressed in cumulative learning processes and the pressure to compete that the companies force on each other. Both of these forces, learning and the pressure to compete, stimulated the continued development of the studied industries.

In the climate of co-existing competition (the negative pole of competition), the dynamics of competition are low, and competition paralyses companies rather that stimulating them. As in the positive pole of competition, the nature of the climate of co-existing competition gives rise to stability and harmony. However, no cumulative learning processes develop, as the stability and harmony is too considerable. There is no direct dependency between the companies, because their relative positions are distant. Threats and pressure from competitors, expressed in the positive pole of competition as dependency and balancing acts between the competitors, are not found in the negative pole of competition. This makes the climate far too stable and harmonious, which in turn gives rise to a form of competitive blindness and complacency which paralyses the companies' abilities to be innovative, as well as the development of the industries.

The transitionary climates of competition, i.e. the climates of evolutionary and revolutionary competition, are more temporaneous in their nature, and are characterised by change and conflict. Changeability can be linked to the increased awareness of the threat from competitors and a will to change the current situation, and conflict can be linked to the lack of acceptance of current conditions. However, conflict can differ between the climates. Conflict in the climate of revolutionary competition is external, and is expressed in destructive action, whereas conflict in the climate of competition is internal, linked to the process whereby awareness of changing conditions for competition progressively develop and spread within the organisation. The actors' conflicting goals are not expressed in active action relative to their competitors, but can instead be described as silent protests through internal re-orientation and mobilisation.

Actors in both of the transitional climates are also involved in inter-dependent relations. In the climate of revolutionary competition, the companies' goals are in conflict with their competitors, and are described as relative to each other; the companies' individual actions therefore directly affect each other. Moreover, uncertainty about the companies' relative positions is considerable due to the complexity of the climate of revolutionary competition and to the indirect competition in the climate of evolutionary competition. Changeability and conflict give rise to accommodative learning processes within the companies, and uncertainty and dependency pressurises the companies to increased watchfulness. These accommodative learning processes are expressed in the mobilisation within the companies, which occurs internally in the climate of evolutionary competition and externally in the climate of revolutionary competition. The companies thereby re-orient their operations, and creativity/innovativeness is stimulated both within the companies and within the industry.

Transitions Over Time between the Climates of Competition

The dynamics of competition are also expressed in the form of the mobility and change that give rise to changes of climate over time. The understanding that has been gained of the nature and dynamics of competition makes it possible to conduct a hypothetical discussion of how competition between proximate actors can contribute to development within an industry.

The climates of competition can fulfil different functions over time, and can therefore together stimulate development within an industry. During stable phases, companies can develop their own strengths and operations within existing areas of operation, whereas periods of turbulence and variation stimulate the companies to creative thinking and to changing the direction and contents of their operations. The development that occurs during such unstable periods can be consolidated during periods of stability.

The climate of the negative pole of competition is not in itself particularly dynamic, but it does make it possible for companies to exploit the stimulation that exists elsewhere in the industrial environment relatively undisturbed. After a period of intensive and, in the short run, destructive competition in the climate of revolutionary competition, change in competition is necessary in order to avoid the short-term destructiveness of competition and to stabilise the conditions for competition. Thereby, the development that is initiated in the climate of revolutionary competition can be continued. However, for this development not to be paralysed, stability must be discontinued and a more turbulent and dynamic climate must develop. If the industry is conservative and a stable and asymmetrical climate of competition becomes dominant for a longer period of time, development can be paralysed.

In the same way as in the climate of co-existing competition, stability in the climate of rivalling competition provides companies with the opportunity to further develop their existing operations under relatively ordered conditions. The difference between these two climates is that interaction between competitors in the climate of rivalling competition stimulates action by the companies. It is, however, questionable whether it is desirable for this climate to exist for a longer period of time, as such a situation would result in further development for which there is no demand; for example, advanced technology can be built into a product which does not even meet potential customer needs. Areas of operations can be developed in some respects *in absurdum*. A change of climate would be desirable in such a situation, from the climate of rivalling competition to a climate of revolutionary competition. In that way, further development could be stimulated in new areas, thus guaranteeing continued development in the industry.

These two climates of competition, and the dynamics that can be observed within them, can also be assumed to fulfil different functions for the development of companies and industries. The climate of revolutionary competition can, to a great extent, be assumed to contribute to the emergence of new sub-industries as a result of the companies' efforts to avoid competition. The climate of evolutionary competition can fulfil an important function by providing a period of respite, in which companies can rebuild their own relative strengths and reconstruct their internal pre-conditions to prepare for active competition in the future.

These two climates can be assumed to be destructive if they become permanent. If the short-term destructive competition that exists in the climate of revolutionary competition is maintained over longer periods of time, competitors can destroy future market opportunities through price wars, and can literally 'fight to the death'. The climate of evolutionary competition can become permanent if the competing companies decide to co-operate instead of competing.

This means that the forming of cartels of different kinds can lead to permanent symmetry and passivity. The dynamics that arise as a result of active competition between competing companies will cease to exist, as will the stimulation that can be assumed to arise from the fluctuation over time between the positive and negative poles of competition via the two transitionary climates.

Three Dimensional Distance Between Competitors

In the discussion of the nature and dynamics of competition in Chapter One, it was stated that the economic theory view of competition only takes into account structural differences that can exist in an industry, excluding geographical space. Studies where the point of departure lies in the geographical space disregard to a great extent other differences between different contexts of competition. This book considers both structural variation and the importance of geographical space. The findings of this book concur in certain aspects both with the descriptions of competition given within economic theory and with Porter's (1990) discussion of geographical proximity between competitors and its importance for further development. This confirms the necessity of including both geographical and structural space as points of departure in the search for increased understanding of the nature and dynamics of competition.

Similarities exist between the structural descriptions of competition that were discussed in Chapter Two and the actions that have been studied in the three industries. The connections that have been studied within the areas of theory covered by Chapter Two can be identified in the three industries. In discussions of competition within an industry or within strategic groups, it is clear that distance between competitors is important. However, it is primarily the proximity that arises from symmetry in important strategic dimensions that is discussed. The importance of psychological and geographical proximity is not dealt with in the same manner.

The importance of geographical proximity was emphasised in the schools of theory that were presented in Chapter One, where national competition was considered to be important, acting as a catalyst or motor in the industrial system. This book shows that interaction between geographically proximous companies is important for the development of an industry. A number of examples has shown that considerable geographical distance between competitors limits awareness of, and surveillability over, competitors. Neither functional proximity nor geographical proximity between competitors can solely explain the dynamics of competition. In the climate of co-existing competition, geographical proximity exists between competitors, but, despite this, the climate of competition is paralytical, because of the functional and psychological distance that exists between the competitors.

Distance between competitors is thus three dimensional. Firstly, geographical proximity/distance can be found, in that the companies can find themselves physically close to each other. Secondly, functional proximity/distance can be found, in that companies operate and undertake similar measures within the same product or market areas. Thirdly, psychological proximity/distance can develop between competitors, where strong attitudes and values of competitors can be expressed in interaction between them. All three dimensions must be integrated in analysis in order to gain an increased understanding of the nature of dynamics of competition. It is through interaction that proximity between competitors can become a catalyst that stimulates further development.

Having summarised the findings of this book, the following sections will present a discussion of the practical implications of this study and the need for continued research within this area of research.

PRACTICAL IMPLICATIONS OF THE STUDY

The understanding of competition that has arisen from this book is of importance both for companies and their actions, and for political decisions at a societal level. This book supports the theories that emphasise the importance of national or domestic competition for development within industry. The dynamics of competition vary between different climates of competition. The findings of the book can therefore be useful as tools of analysis or combined as a theoretical model to asses the dynamics within an industry, making it possible to undertake or restrict competitive moves so that the dynamics of competition can be maintained. If competition is not dynamic, measures can be instigated to either increase competition or to compensate for the lack of competition.

Competition is perceived by companies as being negative and destructive, and co-existence can therefore be perceived as being an ideal state. Companies would then able to develop good relations with customers and other actors undisturbed. The returns on investment in product and market areas would not be reduced as a result of new products being imitated by competitors. Hard and intensive competition would be considered as restricting attempts to achieve profit targets and returns on investment targets. Such arguments are used to justify efforts to reduce competition.

However, companies are stimulated or pressurised through active competition to be constantly alert and to find new solutions. Through interaction with competitors, different kinds of learning processes can arise in companies. Competition stimulates creativity within companies, which is of importance to the long term development of the companies involved and of their industries. The tendency to avoid competition means that public authorities must contribute to the maintenance of competition, which is possible by laws and regulations, and by controlling that these laws and regulations are followed. An understanding of the dynamics of competition is therefore vital in the assessment of infringements on the ban on co-operation that limits competition contained within antitrust-laws, and in the assessment of fusion's between companies operating within the same industry.

Areas of interest, as far as the results of this book are concerned, concern company decisions about integration (e.g. fusions, acquisitions, contracts), contracts of co-operation, and internal conditions for competition in larger corporations. Decisions regarding interaction ought to ensure that a dynamic climate of competition is attained and maintained, which can partly involve that the number of competitors remains as it is, and partly means that competition is not eliminated by the exclusive contracts and other similar arrangements that increase asymmetry between competitors. It ought to be more advantageous for companies interested in developing new areas to integrate with foreign partners rather than to build an expansion on the strategy of first attempting to dominate the domestic market. If a company intends to expand through the acquisition of competitors, it would therefore be better to seek investment abroad, thereby maintaining national competition.

It is particularly important, from a national perspective, to retain a dynamic domestic climate of competition within such industries where strategic functions are concentrated to, in this case, Sweden. If, from an international perspective, the most important and successful product development occurs in Sweden, it is therefore vital that several centres of development are retained within the nation. If such centres do not exist, company management should consider moving product development to countries where competition exists. However, this would bring about negative effects from a national perspective. If Swedish companies integrate with foreign companies, the dynamism within national competition decreases. The use of exclusive contracts and other similar measures, can, on the one hand, increase the pressure on companies to seek new solutions, but can also, on the other hand, lead to the development of a climate of co-existing competition. By analysing operations based on the findings of this book, it is, however, possible to assess which measures would be suitable.

If the current climate is one of co-existence, there is a lack of pressure and opportunities for learning that arise from competition. It would therefore be of interest to compensate for the lack of dynamics. All three industries that have been studied here have developed and retained internationally prominent positions, though one of the industries has mainly been dominated by just one company. The success of this one dominating company can be considered to be a result of the dynamism that is present in relations with other actors, internal dynamism and as a result of external events.[1]

Learning can arise through interaction with related industries. However, companies are not forced to interact with actors from related industries in the same way as with competitors. It would therefore be necessary to act purposefully to bring about a similar form of interaction. Systems can be developed to pick up new ideas and customer needs more effectively. Companies should also strive to establish relations with demanding customers that can offer the pressure and opportunities for learning that are missing in weak national competition. If competitive operations exist within the corporation, an internal climate of competition can develop, which would stimulate creative and innovative action.

To strive seriously to create internal competition is a huge challenge for a corporation's strategic leadership. Short-term goals and required levels of return on investments by stock-holders should perhaps be a subordinate priority if the long term dynamism that internal competition can provide is to be guaranteed. The problem is most likely not as acute during phases where competing departments expand and develop parallel to each other. It is when departments are forced to expand at the cost of other departments that the risk of corporate management regulating competition is considerable, thereby eliminating the possibility of retaining an internal

---

[1] Cf. Porter, 1990, who points out that the industrial environment as a whole stimulates development within an industry.

climate of competition. Further research is needed to improve the understanding of how internal competition works and how partly contradictory demands affects management's action in this area.

THE NEED FOR FURTHER RESEARCH

The ambition of this study has been to develop concepts and generate theory. The findings constitute a substantive theory of the nature and dynamics of competition in three industries, and have stimulated a more general discussion of the nature and dynamics of competition. This book should thus be considered a first step in the further generation and development of theory. However, new methods of study need to be developed for further research into climates of competition. Studies of other industries are also necessary to both widen the understanding for the nature and dynamics of different climates of competition, and to increase the general applicability of the theory developed here.

The Development of Methodology

The methodological point of departure for this book has been inductive; a theoretical perspective has been used to focus the empirical studies rather than to formulate testable hypotheses of the research problem. The empirical material consists of qualitative data gathered from interviews with representatives for the different companies in the studied industries, and the analysis has concentrated on the generation of theory. There are arguments that support and criticise the chosen approach for this book. Two specific issues that are of interest methodologically for further research will be considered in this section. The first regards methods that will enable the aggregation of individual accounts to consistent historical descriptions of different courses of events. The second issue deals with methods for identifying coherent phases in the history of industries and for assessing an industry's characteristics (in terms of symmetry/ asymmetry and activity/passivity) from such descriptions.

The issue regarding the development of methods to make possible historical case descriptions from the different interviewees' accounts involves several problems. The ever-present problem for historical analysis is the reliability of sources. Another problem involves the effects on data arising from the fact that 'sources' are active persons who look back on a development that they themselves have been sometimes intensively, sometimes only partly, involved in. The critique of sources is a very interesting issue that has been well documented and discussed in methodological literature. The latter issue regarding the use of 'perceptual data' that is produced in connection with interviews in creating historical description or longitudinal studies stretching back into the past, however, has been discussed in less detail, and deserves, therefore, further attention.

Possible solutions may lie in different combinations of different descriptions to access convergent or deconvergent points of view, and in different ways of more systematically combining interview material with other data produced at other times and for other purposes (such as newspapers and journals, annual financial reports, books, and company archives). However, such a study does not necessarily have to result in the production of a 'unanimous' description; there is considerable merit in pointing out differences in accounts, as shown by this book. The methodological challenge lies in the ability to systematically gather and analyse such material.

The other issue introduced above involves ways of stating and characterising the development of industries based on different types of concepts. Though linked to the first issue, this issue reflects a more pronounced analytical problem; which requirements can and should be placed on data, in order for it to be used for the periodisation of longer courses of events and the categorisation of entire industries. The problem differs from those research situations that are often assumed to involve so-called naturalistic approaches, where analysis usually deals with an empirical reality that exists, to all extent and purposes, in the present. When the time perspective stretches into the past and involves a number of individuals and companies, the problem becomes different. There is then a need for more stringent systematic expositions of methodological possibilities and difficulties. This is important not least for making available historical data for qualitative analysis.

A Wider Empirical Understanding for the Dynamics of Competition

The industries that have been studied show certain common characteristics. In order to increase the general applicability of the theory generated by this book, it would be natural to focus further studies on industries or situations that exhibit characteristics other than those observed here. This section therefore discusses a number of possible situations.

Branches with a high degree of international integration may differ from the industries that have been studied here. A high degree of international integration means that a company's strategic functions, for example product development and company management, may be located and organised in other countries. Internationally integrated production systems with component manufacturers in different companies may also mean that the company can be assumed to be characterised by international integration. In such industries, it can be assumed that competition may occur in a different way than in the industries studied here. It is of interest to study the different ways that strategic functions based in other national environments contribute to the development of dynamics in competition.

The possibility to compensate for the lack of external competition by creating internal competition is another area that has not been researched. Companies with considerable volume, several competing product brands, operations in different countries, or with several different component manufacturers within a corporation, ought to, one way or another, develop structures facilitating internal competition. This can occur by a company that manufactures a certain component also purchasing that component from external suppliers, thus exposing itself to competition. In such unambiguous competitive situations, and given that company management has been more or less successful in establishing competition, different 'internal' climates of competition ought to develop, creating a pressure to compete on the different 'manufacturers'. Such situations would be of interest to study, not least in order to learn more about how the functions of the 'free market' can be recreated within the corporation.

The existence of cartels and strategic alliances gives topical interest to another area of research. Cartels and strategic alliances between companies involve the neutralisation of competition through agreements or contracts. This can be illegal in certain cases, but in many other cases it is a very appropriate form of achieving efficiency/effectiveness in product development or marketing. Cartels or alliances do not normally occur between all the actors within an industry, but they are significant for the entire industry. The nature and dynamics of competition and the ability to stimulate development within industries that are characterised by the occurrence of one or more 'competitively neutral' blocks should be studied further. It would be important to follow the other competitors' actions relative to cartels and alliances, and to analyse the development of relations between the members of the cartel or alliance.

Stagnating industries are characterised by an increasing struggle for market shares, whereas growth in volume is not possible. Furthermore, the potential for development is low when stagnation in itself can imply that alternative, more modern technologies can come to be used, replacing those products manufactured by the industry. It is also probable that companies will progressively leave stagnating industries. It is therefore of interest to study if the different climates of competition that have been studied here function in different ways in such stagnating industries.

The list of industries and conditions that differ from those studied here can be made long, and several examples have been given above. To increase the generalisation of the tentative theory presented in this book, it is of interest to carry out studies of the nature and dynamics of competition in other industries.

A Deeper Understanding of the Dynamics of Competition

As the above proposals for further research are intended to widen the field of applicability for the tentative theory presented in this book, this next discussion aims to deepen the applicability for analysis of the theory by clarifying the different processes and elements that the analysis is built upon or has led to. This primarily concerns two areas, of which the first refers to the different variables that have been used to determine and characterise the different climates of competition, and the second concerns the internal company processes.

A more in-depth analysis of the constituents or elements and processes of the generated theory is needed. Interaction, relations, learning and the pressure to compete are important elements of the theory that has been generated in this book. It has been stated that these elements are of great importance for the development of dynamism in competition, but a more in-depth analysis of the process of competition can contribute to further knowledge of the nature and dynamics of competition. This can be achieved through a detailed study of individual competitive plays, which would lead to a comprehensive survey of interaction between individuals and groups within the competitive companies. The contribution of, or the restrictions that, psychological proximity has on the development of trust between competitors, should be studied, as should the transition from one climate to another — how they are counteracted or actively encouraged — and the interpretations that actors have of the competitive play in which they are involved. Through stimulating deeper knowledge of the importance of learning and the pressure to compete for the actions of competing companies, a deeper knowledge of the dynamics of competition can be gained.

To study the dynamics of competition at an organisational or individual level it is necessary to illustrate other aspects of the competitive process. Research into how emotional conceptions such as prestige and pride grow in an organisation, and whether individuals within certain units of the organisation are more aware about competitors than others, would be of particular interest. This book has focused on the strategic interaction between competitors. The perceptions that ultimately lie behind organisational action can be considered, however, to be a result of internal processes. Perception can differ between functions and between individuals at different levels in an organisation. The experiences that arise from competition may differ, and the perceptions that spread internally in the organisation can exhibit differing characteristics. It would therefore be interesting to analyse the internal processes that are linked to the relationships among competitors, in order to gain a deeper understanding for the process of competition and the climates of competition that emerge within an industry.

Appendix

APPENDIX 1

Phase 1

R1 and R2: Ålö is larger than the other companies, has more resources, and is a technical and market leader. The companies are therefore assessed to be asymmetrical.

P1: Disintegration, i.e. that different companies manufacture different parts of the product, means that the product offer is asymmetrical.

P2: A few versions of the loader that are similar to each other are provided by every manufacturer. The product range is therefore assumed to be symmetrical.

M1 and M2: Sales occur via SLR or via through the private wholesale market. Distribution channels therefore differ, and the market is divided regionally. The companies are therefore assessed to be asymmetrical in their choice of market.

Phase 2

R1: Ålö is larger than the other companies and has more resources. The companies are therefore assessed to be asymmetrical.

R2: Ålö's technical and market leadership decreases due to the concentration of the industry. The companies therefore are considered to be neither symmetrical not asymmetrical.

P1 and P2: The disintegration decreases as the industry concentrates. The companies' product offers are therefore assessed to be neither symmetrical not asymmetrical. Ålö offered several versions of the product in foreign markets, Trima

Appendix 1   Symmetry Between Actors and Activity in Competitive Play in the Four Phases of the Front-loader Industry

Phases	Symmetrical Actors	Neither Symmetry nor Asymmetry	Asymmetrical Actors	Active Plays	Neither Active nor Passive	Passive Plays
Phase 1 1947–65	P2		R1, R2 P1 M1, M2	Intensive	Imitation	Few areas
Summary	Very asymmetrical			Neither active nor passive		
Phase 2 1966–77		R2 P1, P2	R1 M1, M2			Independent Not intensive Few areas
Summary	Asymmetrical			Very passive		
Phase 3 1978–82	R1 P1	R2 P2 M2	M1			Independent Not intensive Few areas
Summary	Symmetrical			Very passive		
Phase 4 1983–91	R1, R2 P1, P2 M1	M2		Move/ countermove Intensive Considerable scope		
Summary	Very symmetrical			Very active		

expands in a new product segment (industrial loaders) but the products on offer in the domestic market very similar. The product range was therefore neither symmetrical nor asymmetrical.

M1 and M2: Ålö sells its products via SLR in the domestic market and via agents in the international market whereas Trima has its own service organisation in Sweden and sells through the private wholesale market in the domestic market. The companies' choice of market segment therefore differ, as Ålö sells internationally, Trima sells nationally/regionally, and Vreten sells only regionally. The companies are therefore assessed to be asymmetrical, both in their penetration of markets and in their choice of market segment.

Phase 3

R1: As a result of Trima's expansion, two of the companies (Ålö and Trima) become comparable in size and resources. The actors become symmetrical.

R2: Ålö loses its technical and market leadership, but Trima's leadership is only marginal and talked about. The leading positions of the companies are assessed therefore as being neither symmetrical nor asymmetrical.

P1: The companies that remain after the concentration of the industry all manufacture the complete product, which means that their product offers do not differ to any significant degree. The companies are therefore symmetrical.

P2: Ålö offers a wider product range abroad while in the domestic market the company offers a similar product range to the product ranges of the other domestic competitors. The companies are therefore neither symmetrical nor asymmetrical.

M1: Ålö sells via SLR in the domestic market and agents in the international market, whereas Trima has its own service organisation and sells through the domestic wholesale market. through the private wholesale market. Distribution channels therefore differ, and the market is divided regionally. The companies are therefore assessed to be asymmetrical.

M2: The regional division of the Swedish market ceases, Trima to a certain extent sold its products abroad but despite this, the companies differ in international commitment and spread. They companies are neither symmetrical nor asymmetrical.

Phase 4

R1 and R2: Ålö and Trima are similar in resources and size, and both companies describe themselves as technical and market leaders. On the whole, the companies are symmetrical.

P1 and P2: The companies sell the same types of products, and both Trima and Ålö offer a wide range adapted to both the domestic and international markets. The companies are therefore assessed to be symmetrical in their choice of product.

M1: All of the companies are operational both in domestic and in international markets, and both Ålö and Trima sell via SLR and the private wholesaler market, as well as having subsidiaries abroad. The companies are symmetrical.

M2: Ålö penetrates substantially more international market segments and have even established itself in the American market. Trima and Vreten penetrate to a greater extent than Ålö the industrial market. Despite this, many of the companies' markets segments are the same, which means that the companies are neither symmetrical nor asymmetrical.

APPENDIX 2

Phase 1

R1: The organisations very similar in size. Trellex gained no financial or personnel resources from its parent company Trelleborg to any great extent, which meant that the companies are assessed to have been symmetrical in their resources.

R2: Skega is considered to have gained a marginal leadership in technique and market, in that most of the interviewees in both companies considered Skega to be technical and market leader at the same time as an intensive discussion arose about which company should really be seen as leader. As Skega's leadership can be considered marginal, the companies are assessed to be neither symmetrical nor asymmetrical as far as technical and market leadership is concerned.

P1 and P2: The operations of both companies are dominated by mill lining products. Both companies manufacture linings for a number of mills, but the differences between the products are minimal, and much of the time are aired as sales arguments rather than actual differences. The companies are therefore assessed to be symmetrical in their choice of product and product range.

M1 and M2: The biggest market for both companies is the Swedish mining industry, and the customers are approached in the same way. There is therefore considerable symmetry in the companies choice of market.

Phase 2

R1: The organisations are similar in size and have approximately the same amount of financial and/or personnel resources.

Appendix 2 Symmetry Between Actors and Activity in Competitive Play in the Three Phases of the Lining Industry

Phases	Symmetrical Actors	Neither Symmetry nor Asymmetry	Asymmetrical Actors	Active Plays	Neither Active nor Passive	Passive Plays
Phase 1 1960–70	R1 P1, P2 M1, M2	R2		Move/ countermove Intensive Considerable scope		
Summary	Very symmetrical			Very active		
Phase 2 1971–82	R1 P2 M1, M2	R2 P1		Move/ countermove	Medium intensive Several areas	
Summary	Symmetrical			Active		
Phase 3 1983–90		R2	R1 P1, P2 M1, M2	Reactive/ conflictive Intensive Considerable scope		
Summary	Very asymmetrical			Very active		

R2: Skega is considered to have a marginal technical and market leadership in technology. Skega is relatively stronger in the mill lining market, whereas Trellex dominates the screen market. On the whole, however, the companies are assessed to be neither symmetrical nor asymmetrical.

P1 and P2: Both companies are similar in the mill lining product area but differ in the fact that they manufacture different types of screens. The companies are therefore neither symmetrical nor asymmetrical in their product offer. The companies product range symmetrical in that they manufacture lining for the same types of mills and screens.

M1 and M2: The companies are symmetrical in their choice of market segment and their penetration of the Scandinavian market (their biggest market). In their international operations the companies differ, both in choice of market and form of establishment. The companies on the whole are therefore assessed to be neither symmetrical nor asymmetrical in their choice of market.

Phase 3

R1: Trelleborg participates more actively in Trellex's operations and acquires some important actors in the field, such as Boliden and some of the Allis Chalmer companies. Consequently, the companies become asymmetrical.

R2: The issue of leadership (both technical and market) does not change during this phase, and thus the companies remain neither symmetrical nor asymmetrical.

P1 and P2: The asymmetry in the companies choice of product increases in that Trellex expands its range of screens. This increase in Trellex's screen product range leads to an overall expansion for entire screen product area, and screens thus become more important for the industry as a whole.

M1 and M2: The asymmetry in the companies choice of market increases, both as a result of the companies' international expansion and as a result of their penetration of different markets and their different choices of form of establishment.

APPENDIX 3

Phase 1

R1: Alimak is larger than its competitors in the Rack and Pinion product area as a result of the expansion that followed the launch of the company's raise climber. Alimak did, however, have similar financial or personnel resources, which means that the companies are assessed as being neither symmetrical not asymmetrical.

Appendix 3 Symmetry Between Actors and Activity in Competitive Play in the Three Phases of the Rack and Pinion Industry

Phases	Symmetrical Actors	Neither Symmetry nor Asymmetry	Asymmetrical Actors	Active Plays	Neither Active nor Passive	Passive Plays
Phase 1 1955–59	P1, P2 M1, M2	R1	R2			Independent Not intensive Few areas
Summary	Very symmetrical			Very passive		
Phase 2 1960–62	R2 P1 M1	R1 P2 M2		Move/ countermove Intensive		Few areas Few areas
Summary	Symmetrical			Active		
Phase 3 1963–90			R1, R2 P1, P2 M1, M2			Independent Not intensive Few areas
Summary		Very asymmetrical		Very passive		

R2: In that Alimak has both technical and market leading positions, the companies are asymmetrical.

P1 and P2: The companies' operations are dominated by cable-driven hoists and their product offers and ranges are very similar. The companies are therefore symmetrical in both the choice of produxt and in product range.

M1 and M2: The companies' biggest market is the Swedish construction industry, and the customers are all approached in the same way. Symmetry in the companies' choice of market is therefore considerable.

Phase 2

R1: Alimak is still bigger than its competitors in the rack and pinion product areas as a result of its international expansion and the launching of raise climbers. However, the companies have similar financial or personnel resources, resulting in an assessment of neither symmetrical nor asymmetrical actors.

R2: Alimak loses its technical and market leadership, but no other companies assumes leading positions. The companies are therefore symmetrical.

P1: In the companies' biggest product area, cable driven hoists, the companies offer similar products, and are therefore symmetrical.

P2: The companies differ in their product range due to Alimak expanding its range to include raise hoists and rack and pinion driven hoists. This area of the industry's entire operations is still minor, however, which results in neither symmetry or asymmetry in the companies product ranges.

M1: The companies are symmetrical in their style of market penetration, using similar channels of distribution. The companies are therefore assessed to be symmetrical.

M2: On the other hand, the companies chose to penetrate different market segments, in that Alimak sells its products internationally and to the domestic mining industry. These market segments are, however, a small part of the total market. The companies are therefore neither symmetrical not asymmetrical in their choice of market segment.

Phase 3

R1 and R2: Alimak dominates in both relative size and resources, gaining both technical and market leadership. In this respect, the industry is therefore characterised by asymmetry.

P1 and P2: The asymmetry in the companies' choice of product is considerable, in that of the companies, only Alimak expanded its operations to includes four different product areas, offering a significantly wider product range in each of these areas compared to its competitors.

M1 and M2: The competing companies chose different markets to operate within. Alimak distinguishes itself from its competitors by penetrating different customer groups and different regional markets, as well as by establishing subsidiaries in a large number of foreign countries. The other competitors chose to penetrate well-defined nisches. There is therefore considerable symmetry in choice of market.

References

Aghion, B. and Bolton, P. (1987), Contracts and Barriers to Entry *The American Economic Review*, vol. 77 no. 3, pp. 388–401.

Aharoni, Y. (1993), In search for the unique: Can Firm-Specific Advantages be Evaluated? *Journal of Management Studies*, vol. 30, no. 1, Jan pp. 31–49.

Amin, A. and Robins, K. (1990), The Re-Emergence of Regional Economies? The Mythical Geography of Flexible Accumulation. *Environment and Planning D: Society and Space*, vol. 8, pp. 7–34.

Ansoff, H.I. (1965), *Corporate Strategy — An Analytic Approach to Business Policy for Growth and Expansion*. New York: McGraw Hill.

Argyris, C. (1976), Leadership, Learning, and Changing the Status Quo. *Organizational Dynamics*, 4 (Winter), pp. 29–43.

Argyris, C. and Schön, D.A. (1978), *Organizational Learning: A Theory of Action Perspective*, Reading: Addison-Wesley.

Arrow, K.J. (1962), Economic Welfare and the Allocation of Resources for Invention. In Nelson, R.R., (ed.) *The Rate and Direction of Inventive Activity*. Princeton: Princeton University Press.

Asheim, B.T. (1991), Flexible Specialisation, Industrial Districts and Small Firms: A Critical Appraisal, in Ernste, H. (ed.) *Regional Development and Contemporary Industrial Response: Extending Flexible Specialisation*. London: Belhaven Press.

Bain, J.S. (1959), *Industrial Organization*. New York: John Wiley and Sons.

Barnard, C. (1968), *The Function of the Executive*. Cambridge: Cambridge Mass.

Barney, B.B. and Hoskisson, R.E. (1990), Strategic Groups: Untested Assertions and Research Proposals. *Managerial and Decisions Economies*, vol. 11, pp. 187–198.

Bartlett, C.A. (1986), Building and Managing the Multinational. In M.E. Porter (ed.), *Competition in Global Industries*. Boston: Harvard Business School Press.

Bengtsson, M. (1987), Smartac AB. Umeå University.

Bengtsson M. and Bonnedahl K.J. (1993), European Integration and Strategy-implications for the Manufacturing SME — Towards Local and Global Niche-Seeking. Paper presented at *23rd European Small Business Seminar*, Belfast Northern Ireland, September 1993.

Bengtsson, L. and Skärvad, S-H. (1988), *Företagsstrategiska perspektiv*. Lund: Studentlitteratur.

255

Björkegren, D. (1989), *Hur organisationer lär*. Lund: Studentlitteratur.

Bonnedahl, K.J. (1991), *Småföretagen inför EG 1992*. Fe-publikationer: 1991: Nr 125 Umeå Business School.

Bogner, W.C. and Thomas, H. (1993), The Role of Competitive Groups in Industry Formulation: A Dynamic Integration of Two Competing Models. *Journal of Management Studies*, 30:1, January pp. 51–67.

Brunsson, N. (1985), *The Irrational Organization Irrationality as a Basis for Organizational Action and Change*. New York: John Wiley and Sons.

Burgess, R.G. (1984), *In The Field. An Introduction to Field Research*. London: Unwin Hyman.

Burns, T. and Stalker, G. (1961), *The Management of Innovation*. London: Tavistock.

Cartwright, R.W. (1992), Multiple Linked Diamonds and the International Competitiveness of Export-Dependent Industries: The New Zealand Experience. Paper presented *at Academy of International Business Conference*, Brussels, Belgium, November 22.

Carlman, L. (1986), *Kontraktsrelationer/relationskontrakt — om förtro-ende, förväntningar och ekonomisk aktivitet*. Department of Business Administration, Lunds Universitet.

Caves, R.E. (1980), Industrial Organization, Corporate Strategy and Structure. *Journal of Economic Literature*, 18, March pp. 64–92.

Caves, R. and Porter, M.E. (1977), From Entry Barriers to Mobility Barriers: Conjectured Decisions and Contrived Deterrence to New Competition *Quarterly Journal of Economics*, vol. 91, pp. 241–267.

Chakravarthy, B.S. and Doz, Y. (1992), Strategy Process Research: Focusing on Corporate Self-Renewal. *Strategic Management Journal*, vol. 13, pp. 5–14.

Chamberlin, E. (1933), *The Theory of Monopolistic Competition*. Cambridge: Harvard University press.

Chandler, A.E. (1991), The Enduring Logic of Industrial Success. To Compete Globally You Have to Be Big. History Explains Why in Montgomery, C.A., and Porter, M.E., *Strategy — Seeking and Securing Competitive Advantage*. Boston: Harvard business review book series.

Cool, K. and Dierickx, I. (1993), Rivalry, Strategic Groups and Firm Profitability. *Strategic Management Journal*, vol. 14, pp. 47–59.

Couse, R.H. (1937), The Nature of the Firm. *Economica*, 4, pp. 386–405.

Cyert, R. and March, J. (1963), *A Behavioral Theory of the Firm*. Englewood Cliffs: Prentice-Hall.

—— (1988), *Dynamics of Entrepreneurship, Technology and Institutions: A Theoretical and Historical Approach, in Evolution of Technology and Market Structure in an International Context*. Proceedings from the second world congress of the International Joseph A. Schumpeter Society, May 24–27 Siena, Italy.

Delmar, F. (1990), *Trellex och Skega lining — en studie i den subjektiva upplevelsen av rivalitet*. C-Uppsats Umeå University.

DiMaggio, P.P. and Powell, W.W. (1983), *American Sociological Review*, 48, pp. 147–60.

Dosi, G. (1988), Sources, Procedures, and Microeconomic Effects of Innovation. *Journal of Economic Literature*, vol. XXVI, September pp. 1120–1171.

Downey, H.K. and Brief, A.P. (1986), How Cognitive Structures Affect Organizational Design: Implicit Theories of Organizing in Sims Jr, H.P. and Gioia, D.A. and associates. *The Thinking Organization Dynamics of Organizational Social Cognition*. San Francisco: Jossey-Bass.

Dunning, J.H. (1993), Internationalizing Porter's Diamond, *Management International Review* 1993/2.

Durö, R. and Sandström, B. (1986), *Marknadskrigföring, hur man besegrar konkurrenterna i slaget om marknaden.* Malmö: Liber.

Easton, G. (1987), *Relationships Among Competitors.* University of Lancaster, February 1987.

Easton, G. and Araujo, L. (1992), Non-Economic Exchange in Industrial Network in Axelsson, B. and Easton, G. *Industrial Networks A New View of Reality.* London: Routledge.

Enright, M.J. (1992), The geographic Scope of Competitive Advantage. Paper presented at the *VUGS Conference Ultrech Netherlands,* October 1992.

Fiegenbaum, E.A. (1970), Information Processing and Memory i Donald A. Norman (ed.) *Models of Human Memory,* pp. 451–468. New York: Academic Press.

Fiegenbaum, A. and Thomas, H. (1993), Industry and Strategic Group Dynamics: Competitive Strategy in the Insurance Industry, 1970–84. *Journal of Management Studies,* 30:1, January pp. 69–105.

Fiegenbaum, A., Sudharshan, D. and Thomas, H. (1990), Strategic Time Periods and Strategic Group Research: Concepts and an Empirical Example. *Journal of Management Studies,* 27:2, March pp. 131–147.

Forsgren, M. and Olofsson, U. (1989), Power Balancing in an International Business in Forsgren, M. and Johanson, J. (eds.): *Managing Networks in International Business,* Uppsala. Uppsala University, pp. 178–193.

Friedman, J.W. (1983), Advertising in Oligopolistic Equilibrium. *Bell Journal of Economics,* vol. 14, pp. 464–472.

Fumbrun, C.J. and Zajac, E. (1987), "Structural and Perceptual Influences on Intraindustry Stratification." *Academy of Management Journal,* vol. 30, no. 1, pp. 33–50.

Gabrielsson, Å. and Pålsson, M. (1991), *The Mental Dimension in Local Change.* Paper presented with The second European Congress in Psychology, Juli 1991.

Gadde, L.E. and Grant, B. (1984), *Quasi-Integration, Supplier Networks and Technological Cooperation in the Automobile Industry.* Göteborg: CIM-Report NO:84:11.

Gilbert, R.J. (1989), Mobility Barriers and the Value of Incumbency in *Handbook of Industrial Organization,* vol. 1. Amsterdam: Elsevier Science Publishers.

Gioia, D.A. (1986), Symbols, Scripts, and Sensemaking: Creating Meaning in the Organizational Experience, in Sims Jr, H.P., Gioia, D.A. and associates. *The Thinking Organization Dynamics of Organizational Social Cognition.* San Francisco: Jossey-Bass.

Gioia, D.A. and Sims Jr, H.P. (1986), Introduction: Social Cognition in Organizations in Sims Jr, H.P. Gioia, D.A. and associates. *The Thinking Organization Dynamics of Organizational Social Cognition.* San Francisco: Jossey-Bass.

Glaser, B.G. and Strauss, A.L. (1967), *The Discovery of Grounded Theory.* Chicago: Aldine.

Hannan, M.T., and Freeman, J. (1989), "The Population Ecology of Organizations." *American Journal of Sociology,* vol. 82, no. 5, pp. 929–964.

Harrigan, K.R. (1985), An Application for Clustering for Strategic Group Analysis. *Strategic Management Journal,* 6, pp. 55–73.

Hatten, K.J. and Hatten, M.L. (1987), Strategic Groups, Asymmetrical Mobility Barriers and Contestability. *Strategic Management Journal,* vol. 8, pp. 329–342.

Hatten, K.J. and Schendel, D.E. (1977), Heterogeneity Within an Industry. *Journal of Industrial Economics,* 26(2), December pp. 97–113.

Hedberg, B. (1981), *How Organizations Learn and Unlearn,* in Nyström, P.C. and Starbuck, W.H. (ed.) Handbook of Organizational design, vol. 1 Oxford Press.

Hofer, C. and Schendel, D. (1978), *Strategy Formulation: Analytical Concepts.* St. Paul, MN: West.

Hood, N. and Vahlne, J-E. (red.) (1988), *Strategies in Global Competition.* London: Croom Helm.

Hunt, M.S. (1972), *Competition in the Major Home Appliance Industry, 1960–1970.* Unpublished doctoral dissertation. Boston, MA: Harvard University.

Håkansson, H. (ed.) (1982), *International Marketing and Purchasing of Industrial Goods, An Interaction Approach.* New York: John Wiley and Sons.

Håkansson, H. (1982), *Teknisk utveckling och marknadsföring.* MTC-tidskrift.

Håkansson, H. (1987), *Industrial Technological Development A Network Approach.* London: Croon Helm.

Håkansson, H. (1989), *Corporate Technological Behaviour Co-operation and Networks.* London: Routledge.

Håkansson, H. (1992), Evolution Processes in Industrial Networks in Axelsson, B. and Easton, G. *Industrial Networks A New View of Reality.* London: Routledge.

Hägg, I. and Johanson, J. (red) (1982), *Företag i nätverk.* Stockholm: SNS.

Isenberg, D.J. (1986), The Structure and Process of Understanding: Implications for Managerial Action in Sims Jr, H.P. and Gioia, D.A. and associates. *The Thinking Organization Dynamics of Organizational Social Cognition.* San Francisco: Jossey-Bass.

Jarillo, J.C. (1988), On Strategic Networks. *Strategic Management Journal,* vol. 9, pp. 31–41.

Johannisson, B. and Gustavsson, B.Å. (1984), *Småföretagande på småort — nätverksstrategier i informationssamhället.* Småskrift nr, 22. Växjö.

Johansson-Lindfors, M.B. (1989), *Organisationers ideologiska ansikten,* Umeå University. Studier i företagsekonomi ser B nr 30.

—— (1993), *Att utveckla kunskap. Om metodologiska och andra vägval vid samhällsvetenskaplig kunskapsbildning.* Lund: Studentlitteratur.

Johanson, J. and Mattsson, L-G. (1987), *Interorganizational Relations in Industrial Systems — A Network Approach Compared With The Transaction Cost Approach.* Working Paper 1987/7. University of Uppsala.

Kamien, M. and Schwarts, N. (1982), *Market Structure and Innovation.* Cambridge: Cambridge University Press.

Knickerbocker, F.T. (1973), *Oligopolistic Reaction and Multinational Enterprise.* Boston.

Kock, S. (1991), *A Strategic Process for Gaining External Resources Through Long-Lasting Relationship — Examples From two Finnish and two Swedish Industrial Firms.* Helsingfors, Svenska Handels-högskolan, ekonomi och samhälle nr 47.

Kotler, P. (1991), *Marketing Management, Analysis, Planning, Implementation and Control.* Englewood Cliffs: Prentice-Hall.

Krugman, P. (1991), *Geography and Trade.* Cambridge: Mit Press.

Kwoka, E.J. (1979), The Effect of Market Share Distribution on Industry Performance. *Review of Economics and Statistics,* February pp. 101–109.

Kwoka, E.J. and Ravenscraft, D.J. (1986), Cooperation v. Rivalry: Price-Cost Margins by Line of Business. *Economica,* August pp. 351–363.

Lamb, R.B. (ed.) (1984), *Competitive Strategic Management.* Englewood Cliffs, New Jersey: Prentice-Hall, Inc.

Lagnevik, M. et al. (1992), *The Baltic Connection.* ERU-rapport Ds 1992:81. Stockholm: Allmänna förlaget.

Lagnevik, M. (1993), *Det sydsvenska fläskets internationella konkurrenskraft.* Paper presented at The 12th Nordic Conference on Business Studies Lund, 1993.

Lawrence, P.R. and Lorsch, J.W. (1967), *Organization and Environment Managing Differentiation and Integration.* Boston: Harvard University Press.

Lazonick, W. (1991), *Business Organization and the Myth of the Market Economy*. Cambridge: Cambridge University Press.

Leblebici, H. (1985), Transactions and Organizational Form: A Re-analysis. *Organization Studies*, 6(2), pp. 97–115.

Leontiades, J. (1989), Dynamics of Global Industry Structure: A Convergency Theory and Some Results. In *Proceedings of the xvth Annual Conference of the European International Business Association: Dynamics of International Business*, vol. 2.

Lincoln, Y.S. and Guba, E.S. (1985), *Naturalistic Inquiry*. Beverly Hills: Sage.

Loasby, B.J. (1991), *Equilibrium and Evolution, An exploration of connecting principles in economics*. Manchaster: Manchaster University Press.

Louis, M.R. (1981), A Cultural Perspective in Organizations: The Need for and Consequences of Viewing Organizations as Culturebearing Mileux. *Human Systems management*, 2, pp. 246–258.

Macauley, S. (1963), Non-Contractual Relations in Business: A Preliminary Study. *American Sociological Review*, vol. 28, pp. 56–67.

March, J.G. and Olsen, J.P. (red.) (1976), *Ambiguity and Choice in Organizations*. Bergen-Oslo-Tromsö: Universitetsforlaget.

March, J.G. and Simon, H.A. (1958), *Organizations*. New York.

Marshall, A. (1961, 1920), *Principles of Economics*. 9th. edn. Cambridge: University press.

McGee, J. and Thomas, H. (1986), Strategic Groups: Theory, Research and Taxonomy. *Strategic Management*, 7, pp. 141–160.

Melin, L., Alsén, G., Berger, S. and Nilsson, A. (1984), *Kommunerna och näringslivet, ett näringslivspolitiskt dilemma*. Stockholm: Liber förlag.

Miller, D. and Friesen, P. (1980), Momentum and revolution in Organizational Adaptation. *Academy of Management Journal*, 32, 2, pp. 333–52.

—— (1982), Structural Change and Performance: Quantum Versus Piecemeal-Incremental Approaches. *Academy of Management Journal*, 25, 4, pp. 867–92.

Mintzberg, H. (1988), Opening up the Definition of Strategy in Quinn, J.B.

Mintzberg, H. and James, R.M. *The Strategy Process — Concepts, Context, and Cases*. Englewood Cliffs: Prentice-Hall.

—— (1989), *Mintzberg on Management, Inside Our Strange World of Organizations*. London: The Free Press.

Mintzberg, H. and Walters, J. (1982), Tracking Strategy in an Entrepreneurial Firm. *Academy of Management Journal*, vol. 25, no. 3, 465–499.

—— (1984), Researching the Formulation of Strategies: The History of Canadian Lady, 1939–1976 Lamb, R.B. (ed.), *Competitive Strategic Management*, Englewood Cliffs. New Jersey: Prentice-Hall.

Mitchell, J.C. (1973), Networks, Norms and Institutions in Boissevain, J. and Mitchell, J.C. (eds) *Network Analysis*. Mouton: The Hauge.

Montgomery, C.A. and Porter, M.E. (1991), *Strategy — Seeking and Securing Competitive Advantage*. Boston: Harvard business review book series.

Nelson, R.R and Winter, S.G. (1982), *An Evolutionary Theory of Economic Change*. Cambridge, Mass: Harvard University Press.

Newell, A. and Simon, H. (1972), *Human Problem Solving*. Englewood Cliffs, Prentice-Hall.

Newman, H.H. (1978), Strategic Groups and the Structure-Performance Relationship. *Review of Economics and Statistics*, August pp. 417–427.

Nilsson, K. and Nilsson, P. (1992), *Småföretag i flerpartssamverkan. En studie av aktörer, byggstenar och fogmassa vid nätverksbyggande*. Studier i företagsekonomi Serie B nr 32 Umeå Universitet 1992.

Normann, R. (1976), *På spaning efter en metodologi*. Stockholm: SIAR.
Oinas, P. (1992), *Flexibility and Locality — Towards Specifying the Scope of Rival Hypotheses*. Paper presented at the IGU Commission on Industrial Change Residential Conferende, Orlando USA 3–7 augusti.
Oster, S. (1982), Intraindustry Structure and the Ease of Strategic Change. *Review of Economics and Statistics*, 64, pp. 376–83.
Porac, J.F. and Thomas, H. (1990), Taxonomic Mental Models in Competitor Definition. *Academy of Management Review*, vol. 15, no. 2, 224–240.
Porac, J.F., Thomas, H. and Baden-Fuller, C. (1989), Competitive groups as cognitive communities: The case of Scottish knitwear manufacturers. *Journal of Management Studies*, 26:4, July pp. 397–410.
Porter, M.E. (1979), The Structure Within Industries and Companies' Performance. *Review of Economics and Statistics*, May pp. 214–227.
—— (1980), *Competitive Strategy: Techniques for Analyzing Industries and Competitors*. New York: The Free Press.
—— (1983), *Konkurensstrategier*. ISL Uddevalla.
—— (1990), *The Competitive Advantages of Nations*. London: Macmillan Press.
Quinn, J.B. (1980), *Strategies for Change Logical Incrementalism*. Homewood: Irwin.
—— (1988), Strategies for Change in Quinn, J.B., Mintzberg, H. and James, R.M. *The Strategy Process — Concepts, Context, and Cases*. Englewood Cliffs, Prentice-Hall.
Quinn, J.B., Mintzberg, H. and James, R.M. (1988), *The Strategy Process — Concepts, Context, and Cases*. Englewood Cliffs, Prentice-Hall.
Reger, R.K. and Huff, A.S. (1993), Strategic Groups: A Cognitive Perspective. *Strategic Management Journal*, vol. 14, pp. 103–124.
Reich, R.B. (1991), Who is Them? *Harvard Business Review*, March-Aprils, 77–88.
Rumelt, R.P. (1984), Towards a Strategic Theory of the Firm in Lamb, R.B. (ed.) (1984), *Competitive Strategic Management*. Englewood Cliffs, New Jersey: Prentice-Hall.
Sangenberg, W. and Pyke, F. (1991), Small Firm Industrial Districts and Local Economic Regeneration: Research and Policy issues. *Labour and Society*, 16/1, pp. 1–24.
Scherer, F.M. (1980), *Industrial Market, Structure and Economic Performance*. Chicago: Rand McNally College Pub. Co.
Schmalensee, R. (1988), "Industrial Economics: An Overview." *The Economic Journal*, September pp. 643–681.
Schumpeter, J.A. (1942), *Capitalism, Socialism and Democracy*. New York: Harper and Brothers Publishers.
Smircich, L. (1983), Concepts of Culture and Organizational Analysis. *Administrative Science Quarterly*, 28, pp. 339–359.
Smith, A. (1776, 1976), *An Inquiry Into the Nature and Causes of the Wealth of Nations*, 1776, Campbell, R.H. and Skinner, A.S. (eds.) Oxford: Clarendon Press.
Spence, M.A. (1984), Competition, Entry, and Antitrust Policy I. *Competitive Strategic Management*, ed. Lamb, R.B. Englewood Cliffs: Prentice-Hall.
Spender, J-C. (1989), *Industry Recipes — An Inquiry into the Nature and Sources of Managerial Judgement*. Oxford: Basil Blackwell Ltd.
Stoneman, P. (1983), *The Economic Analysis of Technological Change*. Oxford: Oxford University Press.
Söderholm, A. (1991), *Organiseringens logik*. Studier i företagsekonomi. Serie B nr 31 Umeå Universitet.
Sölvell, Ö. (1987), *Entry Barriers and Foreign Penetration — Emerging Patterns of International Competition in two Electrical Engineering Industries*. Stockhom School of Economics.

Sölvell, Ö., Zander, I. and Porter, M.E. (1991), *Advantage Sweden*. Stockholm: Nordstedts.

Taylor, W. (1991), The Logic of Global Business: An Interview With ABB's Percy Barnevik. *Harvard Business Review*, March-Aprils, 91–105.

Tirole, J. (1988), *The Theory of Industrial Organization*. Cambridge: MIT Press.

Thomas, H. and Venkatraman, N. (1988), Research on Strategic Groups: Progress and Prognosis. *Journal of Management Studies*, November 1988, pp. 537–555.

Törnqvist, G. (red) (1986), *Svenskt näringsliv — i geografiskt perspektiv*. Stockholm: Liber.

—— (1990), Det upplösta rummet — begrepp och teoretiska ansatser inom geografin. In Karlqvist (ed.) *Nätverk — Teori och begrepp i samhälls- vetenskapen* Värnamo: Gidlunds.

Weick, K.E. (1979), *The Social Psychology of Organizing*. Reading MA: Addison-Wesley.

Wilson, T. and Bålfors, G. (1993), *International Niching: A Second Opinion on Sweden*. Paper at Umeå Business School.

Williamson, O.E. (1975), *Markets and Hierarchies: Analysis and Antitrust Implications*. New York: The Free Press.

—— (1981), The Modern Corporation: Origins, Evolution, Attributes. *Journal of Economic Literature*, December pp. 1537–1568.

Williamson, O.E. and Ouchi, W.G. (1981), The Markets and Hierarchies Program Research: Orgins, Implications, Prospects in Van de Ven, A.H. and Joyce, W.F. *Perspectives on organization Design and Behavior*, New York: John Wiley and Sons.

Worcester, D.A. (1957), Why Dominant Firms Decline. *Journal of Political Economy*, 65, pp. 338–347.

Wåhlin, N. (1993), Studier av näringsledarnas aktiviteter i nätverk. Utkast till avhandlingsmanus. inst för företagsekonomi. Umeå Universitet.

Yamagishi, T., Gillmore, M.R. and Cook, K.S. (1988), Network Connections and the Distribution of Power in Exchange Networks. *American Journal of Sociology*, vol. 93, no. 4, January 833–51.

Yip, G.S. (1982), *Barriers to Entry*. Lexington Books.

Yu, C-M.J. and Ito, K. (1988), Oligopolistic reaction and foreign Direct Investment: The case of the U.S tire and textiles industries. *Journal of International Business Studies*, Fall, pp. 449–460.

Zander, I. and Sölvell, Ö. (1991), *Transfer and Creation of Knowledge in Local Firm and Industry Clusters — Implications for Innovation in the Global Firm*. IIB, Stockholm School of Economics.

Index

After a page reference, 'app' indicates an appendix, 'f' a figure, 'n' a note and 't' a table.